this
book

belongs 7/4/14
to:
Molly McKeown
From.
May Hairland

MARTHA'S
AMERICAN FOOD

4th

Dear Molly —

Here's to Hurricanes & Happiness!

Thank you for specily this wacky 4th of July
here at the River.

My most treasured friend, enjoy these
recipe treasures!

Love Always,
Mary

8 July 2014

MARTHA'S AMERICAN FOOD

A celebration of our
nation's most treasured dishes,
from coast to coast

Pg 298 lobster
Corn
dog
Pg 383 chicken w
lemon + garlic

Clarkson Potter/Publishers
New York

Copyright © 2012 by
Martha Stewart Living Omnimedia, Inc.

All rights reserved.
Published in the United States by
Clarkson Potter/Publishers, an imprint
of the Crown Publishing Group,
a division of Random House, Inc., New York.
www.crownpublishing.com
www.clarksonpotter.com
www.marthastewart.com

CLARKSON POTTER is a trademark and POTTER
with colophon is a registered trademark
of Random House, Inc.

Some photographs and recipes originally appeared
in *Martha Stewart Living* publications.

Library of Congress Cataloging-in-Publication Data
Stewart, Martha
Martha's American Food.—1st ed.
1. Cooking, American. 2. Cookbooks. I. Title.
  II. Title: American Food.
TX715.S854 2012
641.5973—dc23   2011029172

ISBN 978-0-307-40508-1
eISBN 978-0-7704-3297-3

Printed in China

Photograph credits appear on page 431.

Book design by Jessica Blackham, Yasemin Emory,
and William van Roden

Cover design by William van Roden and
Jessica Blackham

Front cover photograph by Paul Costello
Back cover photograph by Mikkel Vang

10 9 8 7 6 5 4 3 2 1

First Edition

*To everyone who has generously contributed
to the wonderful cuisine we now
recognize as American*

CONTENTS

INTRODUCTION

We are thrilled to have consolidated, in this volume, a collection of recipes that we believe are excellent examples of real American food. What exactly can be categorized as American food is open to lively debate. Since before the explorers discovered the bounty and wonders of this continent, Native Americans have been using indigenous, edible species and abundant wildlife for everyday consumption; corn, crab, lobster, oysters, blueberries, cranberries, turkey, tomatoes, potatoes, pumpkins, squash, and so much more were commonly incorporated into their everyday diets. Early settlers readily adapted to these new foods and used them regularly, supplementing what were unknown, unusual, and sometimes peculiar ingredients with their own more familiar flavorings and seasonings.

This book is divided into regions, each with its particular defining features, as you will discover as you peruse the contents and experiment with the very delicious recipes. The challenge in putting it together was to edit the vast numbers of recipes beloved by so many into a manageable compilation of what we consider the best examples of a genre: chowders, pies, chilis, burgers, cobblers, casseroles, salads, and such. Fish chowder in the Northeast, as an example, is a very different soup from the corn chowder of the Southwest, and cioppino from the Northwest will be very distinguishable from the gumbos of Louisiana. Sauces, salsas, muffins, biscuits, sandwiches—there is great variety and much opportunity to experience a memorable trip around America and through time by cooking as many of these recipes as you can. An added bonus are the many recipes for cocktails and non-alcoholic beverages that also highlight the ingenuity and inventiveness of the people who settled here.

The kitchens at *Martha Stewart Living* are filled with talented and knowledgeable editors who are also excellent recipe developers and food historians. We have all contributed something of what we know and love about American cuisine to this book, and every mouthwatering photograph promises something delightful to serve your families and friends.

I hope you will discover favorites new and old in the following pages. And I hope you read all of the "backstories" that accompany the recipes. I promise you will learn a great deal about who we are as a vast community held inextricably together by wonderful food.

Martha Stewart

ALL-
AMERICAN

In the beginning, American cooking was a crazy quilt of cuisines, all stitched together by common ingredients: wild game, pork, fish, chicken, corn, and wheat from local gristmills, and the bounty from carefully tended kitchen gardens. The forthrightness and utter lack of pretension that are found in our country's earliest cookbooks have echoed through the centuries.

There is still no single, all-encompassing definition of American food, but those same qualities are still true of our quintessential foods today. Meatloaf with a side of creamy, buttery mashed potatoes, the ultimate blue-plate special; a fragrant chicken potpie beneath a burnished pastry crust; an unabashedly generous helping of mac and cheese or juicy, fork-tender pot roast; a tender shortcake piled high with fresh strawberries and sweetened whipped cream; a tall yellow layer cake swathed in chocolate frosting— all of these democratic-with-a-small-*d* dishes spark our appetite, our hunger, whether truly physical or purely metaphorical.

American food has also been influenced by the many immigrant groups that have settled here, each one bringing foods and food memories from their homeland. Pasta, pizza, and artichokes were among the gifts brought by the Italians. Three-bean salad is, in all likelihood, from German settlers; the perfect "go with anything" side, it was popularized as "the salad that men love." And as once-unfamiliar flavors mingled with local tastes and traditions in the various regions, America became a veritable melting pot. It's hard to imagine a time when garlic and spaghetti were considered ethnic ingredients, for instance, or when soy sauce wasn't a staple in kitchens across the land. The end result is an ever-evolving collection of family favorites that transcend regional differences and cross state lines.

The food that is most emblematic of America's psyche, of course, is the hamburger. Although chopped-meat recipes appear in a Roman cookbook of the second century, and a more recent provenance lay in the minced "steak" of Hamburg, Germany, the succulent, beefy patties that sizzle on grills and flattops in mom-and-pop diners, off-ramp franchises, temples of haute cuisine, and suburban backyards across the land are an American invention.

Sustenance is found in eating, of course, but it is found in cooking, too. The recipes in this chapter are powerful. They draw you into the kitchen and allow you to revel in the perfection of small, ordinary tasks: hard-cooking eggs for potato salad, making a satiny gravy for the Thanksgiving turkey, creaming butter and sugar for a batch of oatmeal cookies, or whisking pancake batter in your mother's big ceramic bowl. You might have inherited that bowl a long time ago, but the smell of breakfast—bacon cooking, the hot griddle, fresh coffee—remains exactly the same. And when you teach your children how to crimp the crust of a deep-dish apple pie and then cut steam vents in the top, odds are you are passing down a tradition learned at the side of your mother or grandmother. And those children will remember more than apple-pie aesthetics; they'll remember the apron they were wearing, your hand sprinkling flour on the work surface, and the stories you tell as you help roll out the dough.

Simple and delicious, robust and satisfying, and genuinely heartwarming— these all-American dishes will make you happy and leave you feeling that all is right with the world. They'll remind you of who you are.

RECICES

BLUEBERRY PANCAKES

ALL-AMERICAN

BACKSTORY

*It's something many of us
learn at a very young age:
there is breakfast, and then
there are pancakes. The
humdrum crawl of the typical
week brings the usual cereal,
toast, maybe eggs, or if you are
feeling virtuous, a smoothie.
But on certain days—
weekends, holidays—the
batter gets mixed, the griddle
comes out, and pretty soon
your family is tucking into
a steaming stack of flapjacks,
preferably dripping with
pure maple syrup and melted
butter. Pancakes were first
brought to America by the
earliest English and Dutch
immigrants; these days,
countless variations abound.
Buttermilk makes these
pancakes extra light and
tender, and the addition of
plump blueberries is reason
enough to freeze some of
summer's bounty to enjoy
throughout the year.*

1¾ cups all-purpose flour

3 tablespoons sugar

1 tablespoon baking powder

½ teaspoon coarse salt

1½ cups buttermilk

2 large eggs, room temperature

1 teaspoon pure vanilla extract

1 tablespoon unsalted butter, melted, plus more, softened, for skillet and serving

2 tablespoons plus 2 teaspoons neutral-tasting oil, such as safflower

1 cup fresh blueberries, plus more for garnish

Pure maple syrup, for serving

1 Sift together flour, sugar, baking powder, and salt. In another bowl, whisk buttermilk, eggs, vanilla, melted butter, and 2 tablespoons oil to combine, then whisk into flour mixture (do not overmix; batter should be slightly lumpy). Fold in blueberries.

2 Heat 1 teaspoon softened butter and remaining 2 teaspoons oil in a large nonstick skillet over medium. Working in batches, pour in ⅓ cup batter per pancake. Cook until small bubbles form on the surface, about 3 minutes. Flip; cook until underside is golden brown, about 3 minutes. Add more butter as needed between batches. Serve warm with butter and syrup, garnished with additional blueberries.

MAKES 10

ALEXIS' EGG SALAD SANDWICHES

- 6 hard-cooked large eggs, peeled, whites chopped and yolks crumbled
- ¼ cup mayonnaise, plus more for bread
- ½ teaspoon dry mustard powder
- ¼ teaspoon Dijon mustard
- 1 medium stalk celery, cut into ¼-inch dice (3 tablespoons)

  Coarse salt and freshly ground pepper
- ¼ teaspoon mild Madras curry powder (optional)
- 8 slices pumpernickel bread
- 1 small head radicchio
- 1 small bunch arugula, trimmed

In a bowl, combine eggs, mayonnaise, mustard powder, mustard, and celery; season with salt and pepper. Add curry powder, if using. Gently mix until combined. Egg salad can be refrigerated up to 1 day in an airtight container.

Spread egg salad onto 4 slices of bread, and cover with radicchio, arugula, and remaining slices of bread. Cut each sandwich in half, and serve.

SERVES 4

ALL-AMERICAN

BACKSTORY

At the end of the nineteenth century, the influential cookbook Beverages and Salads, *along with the popularization of delicatessens in New York City and other urban centers, turned egg, chicken, and tuna salads into popular sandwich fillings. One other event contributed to their widespread availability: the introduction of store-bought mayonnaise, most famously by the Hellman family in 1912. Tuna salad was boosted in the early 1900s by a series of cannery-published recipe pamphlets, while chicken salads came to rely on canned meat for a quick and convenient meal (although this version uses poached chicken). Alexis Stewart's egg salad is particularly appealing: mustard powder balances the flavors, and curry powder is an unexpected (and utterly delicious) addition.*

CHICKEN SALAD SANDWICHES

3½   cups chicken broth, preferably homemade
2   boneless, skinless chicken breast
      halves (12 ounces)
1   Granny Smith apple
      Juice of 1 lemon
½   cup diced celery
½   cup mayonnaise
1   tablespoon finely chopped tarragon leaves
      Coarse salt and freshly ground pepper
8   slices white bread, toasted

1 Place stock in a medium saucepan, and bring to a boil. Add the chicken breast, and reduce to a simmer. Cook for about 15 minutes, until the chicken is cooked through. Drain, reserving the stock for another use, and set the chicken aside to cool. When it is cool enough to handle, shred into bite-size pieces.

2 Peel and core the apple, and cut into ¼-inch dice. Place diced apple in a large bowl, and toss with lemon juice to coat. Add the shredded chicken, celery, mayonnaise, and tarragon; season with salt and pepper, and mix to combine. Chicken salad can be refrigerated up to 1 day in an airtight container. Spread chicken salad onto bottom bread halves, and cover with top halves. Cut each sandwich diagonally in half, and serve.

SERVES 4

TUNA SALAD SANDWICHES

2   cans (6 ounces each) solid white tuna,
      packed in water, drained
¼   cup mayonnaise
2   teaspoons Dijon mustard
¼   cup finely chopped celery
2   teaspoons finely grated lemon zest,
      plus 2 teaspoons fresh lemon juice
      Coarse salt and freshly ground pepper
4   rustic rolls, split
½   red onion, very thinly sliced

1 In a bowl, mix tuna, mayonnaise, mustard, celery, and lemon zest and juice with a fork until thoroughly combined. Season with salt and pepper. Tuna salad can be refrigerated up to 1 day in an airtight container.

2 Spread tuna salad onto bottom roll halves, and cover with onions and top halves. Cut each sandwich in half, and serve.

SERVES 4

TOMATOES

Tomato season never comes soon enough. When you're caught up in the languorous rhythms of early summer, spending evenings near the grill and enjoying the longest days of the year, you wonder why you are still faced with lackluster tomatoes in the supermarket. Farmers' markets are selling fresh herbs and all manner of other things that go beautifully with ripe tomatoes—but no tomatoes. Not until mid-July or August do the markets fill with crates of the gorgeous, fleshy fruit. Many of the best farmstand offerings are old-fashioned heirloom varieties; with their complex fusion of sugars and acids, they are bred for flavor. A spectrum of colors as well as tastes makes a large platter of sliced heirlooms a welcome addition to any summer table.

Taking advantage of this sudden abundance is easy because tomatoes are so good just as they are—eaten out of hand, not unlike apples. But there are ways to make ripe tomatoes even better. To keep them at their peak, leave them at room temperature; refrigeration will compromise their flavor. To taste a fresh tomato dish at its most sublime, let it stand for a while. A tomato salad, for instance, should sit for at least an hour at room temperature, the slices absorbing a sprinkling of extra-virgin olive oil, salt (not too much, to avoid draining the tomatoes of all their liquid), and chopped fresh herbs—basil, mint, sweet marjoram, oregano, or lovage. And avoid adding black pepper and an acidic ingredient such as vinegar or lemon juice; let the tomatoes' natural sweet-tart taste come through.

Although it now seems hard to think of spaghetti without marinara or french fries without ketchup, until two hundred years ago tomatoes were viewed with suspicion in Europe. They were a strange tropical fruit from the New World (originally South America) that people thought were poisonous. Even in Italy, they were considered odd when the Spaniards first brought them to Naples. But by the eighteenth century, Neapolitans were dressing pasta and topping pizza with tomato sauce and, in time, changed the way the world—including Americans—ate.

Roasted tomatoes offer concentrated flavor, and they can be stored in the freezer for months, perfect for using to make soups, stews, salsas, and casseroles—and your own pasta or pizza sauce.

ROASTED TOMATOES Preheat oven to 450°F. Divide 8 pounds plum tomatoes (about 45) and 6 sprigs thyme between two shallow baking pans or rimmed baking sheets. Toss with 2 tablespoons extra-virgin olive oil; season with coarse salt and freshly ground pepper. Spread evenly and bake until tomatoes soften and burst, about 45 minutes, rotating pans halfway through. Let cool, then coarsely chop. Refrigerate tomatoes in airtight containers up to 3 days, or freeze (in small portions, as desired) up to 3 months. **MAKES 10 CUPS**

TOMATO SOUP AND GRILLED CHEESE

BACKSTORY

My first memories of sandwiches are warm, crisp, buttery triangles of white or whole wheat bread filled with delectable melted yellow cheese. In the Kostyra household, these were served with bowls of steaming tomato soup for lunch, and we all loved that meal. At some point, tomatoes were added to the sandwich filling, and I loved the mixture of sharp cheddar and tart slabs of homegrown Big Boy tomatoes between the unctuous cheese toast. The sandwich had to be cooked in a big iron skillet, and the bread had to be evenly golden brown and the cheese completely melted. Otherwise, it just wasn't quite right.

FOR THE SOUP

- 2 tablespoons unsalted butter
- 1 onion, finely chopped
- 3 garlic cloves, minced
- 3 cans (28 ounces each) crushed tomatoes (about 10 cups)
- 5¼ cups chicken stock, preferably homemade (page 410)
- 3 sprigs oregano, plus more for garnish (optional)
- ½ cup half-and-half

  Coarse salt and freshly ground pepper

FOR THE SANDWICHES

- 8 slices (½ inch thick) firm white sandwich bread, such as Pullman or pain de mie
- ½ pound cheddar, sliced ⅓ inch thick

  Unsalted butter, softened

1 Make the soup: Melt butter in a medium saucepan over medium-low heat. Cook onion and garlic, stirring occasionally, until translucent, about 8 minutes.

2 Add tomatoes, stock, and oregano, and bring to a boil. Reduce heat and simmer gently until thickened, about 45 minutes. Remove oregano sprigs. Using an immersion blender, purée soup until smooth (or purée in a blender in batches, being careful not to fill the jar more than halfway).

3 Return soup to a simmer over medium-low heat. Gradually add half-and-half, stirring constantly. Season with salt and pepper. Garnish with more oregano sprigs, if desired. Serve hot.

4 Make the sandwiches: Heat a griddle or large cast-iron skillet over medium-low. Cover each of 4 slices of bread with a layer of cheese; top with remaining bread slices, pressing gently to adhere. Generously butter both sides of each sandwich, spreading butter all the way to the edges.

5 Cook two sandwiches at a time until golden brown and cheese has melted, 3 to 4 minutes per side, turning once. Before removing from griddle, flip sandwiches to reheat first side, about 15 seconds. Cut each sandwich diagonally in half and serve immediately.

SERVES 4

HOT CRAB DIP

CARAMELIZED-
ONION DIP

BAKED ARTICHOKE DIP

HOT CRAB DIP

½ cup (1 stick) unsalted butter

1 onion, finely chopped

2 garlic cloves, minced

¼ cup plus 2 tablespoons all-purpose flour

1½ cups milk

¼ teaspoon cayenne

2 teaspoons dry mustard powder

4 ounces sharp white cheddar, shredded (1 cup)

Finely grated zest of 1 lemon, plus
2 tablespoons fresh lemon juice

2 teaspoons Worcestershire sauce

10 ounces lump crabmeat, picked over

2 tablespoons coarsely chopped fresh flat-leaf parsley

Coarse salt and freshly ground pepper

½ small (8-ounce) loaf rustic bread, crusts trimmed,
torn into 1-inch pieces (1 to 2 cups)

Assorted crackers and flatbreads, for serving

1 Preheat oven to 400°F. Melt 6 tablespoons butter in a medium saucepan over medium heat. Add onion and garlic; cook, stirring occasionally, until soft, about 4 minutes. Whisk in flour; cook, whisking constantly, 4 minutes. Whisking constantly, pour in milk in a slow, steady stream. Simmer over medium heat, whisking, until thickened, about 4 minutes. Stir in cayenne and mustard. Gradually whisk in cheese; whisk until melted.

2 Remove from heat. Stir in lemon zest and juice along with Worcestershire to combine. Stir in crabmeat and parsley. Season with salt and pepper. Transfer to a 1-quart ovenproof dish.

3 Melt remaining 2 tablespoons butter; stir into bread pieces. Season with salt and pepper. Arrange bread mixture over crab dip. Bake until heated through and the topping is golden brown, 25 to 30 minutes. Remove from oven. Let stand 10 minutes before serving with crackers and flatbreads.

MAKES 4 CUPS

CARAMELIZED-ONION DIP

2 tablespoons extra-virgin olive oil, plus more for drizzling

3 pounds onions (about 8 large), halved and thinly sliced

Coarse salt and freshly ground pepper

¼ cup red-wine vinegar

1 tablespoon chopped fresh thyme

8 ounces cream cheese, softened

1 cup (8 ounces) sour cream

Assorted chips or crackers, for serving

Crisp Onions, for garnish (optional; recipe follows)

1 Heat olive oil in a medium heavy-bottomed pot over medium-high. Cook onions, stirring occasionally, until soft and golden brown, about 15 minutes. Cover; reduce heat to low. Cook, stirring occasionally, until onions are well caramelized, about 40 minutes.

2 Raise heat to medium, and season onions with salt. Stir in vinegar; simmer until absorbed. Stir in thyme; remove from heat. Let cool; coarsely chop onions.

3 With an electric mixer on medium speed, beat cream cheese until smooth. Fold in sour cream and chopped onions with a flexible spatula; season with salt and pepper. Transfer to a serving dish. Cover with plastic wrap and refrigerate 1 hour (or up to overnight) before serving with chips and crackers, garnished with crisp onions, if desired.

MAKES 4 CUPS

CRISP ONIONS

¼ cup plus 1 tablespoon neutral-tasting oil, such as safflower

1 small onion, very thinly sliced

Heat oil in a medium skillet over high until hot but not smoking. Fry onion in small batches until crisp, about 1 minute. Transfer to a paper towel–lined plate to drain.

MAKES 1½ CUPS

BAKED ARTICHOKE DIP

3 cans (14 ounces each) artichoke hearts in water, drained

6 tablespoons (¾ stick) unsalted butter, softened

¼ cup all-purpose flour

2 cups milk, warmed

⅛ teaspoon cayenne

Coarse salt and freshly ground pepper

1 cup grated parmesan (3 ounces)

1 cup grated pecorino romano (3 ounces)

1 large onion, finely chopped

1 tablespoon fresh thyme leaves, coarsely chopped

3 garlic cloves, minced

1½ teaspoons finely grated lemon zest

¼ cup fresh breadcrumbs (page 408)

Assorted crackers and flatbreads, for serving

1 Remove leaves from 1 artichoke heart; pat dry and reserve. Thinly slice remaining artichoke hearts; pat dry.

2 Preheat oven to 400°F. Melt 4 tablespoons butter in a medium saucepan over medium heat. Add flour and cook, stirring constantly, 2 minutes. Whisk in milk and bring to a boil. Add cayenne and season with salt and pepper. Simmer until thickened, about 2 minutes. Remove from heat and stir in cheeses.

3 Melt remaining 2 tablespoons butter in a medium skillet over medium-high heat. Cook onion, stirring occasionally, until softened, about 3 minutes. Add thyme, garlic, and sliced artichoke hearts and cook, stirring, until heated through, about 3 minutes. Add to cheese mixture along with lemon zest.

4 Transfer to a 2-quart baking dish. Top with reserved artichoke leaves and sprinkle evenly with breadcrumbs. Bake until bubbling and topping is golden, about 15 minutes. Let cool slightly before serving with crackers and flatbreads.

MAKES 6 CUPS

MUSHROOM-AND-BACON DIP

  3 dried porcini mushrooms

  ½ cup boiling water

  8 slices thick-cut bacon

  1 large or 2 small leeks, white and pale-green parts only, halved lengthwise, thinly sliced crosswise, washed well and dried

  4 garlic cloves, finely chopped

  1 pound fresh cremini, button, or shiitake mushrooms, cleaned and chopped, plus 3 mushroom slices, for garnish

     Coarse salt and freshly ground pepper

1½ teaspoons finely chopped fresh thyme

  8 ounces cream cheese, softened

  2 cups (16 ounces) sour cream

  3 tablespoons sliced trimmed scallions (dark green parts only), plus more for garnish

     Crackers or toasted bread slices, for serving

1 In a small bowl, soak porcini in the boiling water until soft, about 20 minutes. Working over the bowl, lift out porcini and squeeze out liquid into bowl. Coarsely chop porcini. Leaving powdery residue at bottom of bowl, pour liquid through a fine sieve into another bowl and reserve.

2 Cook bacon in a large skillet over medium heat until crisp, about 5 minutes per side. Drain on paper towels. Pour off rendered bacon fat, reserving ¼ cup. Wipe skillet clean. Coarsely chop bacon.

3 Return 3 tablespoons bacon fat to skillet. Add leeks and garlic; cook over medium heat, stirring occasionally, until translucent, about 2 minutes. Add porcini and chopped fresh mushrooms, then season with salt and pepper. Raise heat to high; cook, stirring, until mushrooms are tender, 5 to 8 minutes. Add thyme; cook 2 minutes more. Transfer to a plate; let cool. Wipe skillet clean with paper towels.

4 With an electric mixer on medium speed, whisk cream cheese until smooth. Gradually add sour cream, whisking until smooth. Stir in mushroom mixture, three-fourths of the bacon, the scallions, and 2 tablespoons porcini soaking liquid. If necessary, add more porcini liquid to reach desired consistency.

5 Cook sliced mushrooms in remaining 1 tablespoon bacon fat in a medium skillet over medium heat, stirring occasionally, until golden brown, about 2 minutes. Scatter over dip. Garnish dip with scallions and remaining bacon. Serve with crackers or bread.

MAKES 4 CUPS

MEATLOAF

3 slices good-quality white bread,
  torn into large pieces (do not trim crusts)

1 onion, coarsely chopped

2 garlic cloves, coarsely chopped

1 celery stalk, coarsely chopped

1 carrot, coarsely chopped

½ cup fresh flat-leaf parsley

¾ pound ground beef

¾ pound ground pork

¾ pound ground veal

1 large egg

¾ cup ketchup

1 tablespoon Dijon mustard

1 tablespoon Worcestershire sauce

1 tablespoon coarse salt

½ teaspoon freshly ground pepper

2 tablespoons dark-brown sugar

1 Preheat oven to 375°F. Pulse bread in a food processor until finely ground. Transfer to a medium bowl (you should have 2½ cups crumbs).

2 Combine onion, garlic, celery, carrot, and parsley in food processor; pulse until finely chopped. Add to breadcrumbs along with ground meats, egg, ¼ cup ketchup, the mustard, Worcestershire, salt, and pepper; mix gently but thoroughly by hand to combine. Transfer mixture to a 9-by-5-inch loaf pan, pressing to fill in an even layer.

3 Combine remaining ½ cup ketchup and the brown sugar in a bowl and stir until smooth; brush over meatloaf.

4 Place pan on a rimmed baking sheet and bake until an instant-read thermometer inserted in middle of meatloaf registers 160°F, about 1 hour 20 minutes. Let cool slightly before serving.

SERVES 6 TO 8

MASHED POTATOES

4 pounds Yukon Gold potatoes,
  peeled and cut into 1-inch pieces

  Coarse salt and freshly ground pepper

1 cup heavy cream

1 cup milk

½ cup (1 stick) unsalted butter

1 Place potatoes and 2 tablespoons salt in a large saucepan. Cover with cold water by 2 inches and bring to a boil. Reduce heat to medium-low, and simmer until potatoes are tender, 8 to 10 minutes.

2 Meanwhile, heat cream, milk, and butter in a small saucepan over medium-low heat, stirring occasionally, until butter melts.

3 Drain potatoes and pass through a ricer into a heatproof bowl (or mash with a potato masher until smooth). Pour warmed cream mixture over potatoes in a slow, steady stream, and stir until smooth. Season with salt and pepper. Serve immediately, or cover bowl and keep warm over a pan of simmering water up to 2 hours.

SERVES 8 TO 10

ALL-AMERICAN

BACKSTORY

Food historians believe meatloaf to be a direct descendant from European pâtés—the use of ground beef, however, made it a thoroughly New World invention. It is widely acknowledged that a combination of equal parts beef (for flavor), pork (for juiciness), and veal (for tenderness and easy slicing) produces the very best meatloaf; you'll find the combination packaged in supermarkets and labeled "meatloaf mix." Mashed potatoes are, of course, the essential accompaniment. The recipe here produces potatoes with an ultra-creamy texture, especially when passed through a potato ricer; for stiffer mashed potatoes, reduce the combined amount of milk and cream from two cups to one and a half cups. Sautéed broccolini or broccoli adds color to the plate.

ROAST TURKEY

  1 fresh whole turkey (about 20 pounds), giblets
     and neck removed from cavity and reserved
 1½ cups (3 sticks) unsalted butter, melted,
     plus 4 tablespoons, softened
  1 bottle (750 ml) dry white wine, plus 1 cup dry red
     or white wine (or water), for gravy
     Coarse salt and freshly ground pepper
     Cornbread, Bacon, and Leek Stuffing (recipe follows)
     Giblet Stock (recipe follows)

1 Rinse turkey and pat dry with paper towels. Let stand 2 hours
at room temperature.

2 Preheat oven to 450°F, with rack on lowest level. Combine melted butter
and bottle of white wine in a large bowl. Fold a large piece of cheesecloth
into quarters and cut it into a 17-inch, four-layer square. Immerse cheesecloth
in the butter and wine; let soak.

3 Place turkey, breast side up, on a roasting rack in a heavy roasting pan. (If
the turkey comes with a pop-up timer, remove it; an instant-read thermometer
is a much more accurate indication of doneness.) Fold wing tips under turkey.
Season cavities (including neck) with salt and pepper, then fill loosely with
stuffing; do not pack tightly. (Cook any remaining stuffing in a buttered baking
dish at 350°F for 35 minutes.) Tie legs together loosely with kitchen twine. Fold
neck flap under and secure with toothpicks. Rub turkey with the softened butter
and season with salt and pepper.

4 Lift cheesecloth out of the liquid and squeeze it slightly, leaving it very
damp. Drape evenly over the breast and about halfway down the sides of
the turkey. Place turkey, legs first, in oven. Cook 30 minutes. Using a pastry
brush, baste cheesecloth and exposed parts of turkey with some of the
wine mixture. Continue to cook another 2½ hours, basting with more wine
mixture every 30 minutes.

5 Carefully remove and discard cheesecloth. Turn roasting pan so that the
breast is facing the back of the oven. Baste turkey with pan juices. (If there are
not enough juices, continue to use the wine mixture.) The skin becomes fragile
as it browns, so baste carefully. Cook 1 more hour, basting after 30 minutes.

6 After this fourth hour of cooking, insert an instant-read thermometer into
the thickest part of the thigh (avoiding the bone). The temperature should reach
165°F and the turkey should be golden brown (also check the stuffing, which
should be between 140°F and 160°F). The breast does not need to be checked
for temperature. If legs are not yet fully cooked, baste turkey, return to oven,
and cook another 20 to 30 minutes. Transfer turkey to a platter and let rest
30 minutes before carving (see page 32).

(Continued on next page)

BACKSTORY

*It's fun to think back on all
the different turkeys I have
prepared over many years
of hosting Thanksgiving, the
most celebrated American
meal. I've tried every
technique under the sun:
brining, dry-brining, rubbing,
deep-frying, grilling, and
of course, roasting—quick
roasting at high temperatures,
slow roasting at lower
temperatures, and everywhere
in between. There were subtle
and sometimes not-so-
subtle differences that made
each a unique experience.
Yet the tried-and-true method
I like best requires covering
the bird with a butter-
and-wine–soaked cheesecloth
as it roasts; the result is
an exceptionally moist
and flavorful turkey that
has developed a very loyal
following among* Martha
Stewart Living *readers since
the recipe was first published
in the mid-1990s.*

7 Meanwhile, make gravy. Pour off pan juices into a large glass measuring cup (or a fat separator). Let stand until fat rises to the surface, about 10 minutes, then skim off and discard. Place the roasting pan over medium-high heat. Add remaining 1 cup wine and bring to a boil; deglaze pan, scraping up browned bits from the bottom with a wooden spoon. Cook until most of the wine has evaporated. Add giblet stock to pan. Stir well and bring back to a boil. Cook until liquid has reduced by half, about 10 minutes. Add the defatted pan juices and cook over medium-high heat, stirring occasionally, about 10 minutes more. You should have about 2½ cups of gravy. Season with salt and pepper and strain through a fine sieve into a warm gravy boat. Serve with turkey.

SERVES 12 TO 14

Carving a turkey Use your hand to hold the turkey steady on a carving board; a carving fork, while useful for arranging the meat once it is carved, will pierce and tear the flesh and doesn't provide the same grip. With scissors, cut through the trussing, taking care to remove all of the string. Pull each leg away from the body and slice through skin between breast and drumstick. Bend leg back until thigh bone pops out of socket. Cut through joint and skin to detach leg completely. Keeping the blade close to rib cage and using it as your guide, slice along each side of the breastbone to remove breasts. Cut wings off at joint.

Cut between joint to separate thigh from drumstick. Both pieces can now be cut off the bone into slices. Slice breasts crosswise, skin side up, and arrange on a platter with dark meat and wings. Scoop stuffing from cavity.

GIBLET STOCK

Giblets (heart, gizzard, and liver) and neck reserved from turkey

4 tablespoons unsalted butter

1 onion, cut into ¼-inch dice

1 celery stalk with leaves, stalk cut into ¼-inch dice, leaves coarsely chopped

1 small leek, white and pale green parts only, cut into ¼-inch dice, washed well and drained

Coarse salt and freshly ground pepper

4 cups water

1 dried bay leaf

1 Trim any fat or membrane from giblets. The liver should not have the gallbladder, a small green sac, attached. If it does, trim gallbladder off carefully, removing part of the liver if necessary. Do not pierce the sac; it contains very bitter liquid. Rinse giblets and neck and pat dry.

2 In a medium saucepan, melt 3 tablespoons butter over medium heat. Add onion, celery (stalk and leaves), and leek. Cook, stirring occasionally, until onion is translucent, about 6 minutes. Season with salt and pepper and cook another 5 minutes. Add the water, bay leaf, gizzard, heart, and neck (do not add liver; it needs to be cooked separately or it makes the stock bitter). Bring to a boil, then reduce to a rapid simmer. Cook 45 minutes, or until gizzard is tender when pierced with the tip of a sharp knife.

3 Meanwhile, chop the liver finely. Melt remaining 1 tablespoon butter in a small skillet over medium-low heat. Add liver and cook, stirring constantly, 4 to 6 minutes, or until liver no longer releases any blood and is fully cooked.

4 Remove gizzard, heart, and neck from pot. Strain liquid from pot through a fine sieve into another pot; discard solids. Chop gizzard and heart very fine and add to strained broth, along with chopped liver. Pick meat off neck and add to broth. Stock can be refrigerated up to 2 days in an airtight container; let cool completely before storing.

MAKES ABOUT 2 CUPS

CORNBREAD, BACON, AND LEEK STUFFING

- 2 cups pecans (8 ounces), toasted (page 408) and coarsely chopped
- 2 recipes Skillet Cornbread (page 322; omit jalapeño chiles), coarsely broken into 2-inch pieces (16 cups)
- 8 slices smoked bacon, chopped into ½-inch pieces
- 4 celery stalks, chopped into ½-inch pieces
- 4 leeks, white and pale green parts only, chopped into ½-inch pieces, washed well and dried
- 1 tablespoon plus 1 teaspoon chopped fresh thyme

  Coarse salt and freshly ground pepper
- 2½ cups chicken stock, preferably homemade (page 410)
- 4 large eggs, lightly beaten

1 Mix pecans and cornbread in a large bowl. Cook bacon in a large high-sided skillet over medium-high heat until almost crisp, about 3 minutes. Reduce heat to medium and add celery and leeks. Cook until vegetables are tender, stirring occasionally, about 10 minutes. Stir in thyme and season with salt and pepper. Transfer mixture to a large bowl.

2 Return skillet to medium-high heat. Add stock and bring to a simmer; deglaze pan, scraping up browned bits from the bottom with a wooden spoon, then transfer to bowl with bacon-vegetable mixture. Stir in eggs. Gently mix in cornbread mixture (do not overmix). Let cool completely before using to stuff turkey.

Note If you do not plan on using as a stuffing for turkey, place in a buttered 9-by-13-inch baking dish, dot evenly with 3 tablespoons unsalted butter, cut into small pieces, and bake at 350°F until top is golden brown, about 35 minutes. Serve hot.

SERVES 10 TO 12

ALL-AMERICAN

BACKSTORY

Around the country, you may find a few significant variations on the way the Thanksgiving turkey is cooked, but its stuffing will likely give you a clue as to which region the cook hails from—wild rice in Minnesota, chopped cranberries among the bread cubes in New England, oyster "dressing" in New Orleans, and mashed potatoes and bread in Pennsylvania Dutch country. I have particularly fond memories of my mother's stuffing, which was always made from two-day-old sliced white bread cut into one-inch squares, mixed with freshly roasted chestnuts (prepared by Dad the night before), sausage meat, lots of chopped celery, apples, onions, fresh parsley, dried sage, eggs, salt, pepper, and most important, the inimitable Bell's Seasoning. The version here—made with cornbread, bacon, and pecans—has roots in the South, but the winning combination of flavors (and textures, thanks to the crunchy nuts) makes it universally appealing.

HAMBURGERS

A hamburger recipe may not seem terribly compelling—after all, grocery-store habits suggest that most people from coast to coast simply buy preformed patties and leave it at that. But over the years, as I've grilled and panfried untold numbers of burgers at Martha Stewart Living *for our magazines and on television, I've learned more than a thing or two about how to improve upon the standard. So many chefs have taken up the challenge of making the perfect burger, and I've sampled many of their efforts, in every part of the country. In New York City alone I've enjoyed delicious burgers at Daniel Boulud's DB Bistro Moderne, Shake Shack, and the venerable Peter Luger in Brooklyn, where it's available only at lunchtime. In all of this experimenting and tasting and testing, I've discovered that how the hamburger was invented and by whom is irrelevant—what matters is only the burger before you.*

1¼ pounds ground beef chuck
1¼ pounds ground sirloin
     Neutral-tasting oil, such as safflower, for grill and drizzling
     Coarse salt and freshly ground pepper
  6 thin slices sharp cheddar
  6 hamburger buns, split
  1 white onion, sliced ¼ inch thick
  ¼ cup Dijon mustard
  ¼ cup whole-grain mustard
  6 Boston lettuce leaves
  1 ripe beefsteak tomato, sliced

1 Gently mix beef chuck and sirloin by hand and shape into six 1-inch-thick patties. Cover and refrigerate until cold and firm, about 30 minutes.

2 Heat grill to medium-high. (If you are using a charcoal grill, the coals are ready when you can hold your hand 4 inches above the grill for just 3 to 4 seconds.) When grill is ready, brush grates with oil. Generously season both sides of patties with salt and pepper. Grill, flipping once, until burgers are cooked to desired doneness, about 5 minutes per side for medium-rare. Top each burger with a cheese slice during the final 30 seconds of cooking. Transfer burgers to a platter.

3 Meanwhile, grill buns, cut sides down, until lightly toasted, about 30 seconds. Lightly drizzle onion with oil and toss to coat. Season with salt and pepper. Grill, turning once, until tender, about 2 minutes.

4 Combine mustards in a small bowl, then spread mixture on buns, dividing evenly. Layer bottom halves with lettuce, burgers, tomato, and onion. Sandwich with top halves and serve.

SERVES 6

FRENCH FRIES

6 russet potatoes, peeled and cut into ½-inch-thick wedges
8 cups neutral-tasting oil, such as safflower
Coarse salt

1 Place potatoes in a large bowl and cover with cold water. Refrigerate 8 hours. Drain, rinse, and pat dry.

2 Heat oil in a large pot over medium until it registers 310°F on a deep-fry thermometer. Line two baking sheets with paper towels. Carefully add potatoes to oil in small batches. Cook 3 to 4 minutes, turning occasionally (they will not color much). Using a slotted spoon or a mesh spider, transfer fries to a paper towel–lined baking sheet to drain. Let cool.

3 Increase heat until oil reaches 350°F. Fry potatoes in small batches until golden brown, 3 to 4 minutes. Transfer fries to paper towels to drain. Season with salt and serve immediately.

SERVES 6

QUICK KETCHUP

1 cup canned crushed tomatoes
2½ teaspoons light-brown sugar
2½ teaspoons cider vinegar
⅛ teaspoon ground cloves

In a small saucepan over medium heat, stir together tomatoes, brown sugar, vinegar, and cloves. Bring to a boil, reduce heat, and simmer until thickened, 2 to 3 minutes. Let cool completely before serving or storing. Ketchup can be refrigerated in an airtight container up to 2 weeks.

MAKES 1 CUP

ALL-AMERICAN

BACKSTORY

French Fries are a must with burgers, of course. And, like burgers, they might not top the list of restaurant standbys that home cooks are eager to tackle. But it takes just one time cooking them at home before you're hooked. There is, of course, the deep-frying involved. And in order to produce the very best, crisp-on-the-outside, tender-on-the-inside fries, you need to cook them once at a lower temperature, then drain and fry them a second time at a higher temperature until golden brown. They are definitely worth any extra time and effort, and all you need is a deep, sturdy pot and a deep-fry thermometer. In this recipe, the potatoes are cut into thick wedges to produce "steak fries." Once you get the hang of deep-frying, however, you can experiment by cutting the potatoes into different shapes and sizes—shoestrings, cottage fries, or anything else that suits your fancy.

LASAGNA

Olive oil, for baking dish

3 pounds ricotta

3 large egg yolks

1 cup freshly grated parmesan (3 ounces)

¼ teaspoon freshly grated nutmeg

Coarse salt and freshly ground pepper

1 pound lasagna noodles

3 quarts Meat Sauce (recipe follows) or Marinara Sauce (page 411)

1 pound fresh mozzarella, sliced ½ inch thick

1 Preheat oven to 400°F. Brush an 11-by-14-inch baking dish with olive oil. In a large bowl, combine ricotta, egg yolks, parmesan, and nutmeg; season with salt and pepper and whisk to combine. Cover with plastic wrap and refrigerate.

2 Bring a large pot of water to a boil; add salt. Cook noodles, several at a time, 2 to 3 minutes less than package instructions. Transfer noodles to a colander to drain.

3 Spread 3 cups sauce evenly in bottom of prepared dish. Layer with one-third of the noodles, then spread with 2 cups sauce followed by half the ricotta mixture. Repeat to make another layer of noodles, sauce, and ricotta. Finish with remaining noodles and sauce; arrange mozzarella slices on top.

4 Bake until sauce is bubbling around edges of dish and top is browned in spots, about 1 hour. (If cheese starts to brown too quickly, tent dish with foil.) Let stand 10 to 15 minutes before serving.

SERVES 10 TO 12

MEAT SAUCE

¼ cup olive oil

2 onions, finely chopped

4 garlic cloves, minced

Coarse salt and freshly ground pepper

3 pounds ground beef chuck

1 can (6 ounces) tomato paste

2 cans (28 ounces each) whole peeled plum tomatoes with juice

1 Heat olive oil in a large skillet over medium-high. Add onions and garlic; season with salt and pepper. Cook, stirring occasionally, until onions are softened, about 5 minutes.

2 Add beef and cook, breaking it up with a spoon, until no longer pink, 4 to 5 minutes. Add tomato paste and cook, stirring, 1 to 2 minutes.

3 Reduce heat to medium. Add tomatoes, breaking them up with your hands as you go, along with their juice. Simmer until thickened, stirring occasionally, 45 to 60 minutes. Season with salt and pepper. (If not using immediately, cool the sauce completely and refrigerate in an airtight container up to 2 days or freeze up to 1 month; thaw the sauce overnight in refrigerator.)

MAKES ABOUT 3 QUARTS

ALL-AMERICAN

BACKSTORY

Any Italian will tell you that a classic lasagne bolognese is more about satiny homemade pasta than it is about meat sauce. That is true, but not for this Americanized version. This dish was created by early Italian American restaurateurs, who came from a country where meat was scarce; it was an economical way to incorporate the meat that Americans expected on their plate. And what was not to love? The rich cheese- and beef-laden pasta quickly became a fixture on dinner tables across the country, regardless of family heritage. Easily made ahead and highly portable, it continues to serve as the go-to potluck dish for generations of home cooks.

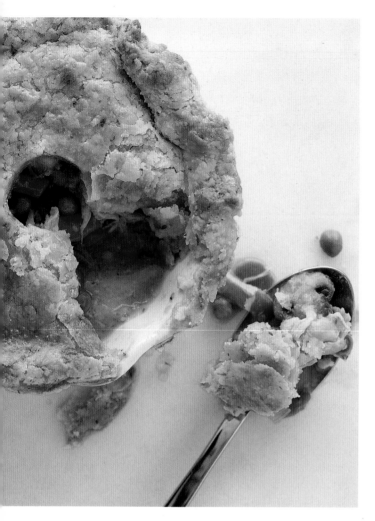

CHICKEN POTPIES

2　dried bay leaves

2　sprigs flat-leaf parsley, plus 2 tablespoons coarsely chopped leaves

2　sprigs thyme, plus 2 tablespoons finely chopped leaves

1　whole chicken (3 to 4 pounds), cut into 8 parts

1　parsnip, cut into 1-inch pieces

3　celery stalks, 1 cut into 1-inch pieces, the rest cut into ½-inch dice

1　onion, sliced

¼　teaspoon black peppercorns

6　to 8 cups chicken stock, preferably homemade (page 410), or water

6　ounces pearl onions

5　tablespoons unsalted butter

2　carrots, sliced into ½-inch rounds

8　ounces cremini mushrooms, trimmed and quartered or halved if large

¼　cup all-purpose flour, plus more for dusting
　　Coarse salt and freshly ground pepper

½　cup frozen green peas (do not thaw)

1　recipe Basic Pie Dough, herbed variation (page 412)

1　large egg, for egg wash

ALL-AMERICAN

BACKSTORY

A humble dish if ever there was one, potpie has undergone an image makeover in recent years. What was once viewed as a homey (and homemade) meal is now considered a rare treat, and worthy of appearing on many restaurant menus. There you might find lengthy descriptions of potpies filled with unexpected ingredients, such as lobster or shrimp, hearty meats like beef or lamb, or a combination of vegetables. Chicken potpie remains the standard, however, especially for home cooks. The recipe for "chicken pie" in Amelia Simmons's American Cookery, *published in 1796, requires baking whole chicken pieces, bones and all, right under the crust. Here, the filling (boneless, thankfully) is divided among small dishes to make single servings, but you can make one large pie for convenience, if you wish (see variation, opposite). The recipe strays from tradition only with the fresh herbs mixed into the pastry crust—a nice update, indeed.*

1 Using kitchen twine, tie together bay leaves and parsley and thyme sprigs for a bouquet garni. Place chicken in a large stockpot (it should be just large enough to hold chicken with 3 inches of room on top). Add bouquet garni, parsnip, celery pieces, onion, peppercorns, and enough stock or water to just cover chicken. Bring to a boil over high heat, skimming foam from surface as necessary; reduce heat and simmer until chicken is just cooked through (juices should run clear when meat is pierced), 7 to 10 minutes for breast and 15 to 20 minutes for thighs. Use tongs to remove each part as soon as it is finished cooking. Once the chicken is cool enough to handle, pull off and discard the skin, separate the meat from the bones, and tear it into bite-size pieces. You will need about 2 cups meat; save any remaining for another use. Strain liquid from pot through a fine sieve, pressing on solids; reserve 2½ cups strained broth and discard solids.

2 While chicken is cooking, prepare an ice-water bath. Bring a pot of water to a boil. Add pearl onions; blanch 1 minute. Using a slotted spoon, transfer onions to the ice-water bath until cool enough to handle, then remove. With a paring knife, cut off the root ends and squeeze onions from skins.

3 Melt butter in a large saucepan over medium-high heat, then add carrots, diced celery, and the mushrooms. Cook until vegetables start to soften, stirring occasionally, 2 to 3 minutes. Add flour and chopped thyme to make a roux; cook, stirring constantly, 1 minute. Stir in reserved broth and season with salt. Bring to a boil; reduce heat and simmer 8 minutes. Add reserved chicken along with the pearl onions and green peas. Return to a boil, then reduce heat and simmer until vegetables are tender and peas are bright green, about 2 minutes. Remove from heat and stir in chopped parsley. Season with salt and pepper. Let cool completely.

4 Set out eight 8-ounce ovenproof dishes. On a lightly floured surface, roll out pie dough until it is about ⅛ inch thick. (Chill dough after rolling if it becomes too soft to work with or starts to shrink.) Invert one of the dishes onto the dough and lightly mark a circle about 1 inch larger than the dish. Repeat to mark seven more circles, then use a pastry wheel or sharp knife to cut out each. Make vents by cutting a 1-inch circle in the center of each with a cookie cutter (or make several slits with a paring knife). Ladle about 1½ cups filling into each dish. Drape dough over the filled dishes, crimping edges to seal as desired. Place on a parchment-lined baking sheet and chill until dough is firm, about 20 minutes. Preheat oven to 350°F.

5 Using a pastry brush, lightly coat dough with egg wash and bake, rotating halfway through, until crust is golden and juices are bubbling in center, about 1 hour. Let potpies cool 20 minutes before serving.

MAKES 8 INDIVIDUAL POTPIES

VARIATION

To make one large pie, roll out dough to a 12-inch round on a lightly floured surface. Ladle all of the filling into a 10-inch cast-iron skillet (or 2-quart baking dish). Drape dough over the skillet, crimping edges to seal as desired and making slits in middle of dough to allow steam to escape. Then chill, brush dough with egg, and bake as directed, cooking for the same amount of time.

TUNA NOODLE CASEROLE

ALL-AMERICAN

BACKSTORY

Your mom's tuna noodle casserole may not have included artichokes, anchovies, or capers, but odds are it was just what was needed after a long day at school or a tough loss on the Little League field. This sort of creamy casserole made of meat, white sauce, and noodles or rice has existed for centuries, but in all likelihood, tuna noodle casserole sprang from one of the cookbooks published by the Campbell's Soup Company in the 1930s. Marketed as a quick, economical meal assembled from packaged or canned foods, the casserole struck a chord with home cooks during the Great Depression. Our version has been tweaked to suit the modern palate—with ingredients readily accessible in the modern supermarket— but its comfort-food quotient remains just as high as ever.

½ cup plus 2 tablespoons extra-virgin olive oil, plus more for dish

1 pound elbow macaroni

   Coarse salt and freshly ground pepper

½ onion, coarsely chopped

1 tin (2 ounces) of anchovies packed in olive oil (about 10 fillets), drained

1½ cans (14 ounces each) artichoke hearts in water, drained (about 11 hearts)

2 tablespoons capers, drained and rinsed

¾ cup finely grated parmesan

3 cans (6 ounces each) water-packed chunk light tuna, drained, ⅔ cup water reserved

1½ teaspoons finely grated lemon zest

¼ cup finely chopped fresh flat-leaf parsley

⅓ cup plain fresh breadcrumbs (page 408)

1 Preheat oven to 350°F. Lightly oil a 2- to 2½-quart soufflé or casserole dish. Cook pasta in a large pot of boiling salted water until barely al dente, about 5 minutes. Drain and rinse with cold water.

2 Purée onion, anchovies, artichoke hearts, and capers in a food processor until smooth. Add parmesan and reserved tuna water, and pulse to combine. With machine running, slowly add ½ cup olive oil and process until emulsified. Season with pepper. Transfer to a large bowl and stir in drained tuna, lemon zest, parsley, and pasta. Season with salt and pepper.

3 Transfer pasta mixture to prepared dish. Sprinkle breadcrumbs on top and drizzle with remaining 2 tablespoons olive oil. Cover with parchment, then foil, and bake until heated through, 40 to 45 minutes. Uncover and cook until breadcrumbs are lightly browned, 15 to 20 minutes more. Let stand 15 minutes before serving.

SERVES 6

POT ROAST

- 5 large russet potatoes, peeled and quartered
- ¼ cup plus 1 tablespoon extra-virgin olive oil
  Coarse salt and freshly ground pepper
- 5 sprigs flat-leaf parsley
- 5 sprigs thyme
- 1 dried bay leaf
- 1 tablespoon all-purpose flour
- ½ teaspoon paprika
- ½ teaspoon ground allspice
- 1 beef rump roast (3¼ to 3½ pounds)
- 4 medium leeks, white and pale-green parts only, halved lengthwise, sliced 1 inch thick crosswise, washed well and dried
- 3 garlic cloves, thinly sliced
- 1 cup dry red wine
- 2 tablespoons tomato paste
- 6 cups beef stock, preferably homemade (page 411)
- 6 large carrots, cut into 3-inch pieces

1 Preheat oven to 400°F. Place potatoes in a large roasting pan; toss with 3 tablespoons olive oil. Season with salt and pepper. Spread in an even layer. Roast until golden brown and crisp, 30 to 40 minutes. Remove pan from oven. Reduce heat to 350°F.

2 Bundle parsley, thyme, and bay leaf in a piece of cheesecloth; tie with kitchen twine. In a bowl, combine flour, paprika, and allspice; season with salt and pepper. Pat beef dry; sprinkle with flour mixture, patting to coat.

3 In a large Dutch oven (about 7 quarts), heat remaining 2 tablespoons olive oil over medium until hot but not smoking. Sear roast on all sides until golden brown, about 2 minutes per side. Transfer to a plate.

4 Reduce heat to medium-low. Add leeks and garlic; cook, stirring occasionally, until leeks are just softened, about 3 minutes. Add wine and bring to a boil; deglaze pan, scraping up any browned bits from the bottom with a wooden spoon. Cook until most of the wine has evaporated. Add tomato paste and cook until caramelized, about 1 minute. Add herb bundle and reserved roast along with

any accumulated juices, and the beef stock. Cover and transfer to oven; cook 30 minutes. Turn over roast and cook 30 minutes more.

5 Add carrots, cover, and cook 1½ hours, turning over roast every 30 minutes. Add potatoes, submerging them halfway in the liquid (so they turn crisp yet tender). Return pan to oven and cook (uncovered) to let some liquid evaporate, about 30 minutes more. Season with salt and pepper.

6 Transfer roast to a carving board and let rest 5 minutes before removing string and slicing meat. Serve with vegetables and pan gravy on the side.

SERVES 6 TO 8

ALL-AMERICAN

BACKSTORY

We have mothers to thank for pot roast—generations of women who fed their families on a budget. Long, slow braising allowed these frugal cooks to transform inexpensive cuts of meat and basic root vegetables into feasts fit for Sunday dinner. If unexpected guests showed up, Mom could always throw in a few more potatoes and carrots to stretch the meal. This delectable dish long ago outgrew its association with large families and thrift, however. On a chilly day, it is simply more appealing than many other possibilities, no matter how fancy. Pot roasting involves browning the beef and then cooking it in a covered pot with a small amount of liquid. This moist cooking process transforms collagen (the connective tissue that can make meat tough) into gelatin, thereby tenderizing the beef. For this reason, inexpensive cuts with high collagen content, such as chuck and rump roasts, are best; higher grade meats that perform well when broiled, grilled, or quickly oven-roasted would dry out with this method. When shopping, tell the butcher you are making pot roast, and he will guide you to an appropriate piece of meat. And ask him to tie the roast; this will keep it from falling apart as it cooks. Pot roast should be so meltingly tender that you can cut it with a fork. And the whole meal is prepared in a single vessel, so the vegetables—potatoes and carrots are used here, but turnips and pearl onions are other good options— cook in the meat juices. Moreover, the flavors of pot roast are even better the next day, especially in a sandwich.

MACARONI AND CHEESE

A recipe for a casserole of macaroni, white sauce, and grated yellow cheese was recorded in the Boston Cooking School Cookbook *in 1896, and Americans have enjoyed this homespun classic ever since. When Kraft introduced its macaroni and cheese dinner in 1937 as a way to market processed American cheese and Tenderoni pasta, it quickly swept the nation, and boxed and frozen varieties became a staple of the national diet. Today, learning to make this dish completely from scratch is well worth your time. To begin, you need to make a béchamel (white sauce) of melted butter, flour, and milk, which thickens on the stovetop, and then cheese and seasonings are stirred in. A combination of pungent cheeses, such as sharp white cheddar mixed with Gruyère or pecorino romano, provides the best balance of flavors. Undercook the pasta so that it retains a slight crunch in the center (it will become tender as it bakes), then rinse under cold water to stop the cooking. Finally, toss the pasta with the cheese sauce, and finish with an even layer of buttered breadcrumbs. The sum of all these disparate parts bakes into a truly memorable dish with a crisp, browned top that contrasts beautifully with the creamy molten center. Nothing from a boxed mix can hold a candle to that.*

½ cup (1 stick) unsalted butter, plus more, softened, for baking dish

6 slices good-quality white bread, trimmed of crusts and torn into ¼- to ½-inch pieces

5½ cups milk

½ cup all-purpose flour

2 teaspoons coarse salt

¼ teaspoon freshly grated nutmeg

¼ teaspoon freshly ground pepper

¼ teaspoon cayenne, or to taste

4½ cups grated sharp white cheddar (about 1¼ pounds)

2 cups grated Gruyère (about 8 ounces)

1 pound elbow macaroni

1 Preheat oven to 375°F. Butter a 3-quart casserole dish. Place bread in a medium bowl. Melt 2 tablespoons butter in a small saucepan over medium heat; pour into bowl with bread, and toss to coat.

2 Heat milk in a medium saucepan over medium. Melt remaining 6 tablespoons butter in a high-sided skillet over medium heat. Add flour to make a roux, and cook, stirring, 1 minute (do not let brown). While whisking, gradually pour in hot milk. Continue cooking, whisking constantly, until the mixture bubbles and thickens. Remove the pan from heat. Stir in salt, nutmeg, pepper, cayenne, 3 cups cheddar, and 1½ cups Gruyère.

3 Cook the pasta in a large pot of boiling water 2 to 3 minutes less than the manufacturer's directions. Drain macaroni, rinse under cold running water, and drain again. Stir macaroni into cheese sauce.

4 Pour mixture into prepared dish. Sprinkle evenly with remaining 1½ cups cheddar and ½ cup Gruyère, then top with bread pieces. Bake until heated through and topping is browned, about 30 minutes. Transfer to a wire rack to cool 5 minutes before serving.

SERVES 10 TO 12

CLASSIC POTATO SALAD

4 pounds russet potatoes (about 8 medium)

Coarse salt

3 tablespoons cider vinegar

3 large eggs

1 cup mayonnaise

½ teaspoon celery seeds

1 teaspoon dry mustard powder

½ teaspoon freshly ground pepper

3 celery stalks, cut into ¼-inch dice

1 small onion, cut into ¼-inch dice

10 cornichons, cut into ¼-inch dice

3 scallions, trimmed and thinly sliced

2 tablespoons coarsely chopped fresh flat-leaf parsley

1 teaspoon sweet paprika

1 In a large saucepan, cover potatoes with water by several inches. Bring to a boil, then add 1 tablespoon salt. Reduce heat and gently boil until potatoes are tender when pierced with the tip of a sharp knife, about 25 minutes. Drain. Peel potatoes while still hot, using paper towels to protect hands; cut into 1-inch pieces. Transfer potatoes to a bowl and drizzle with vinegar; let cool.

2 Place eggs in a small saucepan; fill with enough cold water to cover by 1 inch. Bring to a boil; turn off heat. Cover; let stand 11 minutes. Transfer to a bowl and cover with cold water; let cool and peel. Cut 2 eggs into ¼-inch dice. Slice remaining egg into ¼-inch-thick rounds; reserve for garnish.

3 Combine diced eggs, mayonnaise, celery seeds, and dry mustard in a large bowl; season with salt and pepper, and whisk to combine. Stir in potatoes, celery, onion, cornichons, scallions, and parsley. Refrigerate at least 30 minutes or up to 1 day. Just before serving, garnish with paprika and egg rounds.

SERVES 10 TO 12

ALL-AMERICAN

BACKSTORY

Part of the charm of a picnic is its informality, whether you are in a sunny glade or right in your own backyard. No matter where you are, you want something to eat that isn't difficult to make, that travels well, and that tastes— and looks—great some hours after it's prepared. Sandwiches made with thick, crusty bread fit the bill nicely, as does cold fried chicken. But what people tend to indulge in most are the sides. "I can't remember the last time I had homemade coleslaw!" someone will say. "I need your recipe for three-bean salad," someone else will ask. "It's the best I've ever had." (Chalk one up for its distinctive mustardy dressing.) The only quiet one in the bunch, you will notice, is on his third helping of potato salad. In short, you should keep the following three recipes in heavy rotation at all times. And remember to make lots.

THREE-BEAN SALAD

8 ounces green beans, stem ends removed, halved on the diagonal

4 ounces wax beans, stem ends removed, halved on the diagonal

2 tablespoons Dijon mustard

2 tablespoons red-wine vinegar

2 tablespoons olive oil

Coarse salt and freshly ground pepper

1 can (15.5 ounces) kidney beans, drained and rinsed

1 Prepare an ice-water bath. Fill a large pot with 2 inches of water; set a steamer basket (or colander) inside. Bring to a boil. Place green and wax beans in basket; reduce heat to a simmer. Cover pot and steam until beans are bright and crisp-tender, 6 to 8 minutes. With tongs or a slotted spoon, transfer beans to the ice bath to stop the cooking, then drain.

2 In a medium bowl, whisk together mustard, vinegar, and olive oil; season with salt and pepper. Add steamed beans and kidney beans; toss to coat. (Bean salad can be refrigerated, covered, up to 1 day; bring to room temperature before serving.)

SERVES 4

CREAMY COLESLAW

1 tablespoon Dijon mustard

1 tablespoon cider vinegar

1 tablespoon fresh lemon juice

1 tablespoon sugar

½ cup mayonnaise

¼ cup sour cream

Coarse salt

1 small green cabbage (about 1¾ pounds), finely shredded

2 carrots, cut into ⅛-inch-thick matchsticks or coarsely grated

½ small onion, coarsely grated (optional)

1 Whisk together mustard, vinegar, lemon juice, sugar, mayonnaise, and sour cream in a small bowl; season with salt. Cover and refrigerate dressing until ready to use, up to 2 days.

2 Combine cabbage, carrots, and onion (if using) in a large bowl. Pour in dressing, and toss thoroughly to coat. Refrigerate, covered, until slaw begins to soften, 1 to 2 hours or up to 2 days. Before serving, toss coleslaw again.

SERVES 6 TO 8

THREE-BEAN SALAD

CREAMY COLESLAW

GREEN BEAN CASSEROLE

6 tablespoons unsalted butter, plus more, softened, for baking dish

1 onion, cut into ¼-inch dice

1 pound button mushrooms, stems trimmed, quartered

Coarse salt and freshly ground pepper

1½ pounds green beans, trimmed and cut into 2-inch pieces

¼ cup plus 2 tablespoons all-purpose flour

2 cups milk

Pinch of cayenne

Pinch of freshly grated nutmeg

1 cup grated parmesan (3 ounces)

¼ cup breadcrumbs

½ cup neutral-tasting oil, such as safflower

3 shallots, cut crosswise into ⅛-inch rings

1 In a large skillet, melt 2 tablespoons butter over medium heat. Sauté onion, stirring occasionally, until it begins to soften, about 4 minutes. Add mushrooms and cook until softened and most of the liquid has evaporated, stirring occasionally, about 8 minutes. Season with salt and pepper. Let cool.

2 Prepare an ice-water bath. Bring a large saucepan of water to a boil; add 1 tablespoon salt. Blanch beans until bright and just tender, 4 to 5 minutes. Drain; plunge into ice bath. Drain beans; toss with mushroom mixture.

3 In a medium saucepan over medium heat, melt the remaining 4 tablespoons butter. Add ¼ cup flour, and whisk constantly until mixture begins to turn golden, 2 to 3 minutes. Whisking constantly, gradually pour in milk, and continue whisking until mixture has thickened, about 3 minutes. Stir in cayenne and nutmeg, and season with salt and pepper. Let cool completely, stirring occasionally. Pour over bean mixture; toss to combine.

4 Preheat oven to 375°F. Butter a 2-quart glass or ceramic baking dish. Spread half the bean mixture over the bottom. Sprinkle with half the parmesan, and layer with remaining green beans. Combine the remaining parmesan and the breadcrumbs, and sprinkle on top. Cover casserole with foil and bake until mixture is bubbly and heated through, about 55 minutes. Uncover and cook until top is golden brown, about 15 minutes more.

5 Meanwhile, heat oil in a medium skillet over medium-high. Toss shallot rings with remaining 2 tablespoons flour; fry in batches, turning frequently, until golden brown. Using a slotted spatula, transfer to paper towels to drain.

6 Once casserole has finished baking, remove from oven; top with shallots and let cool slightly before serving.

SERVES 8

ALL-AMERICAN

BACKSTORY

Created by the Campbell's Soup test kitchen in 1955 as a way to promote its cream soups, green bean casserole grew wildly popular, and eventually became an essential part of a Thanksgiving spread for many American families. The original recipe called for just five ingredients, most of which were commercially packaged and readily available: canned green beans, cream of mushroom soup, milk, soy sauce, and fried onions in a can. Like all nostalgic dishes, the recipe can be tinkered with just so much, lest the outcome be too different from the one fondly remembered. Here, fresh green beans and mushrooms, a simple white sauce that holds everything together, and a topping of quick-fried shallots create a flavorful update that nevertheless manages to honor the original. The casserole can be assembled up to two days ahead, then topped with parmesan and breadcrumbs before baking; keep, covered, in the refrigerator until ready to cook.

CHOCOLATE CHIP COOKIES

2¾ cups all-purpose flour

1¼ teaspoons salt

1 teaspoon baking powder

1 teaspoon baking soda

1¼ cups (2½ sticks) unsalted butter, softened

¾ cup granulated sugar

1¼ cups dark-brown sugar

2 large eggs

1 teaspoon pure vanilla extract

1½ cups semisweet chocolate chips

1 Preheat oven to 350°F, with racks in upper and lower thirds. Sift together flour, salt, baking powder, and baking soda into a medium bowl.

2 With an electric mixer on medium speed, cream butter with both sugars until fluffy. Add eggs, one at a time, then vanilla, beating until combined and scraping down sides of bowl as needed. Reduce speed to low. Add flour mixture; mix until just combined. Mix in chocolate chips just to distribute evenly.

3 Using a 1½-inch ice cream scoop, drop dough onto parchment-lined baking sheets, about 2 inches apart. Bake, rotating sheets halfway through, until cookies are golden around the edges but still soft in the middle, about 15 minutes. Let cool on sheets 5 minutes, then transfer to wire racks to cool completely. (Cookies can be stored up to 3 days at room temperature in airtight containers.)

MAKES ABOUT 3 DOZEN

ALL-AMERICAN

BACKSTORY

Cookies are not an American invention. Indeed, "American" cookies bear the imprint of many cultures, and most would be called "biscuits" in Europe. Yet cookies are certainly American in spirit, particularly the all-stars pictured opposite. In general, our cookies tend to be sweeter than their European counterparts, with a truly democratic variety of textures—crisp, crumbly, chunky, nutty, chewy, or cakey. These distinctions— and the preferences of home bakers for one texture over another—have led to the creation of untold numbers of cookies in America over the course of our history. Of all the varieties that have been developed over many years in the test kitchens at Martha Stewart Living, *these four (including brownies, the quintessential bar cookie) are continually requested, searched for, baked, and enjoyed by millions. There are no newfangled interpretations or clever twists here—just pure and simple recipes for the cookies that all Americans seem to love most.*

PEANUT BUTTER COOKIES

CHOCOLATE CHIP COOKIES

OATMEAL RAISIN COOKIES

OATMEAL RAISIN COOKIES

    3   cups old-fashioned rolled oats
        (not instant or quick-cooking)
    1   cup plus 2 tablespoons all-purpose flour
   ½   cup toasted wheat germ
    1   teaspoon baking soda
    1   teaspoon baking powder
   ½   teaspoon ground cinnamon
   ½   teaspoon salt
    1   cup (2 sticks) unsalted butter, softened
    1   cup granulated sugar
    1   cup packed light-brown sugar
    2   large eggs
    1   teaspoon pure vanilla extract
   1½   cups raisins

1 Preheat oven to 350°F, with racks in upper and lower thirds. Whisk together oats, flour, wheat germ, baking soda, baking powder, cinnamon, and salt in a large bowl.

2 With an electric mixer on medium speed, cream butter and both sugars until fluffy. Mix in eggs and vanilla, beating until combined and scraping down sides of bowl as needed. Reduce speed to low. Add oat mixture; mix until just combined. Mix in raisins just to distribute evenly.

3 Using a 1½-inch ice cream scoop, drop dough onto parchment-lined baking sheets, about 2 inches apart. Bake, rotating sheets halfway through, until cookies are golden and just set, 12 to 14 minutes. Let cool on sheets 5 minutes, then transfer cookies to wire racks to cool completely. (Cookies can be stored up to 3 days at room temperature in airtight containers.)

MAKES ABOUT 5 DOZEN

PEANUT BUTTER COOKIES

   2½   cups all-purpose flour
   1½   teaspoons baking soda
   ½   teaspoon salt
    1   cup (2 sticks) unsalted butter, softened
    1   cup granulated sugar
    1   cup packed light-brown sugar
    2   large eggs
   1½   cups smooth peanut butter

1 Preheat oven to 350°F. Whisk together the flour, baking soda, and salt in a medium bowl.

2 With an electric mixer on medium speed, cream butter and both sugars until fluffy. Mix in eggs, then peanut butter, scraping down sides of bowl as needed. Reduce speed to low. Add flour mixture in three batches, mixing until just combined after each addition. Cover with plastic wrap and refrigerate 30 minutes.

3 Using a 1½-inch ice cream scoop, drop dough onto parchment-lined baking sheets, about 1½ inches apart. Press dough with fork tines to flatten and create a crosshatch pattern. Bake, rotating sheets halfway through, until cookies are golden brown, about 15 minutes. Let cool on sheets 5 minutes, then transfer cookies to wire racks to cool completely. (Cookies can be stored up to 3 days at room temperature in airtight containers.)

MAKES ABOUT 4 DOZEN

BROWNIES

½ cup (1 stick) unsalted butter, cut into pieces

6 ounces bittersweet chocolate, finely chopped

1½ cups sugar

3 large eggs

¼ cup unsweetened cocoa powder

½ teaspoon salt

½ cup plus 2 tablespoons all-purpose flour, sifted

1 Preheat oven to 350°F. Line an 8-inch baking pan with parchment, leaving an overhang on all sides. Combine butter and chocolate in a heatproof bowl set over (not in) a pan of simmering water; stir occasionally until melted and smooth.

2 Remove bowl from heat and whisk in sugar. Add eggs, one at a time, whisking until incorporated. Whisk in cocoa and salt. Add flour and fold in with a flexible spatula until just combined.

3 Pour batter into prepared baking pan. Bake until set and a cake tester inserted in the center comes out with just a few moist crumbs attached, 35 to 40 minutes. Transfer the pan to a wire rack and let cool about 15 minutes. Using the paper overhang, lift brownies from the pan and let cool completely on the rack before cutting into 2-inch squares. (Brownies can be stored up to 3 days at room temperature in an airtight container.)

MAKES 8

ICED SUGAR COOKIES

  4 cups all-purpose flour, plus more for surface
  1 teaspoon baking powder
  ½ teaspoon coarse salt
  2 sticks unsalted butter, softened
  2 cups sugar
  2 large eggs
  2 teaspoons pure vanilla extract
     Royal Icing (page 414; leave two-thirds of icing white,
     divide remaining icing in half and tint one half using gel-paste
     food coloring in Red Red and tint other half using both
     Royal Blue and Navy Blue gel-paste)

1 Sift flour, baking powder, and salt into a large bowl.

2 Beat butter and sugar with a mixer on medium-high speed until pale and fluffy, about 3 minutes. Beat in eggs, 1 at a time. Reduce speed to low. Add flour mixture, then vanilla. Refrigerate dough, wrapped in plastic wrap, for at least 1 hour. (Cookie dough can be refrigerated for up to 5 days or frozen for up to 1 month; thaw before using.)

3 Preheat oven to 325°F. Roll out dough to a scant ¼-inch thickness on a floured surface. Cut out cookies using 1¾-, 2¼-, 2¾-, or 3½-inch round cookie cutters, rerolling scraps once. Transfer to a baking sheet. Refrigerate until firm, about 30 minutes.

4 Bake until edges just start to brown, 17 to 19 minutes. Transfer cookies to a wire rack, and let cool completely.

5 To decorate the cookies, pipe an outline of white icing around edge of one cookie, leaving a ¼-inch border, then "flood" with more white icing to cover. Immediately pipe a red or blue dot in the center of cookie. Then pipe concentric rings of colors around the center dot (using the same color as the dot, or alternating colors).

6 Working quickly, drag a toothpick through the colors to create bursts, starting from the center dot and working toward the edge, then alternate dragging inward and outward as you work around the cookie. (Or drag around the cookie in one direction or curve the lines for a pinwheel effect.) Let dry. Repeat with remaining cookies and icings. Decorated cookies can be stored in an airtight container at room temperature up to 3 days.

MAKES ABOUT 7 DOZEN 1¾-INCH COOKIES, 5 DOZEN 2¼-INCH COOKIES, THIRTY 2¾-INCH COOKIES, OR THIRTEEN 3½-INCH COOKIES

ALL-AMERICAN

BACKSTORY

Iced sugar cookies occupy a well-deserved spot in the American cookie jar. Their rolled-and-cut-out profile offers a blank canvas on which to decorate shapes for nearly any occasion, any time of year. I have a huge variety of cookie cutters and am forever adding new shapes from cookware stores, catalogs, or antiques shops. Even so, I sometimes make my own cookie shapes by cutting out cardboard forms, then cutting cookie dough around them. Because the dough calls for basic pantry ingredients and comes together quickly, it's a home baker's dream. Chilling (first after mixing, then again after cutting into shapes) is essential, as it leads to easier rolling and cutting, and helps the dough retain its shape as it bakes. The cookies are just plain wonderful—and simplest—when sprinkled with colorful sanding sugars before or after baking. But they become truly spectacular when given the royal-icing treatment, such as patriotic red-white-and-blue bursts— achieved with a squeeze bottle and a toothpick—that adorn the Fourth of July ones shown here. Of course, the cookies can be cut into shapes other than round, and decorated to suit other holidays or special occasions— or your personal whim.

STRAWBERRIES

At their best, they have a deep sweetness and a beguiling aroma—in fact, their genus name is derived from the Latin word *fragrans*, or "fragrant." The large scarlet strawberry we are all familiar with today is actually the progeny of an accidental cross between Chilean and Virginian varieties that took place in an eighteenth-century French garden. It inherited its large size from the Chilean berry and its brilliant color, bright flavor, and hardy nature from the Virginia berry. In America, commercial cultivation of these modern strawberries began in the mid-nineteenth century, and today, they are grown in all fifty states. California farmers, who can harvest almost year-round, dominate much of the country's crop.

Because they don't sweeten after harvest, strawberries must be picked fully ripe for the best flavor; they are also sweeter after ripening during hot, sunny days. That's why your best bet is to buy from farmers' markets, in season. If you can find organic strawberries, snap them up: conventional varieties are among the fruits most contaminated by pesticides, and washing merely reduces (rather than eliminates) the residue.

At some farmers' markets, you may even find what are known in France as *fraises des bois, or* "strawberries of the woods." (Or even better, grow them yourself.) They are tiny and more intensely fragrant than cultivated strawberries. Once picked, eat them as soon as you possibly can—they are very fragile and their perfume fades quickly. No matter what kind of strawberries you choose, let your nose be your guide—the rich, intoxicating scent of ripe fruit is what you're after.

And no matter how you plan to serve the berries, let the fruit speak for itself. Because some varieties are low in acid, they pair well with acidic ingredients, such as a spritz of lemon juice and even a drizzle of good-quality balsamic vinegar. Don't fuss, in other words, and you'll find even the most basic desserts—such as old-fashioned strawberry shortcake or a bowl of strawberry ice cream—to be as welcome as the warmth of a sunny day.

STRAWBERRIES AND CREAM A bowl of plump, ripe strawberries doused with cream makes an unexpectedly elegant dessert (or a delectable breakfast). Buy strawberries that are bright red (with no white or green at the stem end), fragrant, and plump, with no soft spots. If using right away, it's best not to refrigerate them. Otherwise, lay the berries flat on a paper towel–lined plate and refrigerate for up to two days. Just before using, wash berries, then hull: Hold a berry in one hand and with the other hand, insert the tip of a paring knife, slightly angled toward the center, close to the leaves. Gently cut all the way around; pull out the stem end and core. Halve or quarter any large ones and place in a bowl. Pour heavy cream over and serve.

STRAWBERRY SHORTCAKE

FOR THE BERRIES

2   pints fresh strawberries, rinsed and hulled

    Juice of 1 lemon

¼   cup sugar

FOR THE BISCUITS

2   cups all-purpose flour, plus more for dusting

¼   cup plus 2 tablespoons sugar

1   tablespoon baking powder

½   teaspoon salt

6   tablespoons cold unsalted butter, cut into small pieces

1   cup plus 1 tablespoon heavy cream

1   large egg

FOR SERVING

½   cup cold heavy cream

ALL-AMERICAN

BACKSTORY

Strawberry shortcake is often cited as the single most popular dessert across the country, and for good reason. The combination of sugared fresh fruit, sweet biscuit, and whipped cream makes for a delightful jumble of contrasting tastes, textures, and flavors in every spoonful. The recipe can be adapted to use any summer fruits at their glorious peak, including stone fruits (peaches, apricots, plums, or cherries) or other berries, or try a combination of both, such as nectarines and blackberries.

1 Prepare the berries: Toss the strawberries with lemon juice and sugar to combine. Let macerate at room temperature 1 hour.

2 Meanwhile, make the biscuits: Preheat oven to 375°F. Whisk to combine flour, sugar, baking powder, and salt in a medium bowl. Using a pastry blender or two knives, cut the butter into the flour mixture until mixture resembles coarse meal. Add 1 cup cream and stir with a fork just until dough starts to come together but is still crumbly.

3 Turn out dough onto a lightly floured surface and pat into a rough 6-inch square, about 1 inch thick. With a 2½-inch round cutter dipped in flour, cut four biscuits from dough and place them, evenly spaced, on a parchment-lined baking sheet. Gather dough scraps together, fold once, and gently pat into a rectangle; cut out two more biscuits. Whisk egg and remaining 1 tablespoon cream, then brush egg wash over tops of dough rounds.

4 Bake until tops are golden brown, rotating sheet halfway through, about 25 minutes. Transfer biscuits to a wire rack and let cool slightly.

5 When ready to serve, whip cream in a chilled bowl until soft peaks form. Split biscuits in half, and place a bottom half on each plate. Top generously with berries and their juice, then with remaining biscuit halves and dollops of whipped cream. Scatter a few more strawberries on top and around each plate.

SERVES 6

YELLOW LAYER CAKE

　1　cup (2 sticks) unsalted butter, softened, plus more for pans
1½　cups all-purpose flour, plus more for pans
1½　cups cake flour (not self-rising)
　1　tablespoon baking powder
　½　teaspoon salt
1¾　cups sugar
　4　large eggs
　2　teaspoons pure vanilla extract
1¼　cups milk
　　　Chocolate Frosting (page 414)

1 Preheat oven to 350°F. Butter two 8-by-2-inch round cake pans; line bottoms with parchment. Butter parchment and dust with flour; tap out excess. Sift together flours, baking powder, and salt into a medium bowl.

2 With an electric mixer on medium speed, cream the butter and sugar until pale and fluffy, scraping down sides of bowl as needed. Beat in eggs, one at a time, then beat in vanilla. With the mixer on low speed, add the flour mixture in three batches, alternating with the milk and beginning and ending with the flour; beat until combined after each addition.

3 Divide batter between prepared pans and smooth with an offset spatula. Bake, rotating pans halfway through, until tops are golden brown and a cake tester inserted in the centers comes out clean, 30 to 35 minutes. Let cool in pans on a wire rack for 20 minutes. Run a knife around edges of cakes to loosen and turn out cakes onto rack. Let cool completely, top side up.

4 Using a serrated knife, trim tops of cakes to make level. Split each cake horizontally to make four layers total. Place one of the bottom layers on a serving platter and spread with frosting. Place another cake layer on top; spread with frosting. Repeat with another cake layer and more frosting, then place remaining cake layer on top. Spread entire cake with a thin layer of frosting (called a "crumb coat"); refrigerate until firm, about 30 minutes. Spread with a final layer of frosting in a swirling fashion. Refrigerate cake at least 1 hour before slicing. (Cake can be made up to 3 days ahead. Cover and refrigerate; let sit at room temperature before slicing and serving.)

SERVES 8 TO 10

ALL-AMERICAN

BACKSTORY

Close your eyes and imagine a picture-perfect cake, and surely one of the following beauties comes to mind: each consists of layers of rich moist cake filled and generously covered with thick frosting. These cakes represent a real departure from the tradition of cake baking inherited from the Europeans, who relied on whipped egg whites to lend loft to more demure sponge cakes and who used glazes to moisten the airy layers. With the advent of chemical leaveners, American bakers could increase the amount of butter in their cakes and still get a glorious lift—resulting in a new kind of cake with ultra-moist layers. "Butter cakes," such as the ever-popular yellow layered example (opposite), quickly became the American standard, one that is easily adapted to feature other flavors. Just consider carrot cake surrounded by cream cheese frosting, and coconut cake iced with billowy seven-minute frosting; their appeal is all too apparent and impossible to resist. Some people prefer the cake part, others the frosting, but all agree that each is improved by its proximity to the other. Consider these the only three birthday cake recipes you'll ever need—no matter how big your family may be.

CARROT CAKE

1½ cups (3 sticks) unsalted butter, softened, plus more for pans

2½ cups all-purpose flour, plus more for pans

1 teaspoon baking powder

1 teaspoon baking soda

1 teaspoon ground cinnamon

¾ teaspoon coarse salt

½ teaspoon ground ginger

¼ teaspoon freshly grated nutmeg

1 cup packed light-brown sugar

½ cup granulated sugar

3 large eggs

2 teaspoons pure vanilla extract

½ cup water

1 pound carrots (8 to 10 medium), peeled and shredded on a box grater or in a food processor (about 2¾ cups)

2 cups pecans (8 ounces): 1 cup finely chopped for batter, 1 cup coarsely chopped for decorating cake

Cream Cheese Frosting (recipe follows)

1 Preheat oven to 350°F. Butter three 9-inch round cake pans. Line with parchment. Butter parchment and dust with flour; tap out excess. Whisk together flour, baking powder, baking soda, cinnamon, salt, ginger, and nutmeg in a medium bowl.

2 With an electric mixer on medium speed, cream butter and both sugars until fluffy. Add eggs, one at a time, beating well after each addition. Beat 3 minutes more. Add vanilla, the water, and carrots; beat until well combined, about 2 minutes. Reduce speed to low and add flour mixture, then finely chopped pecans, beating just until combined.

3 Divide batter evenly among prepared pans. Bake until tops are golden brown and a cake tester inserted into centers comes out clean, about 30 minutes. Let cool in pans on a wire rack 15 minutes. Run a knife around edges of cakes to loosen and turn out cakes onto rack. Let cool completely, top side up.

4 Using a serrated knife, trim tops of two cakes to make level. Place one trimmed cake, cut side up, on a serving platter. Spread 1 cup frosting over cake. Top with second trimmed cake, cut side down. Spread 1 cup frosting over cake. Top with remaining cake. Spread remaining frosting over top and sides. Gently press coarsely chopped pecans onto sides of cake. Refrigerate 1 hour or up to 1 day (covered), before serving.

SERVES 8 TO 10

CREAM CHEESE FROSTING

16 ounces cream cheese, softened

2 teaspoons pure vanilla extract

1 cup (2 sticks) unsalted butter, cut into small pieces, softened

2 pounds confectioners' sugar, sifted

1 With an electric mixer on medium speed, beat cream cheese and vanilla until creamy. Gradually add butter, beating until incorporated after each addition before adding more.

2 Reduce speed to low. Gradually add confectioners' sugar and beat until fluffy and smooth. (Frosting can be refrigerated in an airtight container up to 2 days; bring to room temperature and stir well before using.)

MAKES ABOUT 4½ CUPS

COCONUT CAKE

1½ cups (3 sticks) unsalted butter, softened, plus more for pans

3½ cups all-purpose flour, plus more for pans

1 tablespoon plus 1 teaspoon baking powder

1 teaspoon salt

2 cups packed sweetened shredded coconut

2⅓ cups sugar

4 large whole eggs, plus 4 large egg whites

3 teaspoons pure vanilla extract

1½ cups canned unsweetened coconut milk
Seven-Minute Frosting (recipe follows)

1 Preheat oven to 350°F. Butter two 9-inch round cake pans, then dust with flour and tap out excess. Sift together flour, baking powder, and salt into a large bowl. Pulse 1 cup coconut in a food processor until finely chopped; stir coconut into flour mixture.

2 With an electric mixer on medium speed, cream butter and sugar until light and fluffy, about 4 minutes. Add whole eggs, whites, and vanilla; beat until fully incorporated. Add flour mixture in three batches, alternating with the coconut milk and starting with the flour; beat until combined after each addition.

3 Divide batter evenly between prepared pans. Bake until golden brown and a cake tester inserted in the centers comes out clean, about 35 minutes. Let cool in pans on a wire rack 30 minutes. Run a knife around edges of cakes to loosen and turn out cakes onto rack. Let cool completely, top side up.

4 Using a serrated knife, trim tops of cake layers to make level, if desired. Transfer one layer to a serving platter and spread top with 1½ cups frosting. Place other cake layer on top. Using an offset spatula, spread remaining frosting over entire cake, swirling to completely cover. Sprinkle evenly with remaining 1 cup coconut.

SERVES 8 TO 10

SEVEN-MINUTE FROSTING

1¾ cups sugar

2 tablespoons light corn syrup

¼ cup water

6 large egg whites

1 teaspoon pure vanilla extract

1 In a small, heavy-bottomed saucepan, cook 1½ cups sugar, the corn syrup, and water over medium heat, stirring constantly, until sugar has dissolved, about 4 minutes. Raise heat; bring to a boil without stirring, washing down sides of pan with a pastry brush dipped in water to prevent crystals from forming. Continue cooking until a candy thermometer registers 230°F, about 5 minutes.

2 Meanwhile, with an electric mixer on medium speed, whisk egg whites until soft peaks form, 2 to 3 minutes. Gradually add remaining ¼ cup sugar. Reduce speed to medium-low. When syrup has reached 230°F, remove from heat; with mixer on low, carefully pour syrup in a steady stream down side of bowl. Continue beating on medium speed until frosting is completely cool, thick, and shiny, about 7 minutes. Beat in vanilla. Use immediately.

MAKES ABOUT 8 CUPS

APPLES

It's sometimes easy to forget that the things we eat all the time became popular because they are so extraordinary. Anyone who needs reminding of that should take one bite of a freshly picked apple on a brisk autumn day.

Apples—for many, an American icon—have actually been adored around the globe for millennia. More than three thousand years ago, Pharaoh Ramses II had orchards on the Nile; in ancient Greece, a young man could propose marriage by tossing an apple to his intended; and in 1665, an apple falling from a tree in England assured Sir Isaac Newton a place in history.

The Pilgrims brought both apple cuttings and seeds to America because the trees were easy to care for and prodigious in their yields, making apples plentiful and affordable when other sweet things were a luxury. Apple pies were served as often as bread—at breakfast, lunch, and dinner—and cider was consumed year-round by virtually every man, woman, and child. Soon, Johnny Appleseed's uniquely American travels, too, became the stuff of legend.

Today, apples are grown in nearly every state. The three biggest producers—Washington, New York, and Michigan—are filled with orchards of scrubby dark brown trees. In the spring, their branches disappear in a cloud of pale pink blossoms; in autumn, they are heavy with deep red Winesap, pale yellow Golden Delicious, and bright green Granny Smith. On your next trip to a farmers' market or roadside stand, try some varieties you haven't tasted before. First-rate eating apples include Empire, Macoun, McIntosh, Northern Spy, Gala, Fuji, Jonathan, and Winesap because they are especially crisp and juicy. For baking in a double-crusted pie, try Rome (sometimes called Rome Beauty), Cortland, Winesap, or Granny Smith, which maintain their flavor and hold their shape even after being exposed to high heat. For applesauce, think about combining two or more apple varieties; you will get a more complex blend of sweetness and tartness that way.

Happily, many growers are nurturing old-fashioned, or "heirloom," varieties and are also developing new ones—such as the Honeycrisp, released in 1991. There is more flavor than ever within reach, so bite into an apple and see for yourself.

CINNAMON APPLESAUCE Once you've tasted homemade applesauce, there's no going back to store-bought versions. Peel and core 3 pounds Granny Smith apples, then cut into 1/2-inch pieces. In a large saucepan, bring apples, 1 cinnamon stick, 1/4 cup sugar, 3/4 cup water, and a pinch of coarse salt to a boil. Reduce heat; cover and simmer, stirring occasionally, until apples are very tender, about 30 minutes. (If sauce begins to stick to bottom of pan, add 2 or 3 more tablespoons water.) Remove from heat and discard cinnamon stick. Stir in 2 teaspoons fresh lemon juice. Mash apples with the back of a spoon for smoother sauce, if desired. Serve warm, room temperature, or chilled. (Applesauce will keep in the refrigerator up to 1 week in an airtight container; cool completely before storing.)
MAKES 1¾ CUPS

MILE-HIGH APPLE PIE

ALL-AMERICAN

BACKSTORY

No dessert quite says "all-American" like a golden brown, perfectly flaky, double-crust apple pie. In fact, even though I enjoy all kinds of desserts, I think I prefer a slice of a delicious pie over anything else. I not only love eating pies, I also love making the crusts, the fillings, and the toppings and baking them to perfection. And more than any other recipe, I love to prepare this one. It has almost twice as many apples as most pie recipes, and its sheer height makes it one of the most impressive things you can prepare in a home kitchen and bring to the table. I can't think of a better way to end a Thanksgiving meal—or any other celebratory occasion. A combination of apples produces a pie with the best flavor; some of my favorite varieties are Empire, Granny Smith, Cortland, and Macoun. This pie is best eaten (with a scoop of vanilla ice cream) the day after baking it, when the juices have had time to thicken properly.

¼ cup plus 2 tablespoons all-purpose flour, plus more for dusting

1 recipe Basic Pie Dough (page 412; Mile-High Pie variation)

5½ pounds firm tart apples (about 16), such as Jonagold, Mutsu, or Granny Smith

Juice of 2 lemons

1 cup granulated sugar

2 teaspoons ground cinnamon

3 tablespoons cold unsalted butter, cut into small pieces

1 large egg yolk

2 tablespoons water

Sanding or granulated sugar, for sprinkling

Vanilla Ice Cream (page 75), for serving (optional)

1 Preheat oven to 450°F. On a lightly floured work surface, roll out smaller of the two large disks of pie dough (for the bottom crust) into a 12-inch round, about ⅛ inch thick, dusting surface with flour as needed to prevent sticking. Brush off excess flour. Fit dough into a deep-dish 9-inch pie plate. Trim to a ¼-inch overhang; reserve trimmings. Cover with plastic wrap; refrigerate 30 minutes.

2 Meanwhile, roll out larger disk of dough (for the top crust) into a 14-inch round. Transfer to a parchment-lined baking sheet; cover with plastic wrap and refrigerate 30 minutes.

3 Peel and core apples and cut into ⅓-inch-thick slices. Place in a large bowl; sprinkle with lemon juice to prevent discoloration. In a small bowl, combine flour, granulated sugar, and cinnamon; add to apple slices and toss to coat.

4 Remove dough from refrigerator; place apple mixture in pie shell, mounding it into a tall pile. Dot filling with butter pieces. Whisk egg yolk with the water; using a pastry brush, lightly coat edge of dough with egg wash. Center and place other dough round over the apples; trim off edge of dough, if necessary. Tuck edge of top dough between bottom dough and rim of pan. Using your fingers, gently press both layers of dough along the edge to seal, and crimp as desired.

5 Using a paring knife, cut several steam vents in top of dough. Lightly brush surface with egg wash; sprinkle with sanding sugar. Place on a rimmed baking sheet and bake 10 minutes (crust will begin to turn golden).

6 Reduce oven to 350°F, rotate pie, and continue baking until crust is golden brown and juices are bubbling, about 1¼ hours (tent with foil if crust is turning too dark). Transfer to a wire rack to cool completely before serving, with ice cream if desired.

MAKES ONE DOUBLE-CRUST 9-INCH PIE

VANILLA ICE CREAM

2½ cups heavy cream

2   cups milk

8   large egg yolks

¾   cup sugar

¼   teaspoon salt

2   teaspoons pure vanilla extract

1 Prepare an ice-water bath. Heat cream and milk in a saucepan over medium until hot (do not let simmer).

2 With an electric mixer, beat egg yolks, sugar, and salt on high speed until mixture has tripled in volume and can hold a ribbon on surface for 2 seconds, about 3 minutes.Reduce speed to medium. Ladle 1 cup hot cream mixture in a slow stream into yolk mixture to temper it (which keeps yolks from curdling). Add another 1 cup cream mixture; beat to combine. Pour mixture into saucepan; cook over medium-high heat, stirring constantly, until it is thick enough to coat the back of a wooden spoon and an instant-read thermometer registers 180°F, 5 to 7 minutes. Pour custard through a medium-mesh sieve into a bowl set in the ice bath. Let cool completely, stirring often, then stir in vanilla.

3 Freeze custard in an ice-cream maker according to manufacturer's instructions. If not serving immediately, transfer to an airtight container and freeze until ready to serve. If frozen for more than 4 hours, let ice cream stand at room temperature 15 to 20 minutes before serving.

MAKES 1½ QUARTS

ALL-AMERICAN

BACKSTORY

Ice cream's wild popularity in America goes way back: George Washington owned an ice-cream maker, and Thomas Jefferson was another ardent fan. Apparently ice cream was always eaten with a spoon in those days; the ice cream cone didn't make its debut until the 1904 World's Fair in St. Louis. Our forefathers might well be astonished at the sheer number of ice-cream flavors now widely available, but vanilla remains America's favorite. In this age of convenience, making homemade batches of ice cream might sound as necessary as churning butter in your own kitchen. But ice cream can be made with surprisingly little effort, and the result is an incomparable, preservative-free treat. Old-fashioned, Philadelphia-style ice cream is the easiest of all: just stir together cream (and perhaps milk), sugar, vanilla, and salt, then freeze. But a stovetop custard base yields a rich taste and deeply luxurious texture (thanks in large part to the egg yolks). Like an artist's canvas, a good-quality vanilla ice cream provides a flawless base for any number of added ingredients—fruit, nuts, extracts, chocolate chips, or chopped candy, to name but a few (see the recipes on page 276 as examples). Vanilla ice cream is also the perfect partner for other desserts, melting onto a warm brownie or a slice of apple pie as though it were made just for them.

NORTHEAST

Blueberries, cranberries, maple syrup, lobsters, clams: the larder of the Northeast is as full of character as one of Winslow Homer's majestic seascapes or an image of a quaint New England village, complete with white-steepled church and pristine green.

Climate, geography, and immigration influenced the foodways of the Northeast, as they have everywhere else. But in many ways, this region is the cultural bedrock for our whole country. Native Americans introduced the early colonists to blueberries and cranberries, two of the few fruits that are indigenous to the region, as well as to their long-established trinity of beans, squash, and corn. Warm, molasses-spiked Indian pudding ("Indian meal" was the vernacular for cornmeal) is one of America's first desserts. Any pudding leftovers, heated up and drizzled with heavy cream, turn breakfast on a snowy morning into something deeply satisfying.

Brown bread, another very old dish (its origins trace to medieval times), is moist—almost pudding-like; it is an authentic hearth bread, once baked in the fireplace ashes before brick ovens were incorporated into New England farmhouses. It often serves as an accompaniment to baked beans, a regional culinary specialty that evolved from the stewed-bean-and-salted-meat dish called "pottage," a staple of the early settlers. New in comparison, but equally authentic, are Parker House rolls, created at Boston's Parker House Hotel in the 1870s. Simple rounds of dough brushed with butter and folded in half, they are easy to make yet elevate beef stew, roasted chicken—and yes, even baked beans—into very special meals.

By the mid-nineteenth century, New England fishermen were renowned the world over and the local economy revolved around their trade. Both fresh and preserved fish were a constant on family tables. The large Atlantic hard-shelled clams called quahogs (*KO-hogs*) have long been considered chowder clams, but they're ideal for stuffing as well. Cup one of these purple-splashed half-shells in your hand and know that the clam's scientific name, *Mercenaria mercenaria* ("wages"), was chosen because Native Americans made wampum out of them.

The clambake was slow to catch on with European settlers, but it eventually took on a symbolism all its own. Although people "from away" think of clambakes as being a Maine tradition, in fact you'll find "the real thing" in every New England state with a coastline. Ultra-traditionalists debate which clams are best and how to check the tenderness of the potatoes; family clambake masters carefully pass their secrets and techniques down to the next generation. And clever modern cooks have devised a way to re-create the experience—in flavor, at least—on the stovetop, so they can satisfy their clambake cravings no matter the time of year.

There is something about shoofly pie that conjures the Pennsylvania Dutch, the descendants of German and Swiss emigrants who settled much of Pennsylvania in the late eighteenth century. (The Amish are just one group in the larger "Dutch" community.) It entered the country's food scene at the American Centennial Exposition in Philadelphia in 1876 as Centennial Cake, and many variations evolved. The most common type, which has a wet, almost under-baked bottom, is considered a breakfast coffee cake in Pennsylvania Dutch country, although in other regions that tangy, sugary delight is preferred later in the day.

As shipping routes in the Northeast expanded, trading hubs like Philadelphia and New York City doubled and even tripled in size. Many of the workers who came there seeking the American Dream were from Italy and became pushcart vendors, food importers, or restaurateurs. It's quite impossible to imagine life without their culinary contributions to the region: a Philly cheesesteak piled high with grilled onions and peppers, for instance, or chicken parmigiana, a New World spin on an Old World dish. There is Yankee ingenuity at work there; you can bet your bottom quahog on it.

RECIPES

CAPE CODDER

BLOODY MARY

MANHATTAN

APPLE BRANDY COCKTAIL

DRINKS

CAPE CODDER

For a relative newcomer, the Cape Codder has a tangled family history. The New England cocktail harks back to a rum and cranberry-juice drink of the 1940s called the Cape Cod Collins, inspired by the cranberry bogs that dot coastal southeastern Massachusetts. In the mid-1960s, the people at Ocean Spray decided to promote a vodka and cranberry-juice drink they called the Cape Codder. Most Cape Codders are made with lime juice or a wedge of lime, or both. Add grapefruit juice to the mix and you have a Sea Breeze, orange juice and you have a Bog Fog.

Combine ½ cup **cranberry juice**, ¼ cup (2 fluid ounces) **vodka**, and 2 tablespoons fresh **lime juice** in a tall glass; stir. Add 1 cup **ice**. Garnish with fresh or frozen **cranberries**, if desired. Serve immediately. **MAKES 1**

MANHATTAN

A perfect balance of sweet, bitter, and aromatic, the Manhattan is a classic and one of the earliest cocktails to include vermouth. The recipe first appeared in a bar book from the 1880s, and the cocktail—at its best when made with rye whiskey rather than bourbon—quickly became an emblem of its namesake city. As with the martini, ordering a Manhattan signifies urban sophistication.

Combine ¼ cup (2 fluid ounces) **rye whiskey** or **bourbon**, 2 tablespoons (1 fluid ounce) **sweet vermouth**, a dash of **bitters**, and 1 cup **ice** in a cocktail shaker; stir to combine. Strain into a chilled martini glass. Garnish with a **maraschino cherry**. Serve immediately. **MAKES 1**

APPLE BRANDY COCKTAIL

Apple brandy and cider go way back—all the way back to the earliest New England colonies. The settlers, who brought apple seeds to the New World from England, much preferred apple cider to water for everyday drinking, and enjoyed apple brandy in punches and hot drinks. In fact, many of the apples planted across the nation by Johnny Appleseed were destined for distilling, not eating. This cocktail features Laird's Applejack, an American apple brandy that traces its roots to 17th-century New Jersey, but you'll find locally produced apple brandies and ciders in almost every part of the country.

Combine ½ cup fresh **apple cider** with ½ cup (4 fluid ounces) **apple brandy**, preferably Applejack, 2 tablespoons (1 fluid ounce) **dry vermouth**, and a few dashes **bitters**. Divide between two ice-filled glasses, and garnish each with an **orange twist**. **MAKES 2**

BLOODY MARY

Anyone who has visited Harry's New York Bar in Paris knows the story behind the creation of the Bloody Mary: the flavorful mix of tomato juice, vodka, horseradish, pepper, and Worcestershire sauce is believed to have been invented there in the 1920s by an expatriate American bartender. Nearly a century later, the drink remains a stand-by at brunch, and with good reason—the vodka is said to make it a hangover cure (the proverbial "hair of the dog"), and the savory seasonings pair nicely with most breakfast dishes, especially eggs and smoked meats. This version can be adjusted to serve a crowd; just be sure to maintain the proportions.

In a pitcher, stir together 3 cups **tomato juice**, 3 tablespoons freshly grated (or drained prepared) **horseradish**, ½ cup (4 fluid ounces) **vodka**, 2 teaspoons **Worcestershire sauce**, 2 tablespoons **soy sauce**, juice of 1 **lemon**, ¼ teaspoon freshly ground **pepper**, and **hot sauce** (such as Tabasco) to taste. Pour into ice-filled glasses. Garnish with **celery stalks**, **scallions** (dark green parts only), and more horseradish, as desired. Serve immediately. **MAKES 4**

GRILLED PROSCIUTTO-WRAPPED SCALLOPS

1 pound paper-thin slices prosciutto

2 pounds medium scallops (about 40)
Extra-virgin olive oil, for drizzling

2 lemons, halved, plus wedges for garnish
Freshly ground pepper

1 Heat grill to high. (If using a charcoal grill, coals are ready when you can hold your hand 4 inches above grates for just 2 to 3 seconds.)

2 Halve one prosciutto slice lengthwise. Fold in half lengthwise, and wrap around side of one scallop, overlapping prosciutto ends. Repeat with remaining prosciutto and scallops. Thread several scallops onto each skewer.

3 Drizzle scallops lightly with olive oil, squeeze lemons over skewers, and season with pepper. Grill scallops, turning once, until just opaque, about 3 minutes per side. Serve with lemon wedges.

SERVES 12

THE NORTHEAST

BACKSTORY

Scallops abound off the coast of New England, where they are prepared in countless traditional ways, including deep-fried, pan-seared, or baked with breadcrumbs. Here, borrowing from the American fascination with bacon-wrapped nibbles, the sweet, succulent scallops are encased in prosciutto (in a nod to a more recent culinary trend) and grilled. Bluefish, another local fish that is often smoked and served as a spread, makes a fitting companion. Up and down the northeastern seaboard, a smear of this smoky, creamy pâté on bread or crackers is as much a part of the landscape as the salty air and rocky shoreline.

SMOKED BLUEFISH PÂTÉ

1 pound smoked bluefish, skin and dark bloodline removed (ask your fishmonger to do this for you)

12 ounces cream cheese, softened

4 tablespoons (½ stick) unsalted butter, softened

¼ cup fresh lemon juice (from 2 lemons)

2 tablespoons freshly grated or drained prepared horseradish

2 teaspoons Dijon mustard

¼ teaspoon cayenne

1 large shallot, trimmed and minced (¼ cup)
Coarse salt and freshly ground pepper
Extra-virgin olive oil, for baking sheet

2 pounds cherry tomatoes, halved

4 garlic cloves

4 sprigs thyme
Crackers, for serving

1 Purée bluefish, cream cheese, and butter in a food processor until smooth. Transfer to a medium bowl; stir in lemon juice, horseradish, mustard, cayenne, and shallot. Season with salt and pepper. Cover with plastic wrap; refrigerate pâté up to 2 hours.

2 Preheat oven to 300°F. Generously coat a rimmed baking sheet with olive oil. In a large bowl, toss tomatoes with garlic and thyme; season with salt and pepper. Arrange tomatoes, cut side down, on sheet. Bake until shriveled and starting to brown, about 1¼ hours. Let cool completely.

3 Transfer tomatoes and juices to a serving dish. Spread pâté on crackers, top each with a roasted tomato half, and drizzle with juices.

MAKES 4 CUPS

CLAMS

A clam tastes like the ocean itself: briny and sweet, with succulent flesh. It's no wonder, then, that on Cape Cod, the arm-shaped peninsula that defines the eastern edge of Massachusetts—where the shellfish industry brings in millions of dollars a year in revenue for the town of Wellfleet alone—clams are still just about the most valuable commodity around.

Both soft-shell, also called steamer, and hard-shell species flourish here. The hard-shells are categorized by size: littlenecks are the smallest (and often priciest), followed by cherrystones and then quahogs, which grow to more than three inches across. Size matters with steamer clams, too, and regulations prohibit taking steamers that are less than two inches—these are considered "seed" clams and are protected to ensure the sustainability of the population.

Harvesting clams is wet work. To find hard-shells, you drag a rake over the sand at low tide until you strike a hard object, then you grab it. Steamer clams are more elusive: You walk along the sand and look for holes, evidence they're just under the surface. Then carefully use a clamming fork to turn over the sand and reveal the clams, without damaging their soft shells, and then dig with your hands to collect them before they burrow away—and this is the tricky part, because they're fast.

Once you have your catch, and have scrubbed it well, the reward makes the labor entirely worth it. Few pleasures are as purely delicious as a fresh soft-shell clam, steamed and dunked in drawn butter. Except maybe hard-shells cooked in a pit dug right on the beach in a classic New England clambake; simmered in a fragrant chowder; stuffed and baked or grilled; or simply served on the half shell, with lemon wedges alongside. Littleneck clams—and their flavorful cooking liquid—are also traditionally served atop spaghetti; or try them in a more robust pan-roast with sausages, potatoes, and fennel.

CLAM PAN ROAST In a heavy skillet, cook 1 minced garlic clove and ½ pound sweet Italian sausage, casings removed, over medium until browned, 5 minutes; transfer to a bowl. Pour off all but 1 tablespoon fat; cook ¼ pound kielbasa, cut into cubes, until crisp, 8 to 10 minutes. Add to bowl. Arrange 12 small halved red potatoes in pan, cut side down; cook until golden brown, 5 to 7 minutes. Turn; cook 5 minutes, until tender. Top with 3 fennel bulbs, trimmed and sliced; cook 10 minutes, stirring often. Add 1 small leek, thinly sliced (washed well and drained), ¼ cup Pernod or other anise-flavored liqueur, and 1½ cups clam juice; season with salt and pepper. Cook, stirring often, until vegetables are tender, 5 minutes. Return sausages to pan; mix to combine. Add 2½ pounds littlenecks (scrubbed). Cover; cook 5 minutes. Add 2 tomatoes, cut into wedges; cook, covered, until clams open, 8 minutes; discard unopened clams. Stir in ¼ cup chopped tarragon, and serve. **SERVES 4**

STUFFED QUAHOGS

  1 baguette, trimmed of crusts and
     cut into ¼-inch cubes (about 4 cups)
 10 quahogs (about 5 pounds)
 ⅔ cup water
 ¼ pound chorizo, cut into ¼-inch dice
 ⅓ cup olive oil
 10 garlic cloves, finely chopped (about ¼ cup)
  2 large onions, finely chopped (about 3 cups)
 ½ teaspoon crushed red-pepper flakes
  2 large eggs
  2 tablespoons finely chopped fresh basil
  1 tablespoon finely chopped fresh oregano
  2 tablespoons finely chopped fresh flat-leaf parsley
     Freshly ground pepper
  2 tablespoons unsalted butter, cut into small pieces

1 Preheat oven to 300°F. Spread bread cubes in a single layer on a rimmed baking
sheet. Toast until dry, tossing halfway through, about 15 minutes.

2 Meanwhile, holding clams under running water, scrub with a stiff sponge or
a vegetable brush. Place clams in a large pot; add ⅔ cup water. Cover; steam
over high heat until clams have opened, 10 to 15 minutes. Use a slotted spoon to
remove clams, discarding any that remain closed. Strain broth through a fine
sieve lined with a coffee filter or paper towel into a large liquid measuring cup.

3 Rinse pot, fill with water, and bring to a boil. Remove clams from shells. Chop
into ¼-inch pieces. Separate shells into halves; add to pot of water and boil until
thoroughly clean, about 5 minutes. Remove shells from pot; let cool.

4 In a large sauté pan over medium-high heat, cook the chorizo, stirring
occasionally, until fat is rendered and chorizo is lightly browned, about
4 minutes. Using a slotted spoon, transfer chorizo to a paper towel–lined plate;
blot dry. Wipe skillet clean with paper towels. Add olive oil and heat over
medium. Cook garlic, onions, and red-pepper flakes, stirring frequently, until
onions are soft and translucent, about 8 minutes. Let cool to room temperature.

5 In a large bowl, beat 1 cup reserved broth into eggs. Add onion mixture,
chopped clams, chorizo, and herbs; toss well. Add bread cubes and fold together
until just combined. Season with pepper.

6 Heat grill to medium-high. (If using a charcoal grill, coals are ready when you
can hold your hand 4 inches above grates for just 3 to 4 seconds.) Fill each
clamshell with stuffing (¼ to ⅓ cup filling per shell). Dot top of each with butter.
Place clams, stuffing side up, on grill; cook, covered, until heated through and
browned on top, about 10 minutes. Transfer to a platter and serve warm.

MAKES 20

BACKSTORY

*Although quahogs are
sometimes called "chowder
clams," stuffing their beautiful
shells with the chopped
clams and seasonings has
earned them another
nickname: "stuffies." In
southeastern Massachusetts
and Rhode Island, local cooks
invariably flavor the dish
with chorizo, an ingredient
brought to the area by the
many Portuguese fishermen
who settled there. If you can't
find quahogs, most any
variety of hard-shell clams
may be used in this recipe.*

NEW ENGLAND CLAM CHOWDER

5 dozen littleneck clams, picked over (discard any with broken shells)

3 cups water

1 ounce salt pork, rinsed well and cut into 2-inch matchsticks

1 tablespoon unsalted butter (optional)

½ large onion, cut into small dice (1 cup)

1 large russet potato, peeled and cut into ½-inch dice (2 cups)

1 sprig thyme

1 dried bay leaf

Coarse salt and freshly ground pepper

½ cup heavy cream

1 Holding clams under cool running water, scrub with a stiff sponge or a vegetable brush. Combine clams and 3 cups water in a medium pot; cover and bring to a boil. Cook until clams have opened, 5 to 6 minutes. Use a slotted spoon to remove clams, discarding any that remain closed. Strain the broth through a fine sieve lined with a coffee filter or a paper towel into a large measuring cup or a bowl; you should have about 4 cups (if not, add more water). When clams are cool enough to handle, remove meat from shells and coarsely chop. Discard shells.

2 Rinse and dry the pot. Cook salt pork over medium heat until light golden and some of the fat has rendered, about 3 minutes. (Add butter if there is not enough fat to coat bottom of pot.) Add onion; cook until translucent, stirring frequently, about 3 minutes.

3 Return strained broth to the pot along with the potato, thyme, and bay leaf; season with salt and pepper. Bring to a boil; reduce to a simmer, and cook until the potato is tender but not falling apart, 6 to 8 minutes (if desired, mash a few against the side of pot to thicken broth slightly). Stir in clams and cream and cook just until heated through, about 1 minute (do not boil). Season with salt and pepper and serve immediately.

SERVES 4 TO 6

THE NORTHEAST

BACKSTORY

Like most of us, chowder has roots that reach elsewhere. Thought to have originated in France (the word chowder *is derived from* chaudière, *the name for the cauldron used by fishermen to cook the day's catch), the hearty stew made its way to Great Britain and then to the Canadian coast before finally arriving on American soil. The first known reference to chowder in America dates from 1732; and about a century later, New England clam chowder began appearing, making excellent use of the plentiful varieties— quahogs, cherrystones, and steamers—available all along the coast. The creamy chowder quickly became, and remains, America's most well-known version.*

LOBSTER CHOWDER

Coarse salt

2 live lobsters (1½ pounds each)

3 tablespoons unsalted butter

1 large leek, halved lengthwise,
half coarsely chopped and half thinly
sliced crosswise, each washed well
and drained (keep separate)

3 cups fresh corn kernels (from 3 ears),
cobs reserved and halved crosswise

1 tablespoon all-purpose flour

1 small zucchini, cut into ¼-inch dice

1 small summer squash, halved lengthwise
and sliced into ¼-inch half-moons

1 cup fresh basil leaves,
thinly sliced, for garnish

1 Fill a large stockpot three-fourths of the way with water. Bring to a boil, then add a generous amount of salt. Plunge lobsters, one at a time, headfirst into the water, and boil (uncovered) until they turn bright red and are cooked throughout, 10 to 15 minutes (depending on their size). Remove lobsters with tongs and set aside until cool enough to handle.

2 Working over a colander set in a large bowl, snip the tip of each lobster claw to release juices into the bowl. Separate lobster meat from shells (see page 96) and cut into bite-size pieces. Reserve meat and shells separately. Strain cooking liquid through a fine sieve lined with cheesecloth into bowl with lobster juices.

3 Melt 2 tablespoons butter in same stockpot over medium-high heat. Add chopped leek, corncobs, and reserved lobster shells. Cook, stirring, 4 minutes. Add reserved lobster liquid and simmer gently 20 minutes. Strain through a cheesecloth-lined sieve. Discard solids.

4 Purée 1 cup lobster broth with 1 cup corn kernels. Melt remaining 1 tablespoon butter in a large pot over low heat. Cook sliced leek, stirring frequently, 2 minutes. Sprinkle in flour and cook, stirring, 1 minute. Stir in puréed corn mixture and cook, stirring often, until broth thickens, about 2 minutes. Add remaining lobster broth and bring to a simmer. Add zucchini and squash and remaining 2 cups corn and cook until squash is tender, about 2 minutes.

5 Stir in reserved lobster meat and heat until warmed through, about 1 minute. Season with salt and garnish with basil. Serve immediately.

SERVES 6 TO 8

THE NORTHEAST

BACKSTORY

In the early 1800s, chowder was so adored across the Northeast that the word picnic became synonymous with chowder parties—great leisurely affairs that brought townspeople to the beach. Pots filled with the day's fresh catch were presided over by a chowder master. In coastal Maine, lobsters were so abundant they could be harvested by hand at low tide. Although times have changed, few things remain as delicious as succulent chunks of lobster meat vying for space in a buttery broth (see photo on page 77); our version brims with tender sweet corn, chopped summer squash, and slivered fresh basil.

BUFFALO CHICKEN WINGS

THE NORTHEAST

BACKSTORY

The Super Bowl party staple was born in the 1960s in Buffalo, New York. Many Buffalo natives will tell you that the Anchor Bar is the site of the dish's origin; the city was subsequently blanketed with bars that specialized in wings. Like the original, this version is bathed in a sauce made with hot sauce (Frank's RedHot is the authentic choice) and butter; add more hot sauce if your preferences lean toward the fiery end of the heat scale. After all, the must-have accompaniments—a creamy blue cheese dip and crunchy celery sticks—are meant for soothing relief.

Neutral-tasting oil, such as safflower, for frying
3 pounds chicken wings
⅔ cup hot sauce, such as Frank's RedHot
4 tablespoons (½ stick) butter, melted
Blue Cheese Dipping Sauce, for serving (recipe follows)
Celery sticks, for serving

1 Preheat oven to 200°F. Fill a large, deep skillet with 1 inch of oil; heat over medium-high until it returns to 375°F on a deep-fry thermometer. Working in batches, fry chicken until golden brown and cooked through, 6 to 7 minutes per side. Transfer to a paper towel–lined baking sheet in oven to keep warm. Adjust heat so oil returns to 375°F between batches.

2 In a large bowl, stir together hot sauce and melted butter. Add chicken and toss to coat. Serve wings with dipping sauce and celery sticks.

SERVES 4

BLUE CHEESE DIPPING SAUCE

1 cup sour cream
2 tablespoons mayonnaise
2 tablespoons milk
½ teaspoon coarse salt
1⅓ cups crumbled blue cheese (5 to 6 ounces)

In a small bowl, stir together sour cream, mayonnaise, milk, and salt. Stir in blue cheese. Refrigerate, covered, until ready to serve, up to 2 days.

MAKES ABOUT 2 CUPS

WALDORF SALAD

¼ cup mayonnaise

3 tablespoons plain yogurt

1 tablespoon unsweetened applesauce
  or apple cider

1 tablespoon fresh lemon juice
  Coarse salt and freshly ground pepper

1 green or red apple, cored and thinly sliced

2 celery stalks, thinly sliced (about 1 cup)

1 cup walnut pieces, toasted (page 408)
  and coarsely chopped

1 cup seedless red grapes, halved

1 head butter lettuce

Whisk together mayonnaise, yogurt, applesauce, and
lemon juice; season with salt and pepper. Toss apple,
celery, walnuts, and half the grapes with dressing. Divide
lettuce among four plates and spoon salad on top. Add
remaining grapes and serve immediately.

SERVES 4

THE NORTHEAST

BACKSTORY

*Replacing some of the mayonnaise in the dressing with
plain yogurt makes for a fresh, modern, healthier take
on a real period piece. The salad—a creamy mixture of
apples, grapes, celery, and walnuts atop a bed of buttery
lettuce—was created by Oscar Tschirky, the influential
maître d'hôtel of New York City's Waldorf-Astoria Hotel
and known simply as "Oscar of the Waldorf" by socialites,
film stars, American presidents, and European royalty.
In this version of the salad, the walnuts are toasted for
additional flavor.*

VICHYSSOISE

- 6 medium leeks (about 2¼ pounds), white parts only, halved lengthwise and thinly sliced crosswise, washed well and drained
- 1 russet potato (about 8 ounces), peeled and diced
- 3¾ cups chicken stock, preferably homemade (page 410)
- 2 cups water, plus more if needed

  Coarse salt
- ¾ cup heavy cream
- ½ cup snipped fresh chives, for garnish

1 In a large saucepan, bring leeks, potato, stock, the water, and 1 teaspoon salt to a boil. Reduce heat to medium-low, and simmer until the vegetables are very tender, 20 to 25 minutes.

2 Working in batches, purée soup in a blender (be careful not to fill jar more than halfway each time). Transfer to a bowl. Stir cream into puréed soup, and season with salt.

3 Cover with plastic wrap and refrigerate until chilled, at least 2 hours or up to 2 days. Before serving, thin with water if necessary to achieve desired consistency, and season with salt. Serve soup in chilled glasses, garnished with chives.

SERVES 4

THE NORTHEAST

BACKSTORY

Like so many beloved American dishes, vichyssoise— invented in New York City in the early 1900s—is thought to be the product of spur-of-the-moment inventiveness. Apparently Louis Diat, the head chef at the Ritz-Carlton Hotel on Madison Avenue, often served a version of his mother's warm potato and leek soup at the restaurant, but on one auspicious occasion, he added cream to the soup and served it cold, garnished with chives. Named in honor of the city (Vichy) where he was born, it soon became a staple on the menu at the Ritz and at many other fashionable restaurants around town. The recipe is simple, yet the result sublime: a soup that is rich and creamy yet refreshing, with a velvety consistency (easily achieved by puréeing in a blender).

STOVETOP CLAMBAKE

THE NORTHEAST

BACKSTORY

A clambake without a beach may seem heretical, but just imagine digging into the best ingredients of a New England summer—clams, lobsters, mussels, corn—without having to dig a fire pit and haul everything to the shore. The classic feast can be traced to pre-colonial times and the Wampanoag Indians, a southeastern Massachusetts tribe that considered cooking seafood and vegetables in a stone-and-seaweed–lined pit a joyous ritual. A clambake is a great way to celebrate the season, but it's no easy feat. Luckily, with a big enough stockpot, you can prepare all of the components right on your stove in under an hour, start to finish. And when you spread everything out on platters—in your backyard or at your kitchen table— you'll have an instant party. Serve the rich cooking liquid from the bottom of the pot for dipping—or sipping.

2 large onions, cut into large wedges

6 garlic cloves

1 bottle pale ale or medium-bodied beer

1 cup water

Fresh seaweed, well rinsed, for layering (optional)

1½ pounds small potatoes (white, red, or a combination)

1 pound dry cured chorizo, cut into ½-inch pieces

Coarse salt

3 live lobsters (1½ pounds each)

36 littleneck clams, scrubbed well

4 ears of corn, husked and halved crosswise

2 pounds mussels, beards removed and shells scrubbed well

1½ pounds large shrimp, shells on

2 tablespoons unsalted butter (optional)

2 lemons, halved

1 Combine onions, garlic, ale, and the water in a 16-quart stockpot. Cover with a layer of seaweed (or place a steamer basket on top of onions). Add potatoes, chorizo, and 1 tablespoon salt. Bring to a boil. Add lobsters; cover and cook over high heat 15 minutes. Add clams and corn; cook, covered, 6 minutes. Add mussels and shrimp; cook, covered, until clams and mussels open and shrimp are opaque throughout, 4 to 8 minutes.

2 Using tongs and a slotted spoon, remove seafood, corn, potatoes, and chorizo; transfer to large platters or rimmed baking sheets. Discard seaweed and any unopened clams and mussels. Strain broth through a fine sieve into a bowl (discard solids); add butter (if using), swirling to melt. Squeeze lemons over seafood and serve with broth alongside.

SERVES 6 TO 8

Removing lobster meat Twist claws with their knuckles from the body, then separate knuckles from claws. Crack knuckles open with a nutcracker; remove meat. Grasp "thumb" and bend it back to snap it off. Crack claw in half; remove meat. Pull off legs, then twist tail from the joint where it meets the body and pull off tail fins. Bend tail backward to crack off end of shell and use your fingers to push tail meat out opposite side; remove with a fork.

CORNED BEEF AND CABBAGE

2   quarts water
1   cup coarse salt
1   tablespoon pink curing salt (sodium nitrite)
½   cup sugar
8   whole cloves
1   teaspoon coriander seeds, crushed
1   teaspoon mustard seeds, crushed
1   teaspoon black peppercorns, crushed
1   cinnamon stick, crushed
4   dried bay leaves, crushed
5   pounds flat-cut beef brisket
1   onion, halved
1   celery stalk, halved
1   carrot, peeled and halved
1   pound baby turnips, peeled and trimmed
1   pound baby carrots, peeled and trimmed
1   head cabbage, cored and cut into 8 wedges
1   pound small red potatoes
    Dijon mustard, for serving

1 Bring the water to a boil in a large pot. Add salts, sugar, spices, and bay leaves; remove from heat. Stir until salts and sugar dissolve. Let cool. Place brisket in a nonreactive container just large enough to hold it. Pour brine over meat. Place two small plates on top to keep meat submerged; cover and refrigerate 2 weeks.

2 Rinse brisket; discard brine. Place in a large pot; add enough water to cover by 2 inches. Add onion, celery, and halved carrot and bring to a boil. Reduce heat, cover, and simmer until meat is very tender, 3 to 3½ hours.

3 Meanwhile, set a steamer basket (or a colander) in a large saucepan filled with 2 inches of water; bring to a boil. Add baby turnips. Reduce heat, cover, and steam until tender, 8 to 10 minutes. Transfer to a bowl. Repeat with baby carrots, steaming 10 to 12 minutes. Add to turnips.

4 Transfer beef to a cutting board. Tent with foil; let rest 30 minutes. Pass broth through a fine sieve into a saucepan (discard solids); bring to a boil. Add cabbage and potatoes; simmer until tender, about 25 minutes. Add turnips and carrots; cook until warmed. Transfer vegetables to a platter; reserve broth. Trim excess fat from beef. Slice thinly against grain and transfer to platter. Serve with broth and mustard.

SERVES 8

THE NORTHEAST

BACKSTORY

There's no need to relegate this hearty dish to a once-a-year Saint Patrick's Day dinner. The medley of tender meat and warm vegetables is the perfect meal for a cold-weather weekend. It's also inexpensive to make, a fact that made it immensely popular with Irish immigrants during the nineteenth century. Corned beef and cabbage isn't unique, though; it's closely related to the New England boiled dinner, which is sometimes made with ham, as well as the Italian bollito misto *and the French* pot-au-feu. *The recipe here includes instructions for brining your own brisket (which takes about two weeks, so plan ahead), but you can also buy corned beef from any butcher. I have loved the tradition of corned beef and cabbage since I was a girl. Here it is supplemented with turnips, carrots, and boiled potatoes. I always serve it with a loaf of freshly baked Irish soda bread.*

CORNED BEEF AND ROOT-VEGETABLE HASH

THE NORTHEAST

BACKSTORY

Invented centuries ago by clever cooks as a way to put leftover meat and potatoes to good use, hash has long been associated with frugality and a satisfyingly hot-from-the-skillet heartiness. However, its enduring appeal on restaurant menus and in home kitchens is not just in its economy, or even in its ability to satiate, but in its almost limitless adaptability. When you embrace this spirit of innovation, the results are always startlingly good. This hash adds caramelized onions, several types of root vegetables, and grainy mustard to the flavor mix. Top the hash with a fried egg and serve for breakfast, brunch, or supper.

3 cups chicken stock, preferably homemade (page 410)

8 ounces Yukon Gold potatoes, peeled and cut into ½-inch dice

8 ounces carrots, peeled and cut into ½-inch dice

8 ounces parsnips, peeled and cut into ½-inch dice

8 ounces turnips, peeled and cut into ½-inch dice

¼ cup plus 1 tablespoon olive oil

1 small onion, halved lengthwise, then cut crosswise into ¼-inch-thick slices

8 ounces Corned Beef, leftover (page 99) or store-bought, cut into ½-inch dice

2 tablespoons whole-grain mustard

4 large eggs

Freshly ground pepper

1 Bring stock, potatoes, carrots, parsnips, and turnips to a boil in a large saucepan. Reduce heat and simmer until vegetables are just tender, about 6 minutes. Drain, reserving ½ cup cooking liquid.

2 Heat 3 tablespoons olive oil in a large skillet over medium. Cook onion, stirring occasionally, until softened, about 6 minutes. Add vegetables and reserved ½ cup cooking liquid. Cook, stirring occasionally, until vegetables are browned, about 25 minutes. Stir in corned beef and mustard.

3 While vegetables are cooking, heat remaining 2 tablespoons olive oil in a large skillet over medium. Crack eggs into skillet, one at a time. Fry until whites are just set, about 2 minutes.

4 To serve, divide hash among shallow bowls, top each with a fried egg, and season with pepper.

SERVES 4

PHILADELPHIA CHEESESTEAK

MEATBALL SUB

PHILADELPHIA CHEESESTEAK

1½ pounds top round steak

¼ cup olive oil, plus more if needed

2 onions, halved and thinly sliced

⅔ pound thinly sliced white provolone

4 soft hero or hoagie buns, warmed and split

   Italian pickled peppers, for serving (optional)

1 Tightly roll the steak into a log, and wrap securely in plastic. Freeze until firm but not frozen, about 45 minutes. Remove plastic and, working quickly, slice the beef into paper-thin strips, almost shaving the beef. Refrigerate until ready to cook.

2 Heat a large cast-iron skillet or griddle over medium-high; add 2 tablespoons olive oil. Cook onions, stirring, until caramelized, about 10 minutes. Transfer to a bowl; cover to keep warm.

3 Add remaining 2 tablespoons olive oil to skillet. Working in batches, if necessary, cook the beef until lightly browned and cooked through, stirring often, 3 to 5 minutes. Add more olive oil between batches, as needed.

4 Stir in the onion mixture to combine, then add cheese and stir until melted and combined. Spoon into buns and serve immediately, with peppers, if desired.

MAKES 4

THE NORTHEAST

BACKSTORY

The City of Brotherly Love is also a sandwich paradise, and has been for as long as enterprising street vendors and restaurateurs have been piling their favorite meats and cheeses onto crusty rolls, starting in the early 1800s. Although local sub shops sell all kinds of sandwiches, two Philly originals stand out—the cheesesteak and the roast pork Italian. For many, nothing says "Philadelphia" like cheesesteak—the combination of thinly sliced beef, fried onions, and gooey cheese reigns supreme. While tourists wait in line for hours to sample authentic cheesesteaks, locals are just as likely to order a "roast pork Italian" (page 104) topped with wilted greens, a true contender for the title of best South Philly sandwich. A meatball sub (page 104) is yet another specialty, especially in neighborhoods where Italian immigrants set down roots. How you order one will depend on where you are: A "hot hoagie" is the term Philadelphians give to any hot sandwich on a long roll; elsewhere in the Northeast you may hear it called a "hero" (New York), "grinder" (New England), and "Italian sandwich" (Maine). You'll need a hefty appetite—and plenty of napkins—to finish one.

MEATBALL SUB

FOR THE MEATBALLS

 2 slices white sandwich bread,
    torn into small pieces

 ½ cup milk

 8 ounces ground beef (85% lean)

 8 ounces ground pork

 4 ounces ground veal

 ½ cup grated pecorino romano (1 ounce)

 1 garlic clove, minced

 1 large egg

 3 tablespoons chopped fresh flat-leaf parsley

 1 teaspoon coarse salt

 4 cups Marinara Sauce (page 411)

FOR THE SANDWICHES

 4 hoagie or hero rolls

 1½ cups grated mozzarella (5 ounces)

 ½ cup grated pecorino romano (1 ounce)

1 Make the meatballs: Soak bread pieces in milk 5 minutes, then transfer to a large bowl. Add remaining ingredients except marinara sauce, and mix gently but thoroughly with your hands to combine. Cover and refrigerate at least 30 minutes or up to overnight.

2 Warm marinara sauce in a large pot. Divide meat mixture into 12 equal pieces. With the palms of your hands, gently roll each piece into a 2-inch ball until meat just holds together. Place on a plate. Add meatballs to sauce and bring to a gentle simmer; cook, partially covered, until meatballs are cooked through, about 25 minutes.

3 Assemble sandwiches: Preheat oven to 400°F. Split rolls, leaving one side intact, and place cut side up on a baking sheet. Spoon three meatballs and some sauce inside each roll and sprinkle evenly with both cheeses. Bake until cheese is melted and bubbly, about 3 minutes. Serve immediately.

MAKES 4

ROAST PORK ITALIAN

 2 pounds boneless pork loin

 3 tablespoons olive oil, plus more for pork
    Coarse salt and freshly ground pepper

 1½ pounds broccoli rabe

 2 garlic cloves, finely chopped

 2 tablespoons crushed red-pepper flakes

 2 loaves soft Italian bread, each halved
    crosswise and split to make 4 buns, or
    4 soft hero or hoagie buns, warmed

 1 pound provolone, thinly sliced

1 Preheat oven to 450°F. Place pork in a roasting pan. Rub with olive oil; season with salt and pepper. Place in oven; reduce oven to 250°F. Roast until an instant-read thermometer inserted in the thickest part of meat registers 145°F and meat is very tender, 1½ to 2 hours (depending on thickness of loin). Remove from oven, and cover loosely with foil; let rest about 10 minutes.

2 Meanwhile, prepare a large ice-water bath. Bring a large pot of water to a boil; add salt. Blanch broccoli rabe until bright green but still crisp-tender, 2 to 3 minutes. Using tongs or a slotted spoon, transfer broccoli rabe to ice bath to stop the cooking. Let cool, then drain and shake off excess water. Coarsely chop.

3 Heat olive oil in a large skillet over medium. Add garlic and red-pepper flakes; cook, stirring, until fragrant, 1 minute. Add broccoli rabe and stir to combine. Cook, tossing occasionally, until wilted, about 4 minutes. Season with salt and pepper and remove from heat.

4 When ready to assemble sandwiches, slice pork very thin against the grain. Fill bread with pork, then top with cheese, dividing evenly. Top with broccoli rabe and serve immediately.

MAKES 4

BOSTON BAKED BEANS

 2 onions, sliced into ¼-inch rounds

½ cup ketchup

⅓ cup Dijon mustard

¾ cup packed dark-brown sugar

 1 teaspoon dry mustard powder

 1 teaspoon coarse salt

⅛ teaspoon freshly ground pepper

 1 pound dried navy beans, sorted and rinsed

¾ cup unsulfured molasses

¼ cup cider vinegar

 4 ounces salt pork, rinsed and cut into ⅛-inch-thick slices

1 Preheat oven to 275°F. Place onion slices in a 5-quart Dutch oven or heavy pot with a tight-fitting lid so they cover the bottom of the pot, then add ketchup and Dijon mustard and sprinkle evenly with brown sugar, dry mustard, salt, and pepper. Top with beans in an even layer; pour molasses, then vinegar over beans. Lay salt pork slices over the beans, covering them completely (slices can come up the edges of the pot a bit since they will shrink in the warm oven). Fill with hot water to come up just to the bottom of the salt pork.

2 Cover pot and bake 8 hours, without stirring; check every few hours to make sure that the liquid level is still above the beans (add more hot water as necessary). Remove lid and cook 1 hour more (9 hours total); the liquid should thicken during this time. Let cool about 20 minutes before serving. (Any leftovers can be refrigerated up to 3 days; allow the beans to cool completely before transferring to airtight containers.)

SERVES 8 TO 10

Dried beans note Be sure dried beans are from a good source, with a high turnover; if they are too old, they will never turn out right, no matter how long you cook them.

THE NORTHEAST

BACKSTORY

Homemade baked beans were a staple in my childhood home. Not "baked" beans out of a can, but dried beans that were carefully picked over, soaked, rinsed three times, boiled three times, then added to an old-fashioned brown pot with all of Mom's favorite enhancements, and slow-baked for hours until the beans were soft to the tooth and the juices in the pot ran thick and rich and brown-sugary. My brothers and sisters and I fought over the small bits of crispy salt pork that mysteriously rose to the top of the pot during baking, and we fought over the small pieces of onion that stayed down at the bottom, but most of all we fought over who would have the last bit of scrapings from around the sides of the pot when there were absolutely no more beans to be had. For this recipe, there's no need to presoak the beans; they cook long enough to reach the proper texture. This definitive "one-pot dish" is a meal on its own, with the customary Boston brown bread on the side and a garnish of piccalilli—a relish of pickled vegetables, also known as chow-chow in Pennsylvania and parts of the South.

BOSTON BROWN BREAD

Unsalted butter, softened, for cans and parchment
1 cup rye flour
1 cup whole-wheat flour
1 cup cornmeal
2 teaspoons baking soda
2 teaspoons coarse salt
¾ cup unsulfured molasses
2 cups buttermilk

1 Fit the bottom of a large pot with a wire rack. Fill pot one-third of the way with water and bring to a boil. Generously butter two large cans, such as 28-ounce tomato cans or 1-pound coffee tins (do not use enamel-lined cans).

2 In a large bowl, whisk together flours, cornmeal, baking soda, and salt until combined. Stir in molasses and buttermilk until just combined.

3 Divide batter between prepared cans. Cover each with a piece of buttered parchment. Place a piece of foil on top and secure with a rubber band. Carefully place cans in the boiling water; the water should come three-fourths of the way up the cans. Cover pot, reduce heat to medium-low, and simmer 1½ hours, adding more hot water to pot if necessary (check every 30 minutes).

4 Preheat oven to 300°F. Using tongs, lift cans from the water. Carefully remove loaves from the cans, and transfer to a parchment-lined baking sheet. Bake 15 minutes, just to allow some of the moisture to evaporate. Remove from oven and let cool before serving.

MAKES 2 LOAVES

PICCALILLI

4 Kirby cucumbers, thinly sliced
1 red onion, thinly sliced
1 red bell pepper, ribs and seeds removed, thinly sliced into 1-inch-long pieces
1 medium, firm green cabbage (about 2½ pounds), cored and thinly sliced
1 small head cauliflower, cut into small florets
½ cup coarse salt
2 cups sugar
2 tablespoons pickling spices, tied in cheesecloth
1 teaspoon turmeric
1 tablespoon celery seeds
2 cups cider vinegar
2 cups water

1 Combine all the vegetables in a large bowl. Add salt, and mix well. Add enough cold water to cover vegetables and let stand at least 8 hours or up to overnight. Drain; rinse well under running water and drain again.

2 In a large nonreactive pot, whisk together remaining ingredients until combined. Bring to a boil, then reduce heat to a simmer. Add vegetable mixture and cook, stirring occasionally, until warmed through, about 15 minutes. Transfer to a nonreactive container to cool completely. Piccalilli can be refrigerated, covered tightly, up to 3 weeks.

MAKES 3 QUARTS

CHICKEN PARMIGIANA

THE **NORTHEAST**

BACKSTORY

Many of the dishes we think of as Italian are actually Italian American, created by immigrant restaurateurs and chefs in urban "Little Italys" rather than in their home country. Chicken Parmigiana is a great example of this. In order to cater to their new clientele's expectations, eggplant parmigiana, a Lenten (meatless) dish, was first redone with veal—then the most inexpensive meat to be had—and eventually with chicken, presently America's most popular protein choice by a long shot. Serving the parmigiana with pasta is a purely American take, one first seen at red-sauce Italian restaurants. The versatile marinara sauce works for the entrée and the side.

2   cups fine plain fresh breadcrumbs (page 408)
¾   cup finely grated pecorino romano or parmesan (1½ ounces)
    Coarse salt and freshly ground pepper
1   cup all-purpose flour
4   large eggs, lightly beaten
1   pound chicken cutlets, pounded to ⅛-inch thickness
¼   cup neutral-tasting oil, such as safflower, plus more if needed
1¾   cups Marinara Sauce (page 411), plus more for serving
1¼   cups coarsely grated mozzarella (5 ounces)
    Cooked spaghetti, for serving

1 Combine breadcrumbs and ½ cup pecorino; season with salt and pepper. Put flour, eggs, and breadcrumb mixture in three separate dishes. Dredge cutlets in flour, shaking off excess, then dip in egg and let excess drip off before dredging in breadcrumbs to coat. Place on a plate and let stand 30 minutes.

2 Heat oil in large straight-sided skillet over medium-high. (Oil is ready when a breadcrumb sizzles when dropped in.) Working in batches, fry cutlets until golden, 3 to 4 minutes per side. Transfer to a paper towel–lined baking sheet. (If at any point oil becomes too filled with blackened bits, discard between batches, and heat an additional ¼ cup.)

3 Preheat oven to 375°F. Spread ¾ cup marinara sauce in the bottom of a 9-by-13-inch baking dish. Arrange a single layer of cutlets on top. Top with 1 cup sauce, spreading to cover each cutlet. Sprinkle evenly with mozzarella and remaining ¼ cup pecorino. Cover with foil and bake until bubbling, about 10 minutes. Meanwhile, toss spaghetti with more marinara sauce. Uncover chicken; bake until cheese melts, about 2 minutes more. Serve immediately, with spaghetti on the side.

SERVES 4

AUTUMN SQUASH WITH SAGE-CREAM SAUCE

3½ pounds (about six) winter squashes, such as acorn, butternut, or dumpling, halved, seeded, stems removed, and bottoms trimmed to sit flat

Coarse salt and freshly ground pepper

1 teaspoon chopped fresh sage

1 cup chicken stock, preferably homemade (page 410)

4 garlic cloves, halved lengthwise

¼ cup heavy cream

1 Preheat oven to 350°F. Arrange squash halves, cut side up, in two 9-by-13-inch baking dishes. Season with salt and pepper. Sprinkle sage over each, dividing evenly. Pour ½ cup stock into each baking dish and scatter garlic around squashes. Cover with parchment, then foil, and bake until squashes are tender when pierced with a fork, 45 to 55 minutes. Remove from oven.

2 Heat broiler with rack about 8 inches from heat source. Use a slotted spoon to transfer garlic to a small bowl. Mash with a fork, then stir in cream and 2 tablespoons liquid from baking dishes. Spoon evenly over squash halves, including edges. Broil until bubbling and golden, 3 to 4 minutes. Serve immediately.

SERVES 12

THE NORTHEAST

BACKSTORY

Native Americans dubbed squash, beans, and corn "the three sisters" because when planted together they supported one another as they grew. The plants were ideal siblings on the table as well as in the garden, and all three appeared at the first Thanksgiving feast at Plimoth Plantation. The word for squash, like the fruit itself, is a regional native; it comes from the Narraganset word askutasquash, *meaning "the green things that may be eaten raw." Of course, in any color, we prefer our squash cooked these days. Roasted slowly with a few fragrant seasonings, maybe a dash of cream, there's hardly a sweeter taste of Americana.*

RED AND GREEN CABBAGE SLAW WITH BACON

½ medium red cabbage (about 1 pound), finely shredded

¼ medium green cabbage (about ½ pound), finely shredded

½ pound smoked bacon (about 8 strips), cut into ¼-inch pieces

1 teaspoon caraway seeds

3 tablespoons olive oil

1 garlic clove, minced

¼ cup plus 3 tablespoons cider vinegar

2 teaspoons sugar

Coarse salt and freshly ground pepper

1 Granny Smith apple

1 Toss both cabbages together in a large bowl. Cook bacon in a medium skillet over medium heat, stirring occasionally, until crisp, about 5 minutes. Transfer with a slotted spoon to paper towels to drain. Pour off all but about 1 tablespoon fat from skillet.

2 Add caraway seeds to skillet; cook over medium heat, shaking skillet often, until seeds begin to pop, about 1 minute. Add oil and garlic; cook, stirring, 10 seconds (do not let garlic brown). Remove from heat; pour in vinegar. Add sugar and stir until dissolved. Pour dressing over cabbage. Season with salt and pepper. Toss thoroughly. Let stand at least 1 hour, or refrigerate, covered, overnight.

3 Just before serving, cut apple into 1/4-inch-thick wedges or matchsticks. Add to dressed cabbage along with bacon, and toss again.

SERVES 6 TO 10

THE NORTHEAST

BACKSTORY

Early German settlers carried cabbage seeds with them to New York, New Jersey, and Pennsylvania, along with an affinity for shredded cabbage salads. Americans have been enjoying these slaws since the late 1700s, when they were typically mixed with a boiled dressing. Today, a sweetened vinegar dressing is the hallmark of most slaws: it can be mayonnaise-based, as in the creamy slaw on page 50, or smoky with bacon, as in this crisp, colorful version of "hot slaw," typical of Pennsylvania Dutch country.

CREAMED SPINACH AND PEARL ONIONS

1¼ pounds spinach, tough stems discarded, leaves rinsed well (do not pat dry)

10 ounces white pearl onions (2½ cups)

5 tablespoons unsalted butter

2 tablespoons all-purpose flour

1¼ cups milk

¾ cup chopped bacon (3 ounces)

½ cup heavy cream

Pinch of freshly grated nutmeg

Coarse salt and freshly ground pepper

2 teaspoons fresh lemon juice

1 Heat a large pot over high. Add spinach (with water still clinging to leaves), cover, and cook until beginning to wilt, about 1 to 2 minutes. Remove from heat and stir spinach until completely wilted. Transfer spinach to a colander; rinse under cold water. Squeeze out excess liquid in a clean kitchen towel. Finely chop spinach.

2 Bring a medium saucepan of water to a boil. Add onions; cook until skins soften, about 3 minutes. Remove onions with a slotted spoon (reserve water in pot); rinse. Trim root ends, and remove skins. Halve onions if large. Return onions to saucepan and cook until tender, about 10 minutes. Drain, and rinse.

3 Wipe pan clean and melt 4 tablespoons butter over medium heat. Add flour, and whisk until smooth. Whisking constantly, pour in milk in a slow, steady stream, and bring to a boil. Continue to boil, whisking constantly, 1 minute. Remove from heat.

4 Melt remaining tablespoon butter in a large saucepan over medium heat. Add bacon; cook, stirring occasionally, until well browned, about 6 minutes. Stir in onions and spinach. Stir in cream and milk mixture. Add nutmeg and season with salt and pepper. Cook, stirring, until heated through and thickened, about 10 minutes (do not boil). Stir in lemon juice. Season with more salt and pepper.

SERVES 6

THE NORTHEAST

BACKSTORY

Visit any of the venerable steakhouses in New York and you will be hard-pressed to find a menu that doesn't offer some version of creamed spinach. It's a hearty side worthy of the most well-marbled porterhouse or rib-eye, and just plain delicious. Creamed spinach is often enhanced with blanched pearl onions; bacon adds even more heft to this holiday-worthy variation.

CRANBERRIES

Cranberries are jewels of life, having nurtured and sustained Native Americans for many generations. Knowing a good thing, they harnessed the fruit's brilliant color for dyes, mashed the berries into poultices, and pounded them into deer-meat pemmican—a must for long winters.

Cranberry growers tend to be proud of their heritage, for there are few of them, and cranberry country is the most rare type of real estate. On Cape Cod, bogs are often family affairs, passed from generation to generation, and are taken care of like gardens. The older bogs, created on original wetlands, are living and growing remnants of another era. They smell of pine, cedar, peat, and low tide, and are beautiful at all times of year. The annual harvest is a crowd-puller. Berry-peeping tourists watch as farmers don waders and make their way into the crimson tide, which covers thousands of acres in southeastern Massachusetts and leaves pockets of several other states in the Northeast, the Midwest, and the Pacific Northwest submerged in color.

Today, the vast majority of cranberries that make their way to market are wet-harvested from the fields, rinsed and sorted, and then juiced, jellied, dried, or otherwise processed. The jolly red berries found fresh in produce aisles are spared the deluge; they are instead carefully dry-harvested—machine-forked from the vines—before being subjected to intense scrutiny. Only those berries that bounce to a certain height are deemed worthy of the Thanksgiving table, a quaint yet effective means of sorting that dates to the late 1800s.

Cranberries have worked their way onto the American table in countless ways. Sweetened with a little sugar and softened over gentle heat, they offer a tempered tartness to unabashedly sweet desserts, as well as the sauces and relishes that accompany the holiday roast turkey. No matter how you choose to prepare them, cranberries are autumn's most stunning arrival.

CRANBERRY BUTTER Post-Thanksgiving, turn leftover cranberry sauce into a delicious spread for biscuits and other breakfast breads and muffins. It also makes a tasty sandwich condiment, especially when paired with leftover turkey. Stir ½ cup (1 stick) of softened butter in a bowl until smooth; fold in ½ cup cranberry sauce until well blended. Store, covered, in the refrigerator for up to 5 days. Serve chilled or at room temperature.

CRANBERRY-ORANGE RELISH

2 blood oranges or navel oranges

2 cups fresh or frozen (thawed) cranberries

¼ cup diced red onion (¼-inch pieces)

1 large jalapeño chile, ribs and seeds removed, finely chopped

2 tablespoons fresh lime juice

2 teaspoons finely grated peeled fresh ginger

½ cup sugar

2 celery stalks, cut into ¼-inch dice

¼ cup pecans, toasted (page 408) and broken into pieces

¼ cup fresh mint leaves, coarsely chopped

1 Using a sharp paring knife, slice off both ends from oranges. Carefully slice downward, following the curve of the fruit to remove rind and bitter white pith. Working over a bowl to catch the juices, cut between membranes to remove whole segments, reserving juices.

2 Pulse cranberries in a food processor just until coarsely chopped. Transfer to a bowl. Add onion, jalapeño, lime juice, orange sections and juice, ginger, sugar, and celery; mix gently. Cover and refrigerate at least 1 hour or up to 2 days. Just before serving, add pecans and mint and toss to combine.

MAKES ABOUT 2 CUPS

THE NORTHEAST

BACKSTORY

The cranberry is one of the most emblematic of New England foods, so it's no surprise that it appears on Thanksgiving tables across the country as a reminder of that first holiday meal at Plymouth. But although the store-bought version of jellied cranberry sauce might be a childhood favorite, make space for the real thing. One of these relishes will be sure to suit. Cranberry-Orange Relish (above, left) requires no cooking whatsoever; it is flavored with jalapeño, lime juice, and mint, and its appealing crunch comes from celery and pecans. This condiment is great with turkey, of course, but it would also be wonderful with pork or chicken. Cranberry-Ginger Jelly (above, center) requires just four ingredients, but the combination will sparkle festively in the serving dish and be equally dazzling at first bite. It can be made a week ahead of time, and any leftovers can be served on a turkey sandwich or as a topping for cream cheese on crackers. One taste of the chunky Cranberry-Pear Chutney (above, right) will inspire you to roll up your sleeves and make multiple batches (up to a month ahead) for holiday giving. Its sweetness and tang are beautifully balanced, making it an ideal accompaniment to everything from turkey or a standing rib roast to a grilled cheese sandwich.

CRANBERRY-GINGER JELLY

  2 cups fresh or frozen (thawed) cranberries
  2 cups sugar
  2 teaspoons finely grated peeled fresh ginger
2½ cups water
  1 tablespoon unflavored powdered gelatin

1 Combine cranberries, sugar, ginger, and 2 cups water in a medium saucepan. Cover and bring to a simmer; cook, stirring occasionally, until berries have burst and softened, about 10 minutes. Pass through a fine sieve into a bowl, pressing on solids with a wooden spoon to extract as much liquid as possible; discard solids.

2 Meanwhile, sprinkle gelatin over remaining ½ cup water in a bowl. Let soften 5 minutes. Add cranberry mixture; stir until gelatin has dissolved. Cover and refrigerate at least 4 hours or up to 1 week.

MAKES ABOUT 2 CUPS

CRANBERRY-PEAR CHUTNEY

  3 ripe but firm pears, peeled, cored, and cut into ½-inch dice
  1 tablespoon finely grated lemon zest, plus 1 tablespoon fresh lemon juice
  3 cups fresh or frozen cranberries (do not thaw)
  1 cup sugar
  ½ cup fresh orange juice (from 1 to 2 oranges)
  ¼ cup golden raisins
  5 pitted dates, preferably Medjool, coarsely chopped (¼ cup)

1 Toss pears with lemon zest and juice in a bowl.

2 In a large saucepan over medium-low heat, cook cranberries and sugar until berries burst and release juices, stirring occasionally, about 8 minutes.

3 Add orange juice, raisins, and dates to saucepan. Raise heat to medium-high. Cook, stirring occasionally, until mixture begins to bubble. Add pears; cook, stirring, until mixture thickens and pears are softened, about 10 minutes. Remove from heat and let cool completely. (Chutney can be refrigerated in an airtight container up to 1 month; serve chilled or at room temperature.)

MAKES ABOUT 6 CUPS

JOHNNYCAKES

1½	cups johnnycake or stone-ground white cornmeal
	Coarse salt
4	cups boiling water, plus more hot water if needed
¼	cup whole milk
	Safflower oil, for griddle

1 Preheat oven to 200°F. Heat a medium skillet over medium. Toast cornmeal, stirring often, until fragrant, about 5 minutes; transfer to a bowl, and whisk in 1¼ teaspoons salt.

2 Pour boiling water into a heatproof bowl; gradually whisk in cornmeal. Stir in milk. Heat a griddle or large cast-iron skillet over medium heat; coat with a thin layer of oil (about 1 tablespoon). Drop batter by the tablespoon onto griddle. (If batter spatters violently, reduce heat to medium-low, so that johnnycakes are gently bubbling when they hit the griddle. You may need to add more hot water, 2 tablespoons at a time, until batter is pourable but still thick.) Cook 4 or 5 johnnycakes at a time, greasing griddle as needed, until bottoms are golden with lacy, crisp edges, about 5 minutes. Flip; cook until bottoms are crisp, 3 to 4 minutes. Transfer to a baking sheet; warm in oven while others cook. Repeat with remaining batter.

MAKES ABOUT 3 DOZEN

THE NORTHEAST

BACKSTORY

Feelings run high in Rhode Island about the unleavened corn pancakes called johnnycakes (perhaps from "journey cake" or "Shawnee cake," for the Native American tribe). Eaten for breakfast— drizzled with maple syrup and served with crisp thick-cut bacon slices—or with a meal (similar to cornbread), the cakes come in two forms. A thin, milky batter, like the one in this recipe, produces the light, crisp cake known as Newport, or East Bay, style. West Bay cakes are thicker, smaller, and softer. Devotees of both types can agree, though, that all true johnnycakes are made with stone-ground Rhode Island whitecap flint cornmeal (available from regional mills or online); if you can't find it, you may use other stone-ground white cornmeal.

CORN MUFFINS

BACKSTORY

The corn muffin was designated the official state muffin of Massachusetts in 1986, in response to a petition by schoolchildren. A descendant of johnnycakes (page 119) and corn pone (a Southern style of cornbread), corn muffins work equally well at breakfast—spread with jam, butter, or honey—or as a side dish at hearty New England suppers.

1 cup plus 2 tablespoons yellow cornmeal

1 cup all-purpose flour

⅔ cup sugar

1 tablespoon baking powder

1¼ teaspoons coarse salt

¼ cup neutral-tasting oil, such as safflower

4 tablespoons unsalted butter, melted

2 tablespoons mild honey, such as acacia or orange blossom, plus more for serving (optional)

2 large eggs, lightly beaten

1 cup milk

1 Preheat oven to 350°F. Line a standard 12-cup muffin tin with paper cups. Whisk cornmeal, flour, sugar, baking powder, and salt in a large bowl. Combine oil, butter, and honey; stir in eggs and milk. Stir oil mixture into cornmeal mixture. Divide batter evenly among prepared cups.

2 Bake until tops are golden and a toothpick inserted into the centers comes out clean, rotating tin halfway through, about 18 minutes. Let cool 10 minutes before turning out of tins. Serve warm or at room temperature, with honey, if desired. (Muffins can be stored in an airtight container at room temperature up to 4 days; reheat in a 300°F oven, if desired.)

MAKES 1 DOZEN

PARKER HOUSE ROLLS

14 tablespoons (1¾ sticks) unsalted butter, cut into small pieces, plus more, softened, for pan and bowl

2 packages active dry yeast (each 1 scant tablespoon)

1¼ cups warm milk (110°F)

3 tablespoons sugar

1¼ teaspoons salt

5½ cups all-purpose flour, plus more for dusting

3 large eggs, lightly beaten

1 Butter a 9-by-13-inch rimmed baking sheet. In a small bowl, sprinkle yeast over ½ cup warm milk; stir to dissolve yeast. Let stand until foamy, about 5 minutes.

2 Bring remaining ¾ cup milk just to a simmer in a medium saucepan. Remove from heat; add 6 tablespoons butter, the sugar, and salt, stirring until butter has completely melted.

3 Place 4½ cups flour in the bowl of a standing electric mixer. Make a well in the center with your hands, and pour in yeast mixture, butter mixture, and eggs. Attach bowl to mixer fitted with the dough hook and beat on low speed until dough just starts to come together, about 2 minutes. Turn out dough onto a lightly floured surface and knead until smooth and no longer sticky, about 5 minutes, adding remaining 1 cup flour as needed. Place dough in a buttered large bowl, turning to coat evenly with butter. Cover with a kitchen towel. Let rise in a warm place until doubled in bulk, about 1½ hours.

4 Punch down dough and let rest 10 minutes, then divide into two equal pieces. Melt remaining 8 tablespoons butter. On a lightly floured surface, roll out one piece of dough into a 12-by-10-inch rectangle, keeping the second piece covered with the towel until rolling it out. Refrigerate dough until well chilled, about 30 minutes. Meanwhile, preheat oven to 400°F.

5 Cut one piece of chilled dough lengthwise into five 2-inch-wide strips. Cut each strip into three 4-inch-long rectangles. With a short side facing you, brush the top half of one rectangle with some of the melted butter and fold over, about one-third of the way. Transfer to prepared baking sheet, wider side down. Repeat with remaining rectangles, arranging in pan so they overlap slightly, making consecutive rows (ultimately six rows of five rectangles each). Repeat with remaining dough. Cover with a kitchen towel. Let rise in a warm place until doubled in bulk, about 30 minutes.

6 Brush melted butter over top of each roll. Bake until golden brown, 15 to 20 minutes. Remove from oven and brush with remaining melted butter. Serve hot or at room temperature.

MAKES 30

THE NORTHEAST

BACKSTORY

Nothing, absolutely nothing, turns a simple meal into a special occasion like homemade rolls. These, which get their richness from butter, were first made during the 1870s at the Parker House Hotel in Boston, and the recipe started appearing in cookbooks a decade later. The reason for their perennial popularity is that they are, in a word, fabulous; the fact that they are also relatively easy to make can't hurt, either.

SOFT PRETZELS

THE NORTHEAST

BACKSTORY

A warm, soft pretzel—with yellow mustard—sold from a cart has long been a favorite street food in New York City. This type of pretzel probably came about as a Lenten bread in Italy during the Middle Ages, subsequently making its way to America from Holland with the Pilgrims. Although forming the pretzels is easy to do, it is virtually impossible to make them all look identical—the dough has a personality all its own. Relax and enjoy the process. Look for pretzel salt, a special type with very coarse grains, from specialty stores and online resources (such as www.spicebarn.com).

1 package active dry yeast (1 scant tablespoon)
¼ teaspoon coarse salt
2 teaspoons sugar
1 cup warm water (about 110°F)
3 cups all-purpose flour, plus more for dusting
   Pinch of cayenne
2 tablespoons unsalted butter, softened
   Vegetable oil, for baking sheets
3 tablespoons baking soda
1 tablespoon pretzel salt
   Assorted mustards, for serving

1 Mix yeast, coarse salt, sugar, and warm water in a small bowl, whisking until sugar dissolves. Let stand until foamy, about 5 minutes.

2 Mix flour and cayenne in a large bowl. Using a pastry blender or your fingertips, work butter into flour until mixture resembles coarse crumbs.

3 Slowly pour yeast mixture over flour mixture, stirring to combine. Using your hands, gather dough together and turn out onto a lightly floured surface; knead until it is no longer sticky, about 5 minutes. Cover loosely with plastic wrap and let rise in a warm place 30 minutes.

4 With a bench scraper, cut dough into 12 equal pieces. With palms of hands, roll each piece into an 18-inch-long rope. Form a *U* shape with one rope and twist ends around each other twice, leaving an inch at the ends. Fold twisted portion backward along center of *U* shape to form a circle, then gently press ends of rope onto dough to seal. Transfer to an oiled baking sheet and repeat to form pretzels with remaining dough. Let rise 20 minutes.

5 Preheat oven to 475°F. Bring a large pot of water to a boil and add baking soda. Boil pretzels in batches until puffed and slightly shiny, 1 to 2 minutes per side, turning with tongs. Transfer to wire racks to drain.

6 Once all pretzels have been boiled and drained, return them to baking sheet; sprinkle with pretzel salt, dividing evenly. Bake until golden brown and cooked through, rotating sheet halfway through, about 15 minutes. (Pretzels will keep, uncovered, at room temperature up to 12 hours. Reheat in a 250°F oven, if desired.) Serve with mustards.

MAKES 12

STICKY BUNS

2 packages active dry yeast (each 1 scant tablespoon)

1 cup plus 2 tablespoons warm milk (about 110°F)

6 cups all-purpose flour

⅓ cup granulated sugar

2 teaspoons salt

4 large eggs

1 pound (4 sticks) unsalted butter, cut into small pieces and softened, plus more for pan

3⅓ cups pecans (about 14 ounces)

2¼ cups light corn syrup

1¼ cups packed light-brown sugar

1½ cups plus 3 tablespoons sour cream

1 tablespoon ground cinnamon

1 Sprinkle yeast over the milk; stir to dissolve yeast. Let stand until foamy, about 10 minutes. With an electric mixer on low speed, beat flour, granulated sugar, and salt to combine. Mix in yeast mixture and eggs until combined.

2 Increase speed to high and add the butter, several pieces at a time; continue mixing the dough until it is smooth and shiny, 8 to 10 minutes. Transfer to a parchment-lined 13-by-18-inch baking pan; use your hands to spread dough to fit the pan. Cover with plastic wrap and refrigerate up to overnight.

3 Preheat oven to 350°F. Generously butter a standard 12-cup muffin tin. Chop 2 cups pecans; break the remaining 1⅓ cups pecans in half lengthwise. Pour 3 tablespoons corn syrup into each prepared cup; top with about 1 tablespoon brown sugar and 2 tablespoons halved pecans.

4 Remove dough from refrigerator and let stand at room temperature until slightly softened, about 15 minutes. Roll out dough lengthwise to form a 15-by-20-inch rectangle about ¼ inch thick. Using a spatula, spread sour cream evenly over dough, leaving a ½-inch border all around. Dust sour cream with cinnamon and sprinkle with ⅔ cup brown sugar. Top evenly with chopped pecans and roll the dough up lengthwise to form a log, about 3 inches in diameter. Trim ends so log is 18 inches.

5 Using a sharp knife, slice log into 1½-inch-thick rounds. Place one in each prepared cup. Cover with plastic wrap and let rise in a warm place until dough is ½ inch above cups, 20 to 30 minutes. Transfer to oven, placing a baking sheet on the rack below to catch any drips. Bake, rotating tins halfway through, until dark golden brown, about 40 minutes. Remove from oven, and immediately turn out buns onto a parchment-lined baking sheet. Replace any pecans that may have fallen off. Let cool on a wire rack before serving; best enjoyed the same day.

MAKES 12

INDIAN PUDDING

BACKSTORY

Indian pudding is an old-fashioned dessert poised for revival. Recipes for the sweet corn-and-molasses spoon bread appear in some of the earliest American cookbooks, especially regional collections from Massachusetts and surrounding New England states. Yet the dish, believed to be a descendant of English hasty puddings, is definitely not as widely known today as it should be. It's scrumptious and comforting, and is very, very easy to make with just a handful of pantry ingredients. If you ever ate Indian pudding as a child, one bite should help the memories come flooding back; if not, prepare it just once and it's bound to become one of your fallback, from-scratch desserts.

4 cups half-and-half

¾ cup unsulfured molasses

4 tablespoons unsalted butter

1 teaspoon ground ginger

1 teaspoon ground cinnamon

1 teaspoon salt

½ cup yellow cornmeal

Lightly sweetened softly whipped cream or Vanilla Ice Cream (page 75), for serving (optional)

1 Preheat oven to 275°F. In a medium saucepan, combine half-and-half, molasses, butter, ginger, cinnamon, and salt. Bring to a boil, stirring to combine. Remove from heat and whisk in cornmeal until batter is smooth.

2 Transfer to an 8-inch square baking dish and bake until pudding is firm but still jiggles slightly in the center when gently shaken, 2 to 2½ hours. Let cool 30 minutes; serve warm or at room temperature, topped with whipped cream or ice cream, as desired.

SERVES 8

BLUEBERRIES

Usually we think of a fruit that grows wild as scarce and scattered, something we'd be lucky to stumble across while on a hike. Yet the wild blueberry, native to North America, grows in abundance in Maine and eastern Canada and ripens right on schedule, between late July and early September. In a place like northeast Maine, a carefully orchestrated effort, akin to a slow waltz with nature, is required to scoop up all of the succulent berries and get them processed during their brief season. Anyone who participates in this harvest does feel fortunate, despite the challenges of picking from what are called "lowbush" blueberries, which are no more than eighteen inches in height.

Every year, thousands of people flock to Maine to help with the harvest. Blueberry rakes in hand, they bend at the waist to scoop up the berries, combing through the plants and trying hard not to crush the fruit as they go. Many people eagerly return year after year, and even generation after generation. For them, it is a family affair, a working vacation repeated every summer.

For anyone in the rest of the country, however, the summer blueberry ritual likely revolves around buying cultivated varieties at a farmers' market or roadside stand. Cultivated blueberries, which are grown throughout the United States, are "highbush" varieties; they are indeed taller (and thus easier to harvest) and produce larger berries.

Both wild and cultivated blueberries are smooth, with a beautiful waxy bloom. They can be used interchangeably, although wild varieties are smaller, bluer, and have a more intense flavor than the cultivated varieties. The blueberry's sweet-tart flavor lends itself to use in all sorts of desserts and simple baked goods. Blueberries have a wonderful affinity for stone fruits such as peaches and nectarines, so think about putting those flavors together in some way. Sturdier than softer berries, such as strawberries or raspberries, blueberries should keep for a week in the refrigerator and are easy to freeze, so you can taste their summer flavor all winter long.

BASIC BLUEBERRY JAM Preheat oven to 250°F. Put a plate in the freezer. With a potato masher or wooden spoon, crush 1 cup blueberries in a heavy-bottomed, nonreactive saucepan. Add another 3 cups berries and ½ cup water; bring to a simmer over medium heat. Cook, stirring occasionally to break up berries, until they are soft, about 6 minutes. Meanwhile, spread 3½ cups sugar on a rimmed baking sheet. Heat in oven until warm, about 5 minutes. Slowly stir sugar into saucepan; return mixture to a simmer, stirring constantly. Reduce heat to medium-low; cook at a slow boil until thickened, 45 minutes to 1 hour. To test for doneness, drop a small amount of jam onto the chilled plate; it should wrinkle when pressed with your finger. Refrigerate jam in airtight containers up to 2 weeks, or store in sealed, sterilized jars (see page 409) up to 6 months. **MAKES ABOUT 3 CUPS**

BLUEBERRY CRISP

FOR THE FILLING

6 cups (3 pints) fresh blueberries

½ cup sugar

1 tablespoon cornstarch

1 teaspoon fresh lemon juice

¼ teaspoon coarse salt

FOR THE TOPPING

¾ cup all-purpose flour

½ cup old-fashioned rolled oats (not instant or quick-cooking)

½ cup chopped nuts, such as almonds (optional)

½ teaspoon baking powder

½ teaspoon coarse salt

6 tablespoons unsalted butter, softened

⅓ cup sugar

1 Preheat oven to 375°F. Make the filling: Mix blueberries, sugar, cornstarch, lemon juice, and salt in a bowl. Transfer to an 8-inch square baking dish.

2 Make the topping: In a medium bowl, stir together flour, oats, nuts, baking powder, and salt. With an electric mixer on medium speed, cream butter and sugar until light and fluffy. Stir flour mixture into butter. Using your hands, squeeze topping pieces together to form clumps.

3 Sprinkle topping evenly over filling. Bake until filling is bubbling in center and topping is golden brown, about 1 hour. Transfer to a wire rack and let cool 30 minutes before serving.

SERVES 8

THE NORTHEAST

BACKSTORY

Nothing beats the taste of fresh blueberries plucked ripe and eaten off the bush. At Cantitoe Corners, in Bedford, I now have a large area devoted to berries of all sorts, and one very long border is planted with highbush blueberries. We chose a variety of sturdy, high-yielding types so we can have ripe berries for the table and for baking from late June through August, and it's a delight to amble through the patch and eat to our hearts' content. Because the berries are so plentiful, a big bowl is easily filled, and I can make pies and jams and scones, as well as cakes and muffins and pancakes and waffles, all summer long. My freezers are always half-filled with frozen berries for the rest of the year. This crisp is among my favorite blueberry desserts—there are few recipes simpler to put together, and fewer still with such widespread appeal.

NEW YORK CHEESECAKE

Who doesn't love classic New York cheesecake? The ultra-smooth, ultra-creamy dessert made its debut in a Manhattan deli in the 1920s, inspiring numerous versions throughout the city—and eventually, all over the country. This recipe produces the most luxurious cheesecake ever, hands down, with an incomparably rich, dense cream cheese and sour cream filling over a tender sugar-cookie crust. It's essential to bake it in a water bath to ensure the proper texture; also, to prevent the cheesecake from cracking on top, turn off the heat after it's finished baking, open the oven door, and let the cake cool in the oven for one hour before removing it.

½ cup all-purpose flour, plus more for dusting
  Cookie-Dough Crust (page 412)
  Unsalted butter, softened, for pans
3½ pounds (seven 8-ounce packages) cream cheese, softened
2¼ cups sugar
5 large eggs, room temperature
1 cup sour cream, room temperature
1½ teaspoons pure vanilla extract

1 Preheat oven to 350°F. On a lightly floured surface, roll out dough to slightly more than ⅛ inch thick. Place the bottom of a 10-inch springform pan on top of dough; using a paring knife, cut out a round about ¼ inch larger in diameter than the pan. Place dough on a baking sheet; freeze 15 minutes. Bake until golden, 12 to 15 minutes. Transfer crust to a wire rack to cool completely.

2 Butter sides of springform pan and, with bottom of pan intact, insert bottom crust. Wrap bottom half of pan in foil. With an electric mixer on medium speed, beat cream cheese until light and fluffy; scrape down sides of bowl. In a small bowl, combine sugar and flour. With mixer on low speed, gradually add sugar mixture to cream cheese; beat until smooth. Add eggs, one at a time, beating until smooth after each and scraping down sides of bowl as needed. Mix in sour cream and vanilla.

3 Pour filling over crust. Set pan inside a roasting pan. Transfer to oven. Carefully ladle boiling water into roasting pan to reach halfway up sides of cake pan. Bake 45 minutes; reduce oven to 325°F. Continue to bake until cake is golden on top but still slightly wobbly in center, about 30 minutes more. Turn off oven; leave cake in oven with door slightly ajar 1 hour.

4 Transfer cake pan to a wire rack; let cool completely. Refrigerate, uncovered, at least 6 hours or up to overnight. Before removing the sides of the pan, run a knife around the edge of the cake.

SERVES 8 TO 10

MAPLE SYRUP

Long before the snow melts in the sugar bush, that part of the woods where the working sugar maples are thick, the sap starts to run. Syrup makers know that spring is on its way by the change in weather and the sound of crows cawing in the woods—an age-old omen of the maple harvest.

There's usually one clear day that initiates the sap flow on the mountain farms of the northeastern United States and nearby Canada. It takes a freezing-cold night followed by a day when the temperature climbs slowly to a "balmy" forty degrees or so. That's when eager farmers look up toward the sugar bush and strain their ears for the faint ping of sap dripping into their recently hung metal buckets.

Roughly forty gallons of clear, watery sap—the seasonal yield of three trees—must be boiled down for one gallon of pure maple syrup. Its grade, according to USDA regulations, is based on color and flavor, although some states use different terms to mean the same grade: "Grade AA Light Amber" and "Fancy Grade," for example, are synonymous. Grade B syrup is not of lesser quality, but simply darker in color and more robust-tasting. In fact, many people prefer its complex depth, especially for baking. Farmers don't really have a say as to what grade (or how much of it) they make in a given year; the weather is in charge, since it triggers the changes in the maple trees as they move from a dormant state to the growth spurt that occurs in spring. Generally speaking, lighter Grade A syrup is produced early on in the season, when it's colder outside, and Grade B is made later, when temperatures rise.

As the trees begin to leaf out for summer, the sap acquires an unpleasant "bud" taste, which means the harvest is over. And just as noisy crows signal the beginning of the harvest, woodpeckers herald the end. When you hear the sound of their beaks banging against the sap buckets, it's time to wash everything down and get ready for next year's run.

MAPLE SYRUP OVER SNOW For centuries, sugar makers have made a kind of taffy by drizzling hot syrup on newly fallen snow. You can re-create this at home: Heat some maple syrup in a heavy-bottomed saucepan over medium until about 240°F on a candy thermometer. Scoop up some freshly fallen snow and pour the hot syrup over. Try using an egg carton as a "bowl."

MAPLE BUNDT CAKE

¾ cup (1½ sticks) unsalted butter, softened, plus more for pan

2 cups all-purpose flour, plus more for dusting

2 teaspoons baking powder

½ teaspoon baking soda

½ teaspoon salt

½ cup packed dark-brown sugar

2 large eggs

½ cup plus 2 tablespoons pure maple syrup, plus more for drizzling

2 teaspoons pure vanilla extract

1 cup sour cream

½ cup cold heavy cream

1 Preheat oven to 350°F. Butter a 10-inch Bundt pan. Dust with flour and tap out excess. Whisk together flour, baking powder, baking soda, and salt in a medium bowl.

2 Cream butter and brown sugar with an electric mixer on medium-high speed until fluffy, 3 to 4 minutes. Add eggs, one at a time, beating well after each addition. Beat in ½ cup maple syrup and the vanilla. Add flour mixture in three additions, alternating with the sour cream and beginning and ending with flour; beat until just combined after each addition.

3 Scrape batter into prepared pan. Bake until golden brown and a tester inserted into middle of cake comes out clean, 35 to 40 minutes. Let cool in pan on a wire rack 15 minutes before turning out onto rack to cool completely.

4 Just before serving, whisk cream until soft peaks form. Add 2 tablespoons maple syrup and whisk until soft peaks return. Spoon whipped cream over cake and drizzle with more maple syrup. Serve immediately.

SERVES 8 TO 10

THE NORTHEAST

BACKSTORY

A moist, tender Bundt cake is infused with genuine Vermont flavor in the form of maple syrup that is used in the batter and, after the cake has baked, drizzled over a halo of maple-infused whipped cream. First introduced by NordicWare in 1950—and popularized in 1966 when a Bundt cake won the Pillsbury Bake-Off— the distinctively shaped pan was designed as a metal version of the ceramic molds used in Europe to bake kugelhopf, a type of yeast cake. The name is a variation on bund, *the German word for* gathering, *which is precisely what American hostesses use them for, then and now.*

BOSTON CREAM PIE

Unsalted butter, softened, for pan

1 cup sifted cake flour (not self-rising), plus more for dusting

¼ teaspoon salt

4 large eggs

1 cup sugar

¼ cup plus 2 tablespoons milk

1 vanilla bean, split lengthwise

Vanilla Pastry Cream (page 414)

Chocolate Ganache Icing (page 414)

1 Preheat oven to 350°F. Butter a 9-inch round cake pan; dust with flour and tap out excess. Line bottom with parchment. Sift together cake flour and salt three times into a medium bowl.

2 In a heatproof mixing bowl set over (not in) a pan of simmering water, whisk together eggs and sugar until warm to the touch and sugar has dissolved, about 6 minutes. Remove from heat. With an electric mixer on high speed, beat until thick and pale, about 6 minutes.

3 Pour milk into a small saucepan; scrape in vanilla seeds and add pod. Heat over medium just until hot; do not let boil. Discard pod. With mixer on low, add milk to egg mixture in a slow, steady stream. Gently fold in flour mixture until combined.

4 Transfer batter to prepared pan and smooth top with an offset spatula. Bake until cake is golden brown and springs back when touched in the center, about 30 minutes. Transfer to a wire rack to cool 15 minutes. Run a sharp knife around edge and invert cake onto rack, then let cool completely, top side up.

5 Using a serrated knife, slice cake horizontally into two even layers. Spread bottom layer with pastry cream. Chill until set, about 30 minutes. Remove cake from refrigerator; top with remaining cake layer. Place cake on a wire rack set on a rimmed baking sheet. Pour ganache over cake. Use an offset spatula to swirl top. Transfer to a serving plate and chill until ready to serve.

SERVES 8 TO 10

THE NORTHEAST

BACKSTORY

Despite what it's called, this "pie" is actually a cake. One theory on how it got its name is that, in nineteenth-century Boston where it originated, the layers were baked in pie tins, which were more common than cake pans. We get a clue as to the dessert's inventor from older cookbooks, which sometimes refer to it as a Parker House chocolate cream pie, after the historic Boston hotel. Today the cake has the honor of being the official dessert of the state of Massachusetts. The ganache topping thickens as it sits; you want it pourable but thick enough to coat the cake.

SHOOFLY PIE

THE NORTHEAST

BACKSTORY

This Pennsylvania Dutch invention could only have happened with the intersection of two different immigrant groups in America: Molasses pie borrows from the English tradition of treacle tarts and the buttery crumb topping is truly a German streusel. The dessert's name, it is said, comes from the fact that the pie is so sweet that you have to chase the flies away before you can take a bite. Cookbook writers often delineate between "wet bottom" and "dry bottom" versions of shoofly pie or cake; the former denotes a gooey pie filling on top of a crust, and the latter is supposedly firm enough that you can dunk a piece into your coffee. This version falls in the former camp.

1 disk Basic Pie Dough (page 412)
1 cup all-purpose flour, plus more for dusting
½ cup packed light-brown sugar
1 teaspoon ground cinnamon
½ teaspoon freshly grated nutmeg
¼ teaspoon plus a pinch of salt
6 tablespoons (¾ stick) cold unsalted butter, cut into ½-inch pieces
1 cup boiling water
½ cup unsulfured molasses
½ cup light corn syrup
1 teaspoon baking soda
1 large egg, lightly beaten

1 Roll out pie dough on a lightly floured work surface to about ⅛ inch thick. Fit into a 9-inch pie plate. Trim edge to leave a 1-inch overhang; fold edge under and crimp with your fingers. Chill pie shell at least 30 minutes or up to overnight.

2 Preheat oven to 325°F. In a medium bowl, whisk together flour, brown sugar, cinnamon, nutmeg, and ¼ teaspoon salt. Work in butter with your fingers until mixture forms fine crumbs.

3 Stir together the boiling water, molasses, and corn syrup in another bowl. Whisk in baking soda, egg, and remaining pinch of salt. Pour molasses mixture into chilled pie shell. Scatter crumb topping evenly over filling.

4 Bake on a rimmed baking sheet until filling is set and topping is deep golden brown, about 50 minutes. Let cool on a wire rack 30 minutes. Serve warm.

MAKES ONE SINGLE-CRUST 9-INCH PIE

HERMIT BARS

2 cups plus 2 tablespoons all-purpose flour

2 teaspoons baking soda

2 teaspoons ground ginger

1¾ teaspoons ground cinnamon

¾ teaspoon ground cloves

¼ teaspoon salt

½ cup (1 stick) plus 1 tablespoon unsalted butter, softened

1 cup loosely packed light-brown sugar

1 large egg, room temperature

¼ cup unsulfured molasses

¾ cup raisins

1 Preheat oven to 375°F. Line a baking sheet with parchment. Into a medium bowl, sift together flour, baking soda, ginger, cinnamon, cloves, and salt.

2 With an electric mixer, cream the butter and brown sugar on medium speed until light and fluffy, about 2 minutes. Add egg; beat until combined, scraping down sides of bowl once. Add molasses; beat until combined, and scrape down sides of bowl. Add the flour mixture and raisins; beat on low speed until dough just comes together, about 1 minute. Cover with plastic wrap; refrigerate 30 minutes.

3 Remove dough from refrigerator, and turn out onto a clean work surface. Divide into two equal pieces, and shape each piece into a 12-inch log. Place on a parchment-lined baking sheet, at least 3 inches apart.

4 Bake until golden but still very soft to the touch, 20 to 22 minutes. The dough will flatten out and lengthen as it bakes and get slightly puffy in the center. Transfer sheet to a wire rack to cool completely. Cut into 2-inch-wide bars. Hermit bars can be stored in an airtight container at room temperature, up to 1 week.

MAKES ABOUT 30

THE NORTHEAST

BACKSTORY

Rich with molasses, hermit bars are spicy, sturdy, time-honored treats that keep extremely well when tucked away (hence their name). In fact, their flavor improves a day or two after baking, so resist the urge to devour one warm from the oven, if you can. They contain the same trio of spices—cinnamon, cloves, and ginger—that flavor so many other American cookies, including ginger snaps, molasses crinkles, and Moravian spice cookies. Hermit bars are as soft and chewy as cookies get, helped in part by the generous dose of raisins mixed into the batter.

WHOOPIE PIES

THE NORTHEAST

BACKSTORY

*They have a winsome name
of unknown origin and
a pedigree almost as hard to
confirm, but one thing is
certain: Whoopie pies have
been a lunchbox staple
for generations. Some say
they were first created in
Pennsylvania Dutch kitchens
as a way to put leftover
chocolate-cake batter and
icing to good use. Regardless
of when they were introduced,
these confections have been
manufactured commercially
since 1927. They became
a popular homemade dessert
during the late forties and
early fifties and still remain a
beloved favorite, especially
in Maine and Pennsylvania.
Today you will find lots of
innovative variations on the
classic recipe (including
pumpkin, red velvet, and
banana, most filled with cream
cheese icing), yet it is hard to
beat the winning combination
of chocolate cakes and fluffy
seven-minute frosting of the
original. A one-ounce
ice cream scoop (also called
a cookie scoop) makes fast
work of forming the batter into
uniform shapes for even
baking—and perfect matching.*

3½ cups all-purpose flour

1½ cups unsweetened cocoa powder

1 tablespoon baking soda

1 teaspoon baking powder

1 teaspoon salt

1 cup (2 sticks) unsalted butter, softened

2 cups sugar

2 large eggs

2 cups buttermilk, room temperature

2 teaspoons pure vanilla extract

½ recipe Seven-Minute Frosting (page 69)

1 Preheat oven to 400°F. Line two baking sheets with nonstick baking mats or parchment. Sift together flour, cocoa powder, baking soda, baking powder, and salt into a bowl.

2 With an electric mixer on medium speed, cream butter and sugar until light and fluffy, about 2 minutes. Add eggs, buttermilk, and vanilla; beat until well combined. With mixer on low speed, gradually add flour mixture and mix until combined.

3 Using a 1-ounce ice cream scoop, place 12 cookies on each prepared baking sheet, spacing 2 inches apart. Bake until cookies spring back to the touch, rotating sheets halfway through, about 12 minutes. Transfer cookies to a wire rack to cool completely. Repeat with remaining batter to make 24 more cookies.

4 Spread 2 tablespoons frosting onto flat side of each of 24 cooled cookies. Sandwich together with remaining 24 cookies. (Whoopie pies can be stored, layered between sheets of parchment, in an airtight container at room temperature up to 3 days.)

MAKES 2 DOZEN PIES

SOUTH

It doesn't take much to fall in love with the cooking of the American South. Biscuits, hot from the oven and light as a feather. Crisp, golden fried chicken that is reason alone to own a cast-iron skillet. Smoky pulled pork washed down with a glass of iced sweet tea. Pristinely fresh shellfish. Just-picked peaches baked into a juicy cobbler. Deviled eggs, lightly sprinkled with paprika and brought with pride to a family reunion or potluck supper.

Of course, any Southerner will tell you that the cooking of the region is more varied than that of any other part of the country, and it's true that a gutsy oyster po'boy seems a world apart from gently flavored pound cake. But the roots of Southern food—which stretch from the hills and hollows of Appalachia to the lush sweep of the Carolina and Georgia Lowcountry down to the balmy Florida Keys—are found in the abundant provisions of an agrarian land.

With European explorers and settlers came pigs, cattle, chickens, wheat, apples, turnips, and, by way of the Caribbean, key limes. New foods like okra, collard greens, black-eyed peas, and watermelons arrived with the slave trade, along with the knowledge of rice cultivation that made a plantation economy possible. Like all who first arrived on these shores, both black and white newcomers relied heavily on Native American ingredients, including corn, beans, and squash. Rich, light spoon bread—a favorite of the landed gentry—is a wonderful example of the complex, bittersweet melding that occurred in the antebellum South. Cornmeal, made from the indigenous staple, is its primary ingredient; the culinary technique is European; and for much of the South's history, the hand that seasoned and stirred the pot was African.

The Lowcountry, the coastal plain of South Carolina and Georgia that begins at the Atlantic and stretches eighty miles inland, is an enormous web of marsh, grassy savannas, and winding tidal creeks that sustain a multitude of shrimp, blue crabs, oysters, clams, and fin fish such as shad and flounder. This seafood is the backbone of the rich cuisine of the aristocratic cities of Charleston and Savannah. If you are from that part of the South, the food most likely to make you pine for home is shrimp and grits, or possibly Hoppin' John, a humble rice-and-bean dish commonly made with black-eyed peas. It's enjoyed anytime, but especially on New Year's Day, when eating it is considered good luck.

The Creole cooks of New Orleans preferred red kidney beans with their rice, and the dish has become so central to the city's identity that native son Louis Armstrong signed his letters, "Red beans and ricely yours." To celebrate Mardi Gras, residents of the Crescent City might well start things off with a Sazerac (or two) before helping themselves from a big pot of gumbo.

The mountain food of Appalachia, arguably the least known Southern cuisine, is tied to the woods, the farm, and the garden. Get anyone from the region to talk about his or her hands-down favorites, and you will hear of chicken and dumplings (commonly made with flat, unleavened dumplings), biscuits of every description, and home-baked fruit pies and cobblers.

So much of Southern food creates a sense of place, no matter where you are. Just as important, the food is about sitting down at a table together— eating, drinking, sharing stories, and finding room for just one more bite.

RECILES

SAZERAC

MINT JULEP

OLD-FASHIONED

SWEET TEA

DRINKS

SAZERAC

No matter where you sip a Sazerac, the flavors should remind you instantly of New Orleans, where the drink was invented more than a century ago. It was created as a way to showcase French Cognac, though now the cocktail is more often made with rye whiskey. Nevertheless, the method of mixing the drink remains the same: Start by chilling a glass with ice, then combine the ingredients and strain into another chilled glass that has been "rinsed" with Pernod (or Herbsaint, a local version of the anise-flavored liqueur). The result is a remarkably smooth cocktail.

Fill two old-fashioned glasses with **ice** to chill. Discard ice from one glass, and add 1 teaspoon **water**, 4 dashes of **bitters**, and ½ teaspoon **sugar**; stir to dissolve. Add ¼ cup (2 fluid ounces) **rye whiskey** and a few ice cubes; stir. Discard ice from remaining glass. Fill with a small amount of **Pernod** and swirl to coat; discard Pernod. Strain into prepared glass. Garnish with a **lemon twist**. Serve immediately. **MAKES 1**

MINT JULEP

Mint Juleps—so popular during horseracing season, from the Kentucky Derby to the Preakness Stakes and then the Belmont Stakes—are among my favorite cocktails to serve. Each year my friends and I get nervous watching the races, and the soothing tart-and-sweet and minty drinks offer a refreshing alternative to nail biting. My Southern friends love the Juleps as much as I do, and I always take my recipe as a true vote of their confidence. Nary a soul has put one of these icy drinks down unfinished.

Combine 2½ cups (20 fluid ounces) **bourbon**, preferably Maker's Mark, and 1 cup packed fresh **mint** leaves in a large pitcher. Cover and refrigerate 12 hours or up to 1 day. Strain, discarding mint. Add 2 to 3 tablespoons **superfine sugar**, stirring to dissolve. Divide among four julep cups or glasses filled with **shaved ice** (or use crushed ice). Garnish each with a **mint** sprig. Serve immediately. **MAKES 4**

OLD-FASHIONED

The story surrounding the birth of the Old-Fashioned is shrouded in mystery and myth, yet many Southerners contend that it was first mixed in Louisville, Kentucky, as a bartender's response to a request for a drink from Colonel James Pepper, the distiller of Old 1776 Bourbon. Although some claim that the original Old-Fashioneds were made with rye whiskey, bourbon has evolved as the spirit of choice.

Put a **sugar cube** in an old-fashioned glass; add a dash of **bitters** and 2 drops of cold **water** and stir to dissolve the sugar. Add **ice cubes** and ¼ cup (2 fluid ounces) **bourbon**; stir to combine. Twist a thin wedge of **orange** over drink to release oils, then drop into the glass. Serve immediately. **MAKES 1**

SWEET TEA

Ordering an iced tea in the South will more often than not get you a glass of "sweet tea," a sugary—but not at all cloying—variation on the brewed refreshment. The key is to completely dissolve the sugar in the hot tea while it's still brewing. This version, redolent of fresh mint, will encourage you to take to the porch with a good book on a hot summer day.

Bring 4 cups of **water** to a boil in a medium saucepan. Remove from heat. Add 6 black **tea bags**; let steep 5 minutes. Remove tea bags and discard. Stir in ¾ cup **sugar** until dissolved. Let cool. Transfer to a pitcher. Cover and refrigerate at least 1 hour or up to 3 days. Serve over **ice**, garnished with **mint** sprigs. **SERVES 4**

PIMIENTO CHEESE

8 ounces sharp yellow cheddar, room temperature

8 ounces Monterey Jack, room temperature

1 jar (4 ounces) pimientos, drained

1 garlic clove, minced

¼ cup plus 2 tablespoons mayonnaise

½ teaspoon dry mustard powder

¼ teaspoon cayenne

Celery sticks, for serving

Grate both cheeses on the large holes of a box grater and combine in a medium bowl. In a food processor, pulse pimientos, garlic, mayonnaise, mustard powder, and cayenne just until pimientos are coarsely chopped. Stir into cheeses until thoroughly combined and mixture is creamy. Cover and refrigerate at least 2 hours or up to 3 days. Serve with celery sticks.

SERVES 6 TO 8

THE SOUTH

BACKSTORY

No one knows how or when grated sharp cheddar and the long red chile called "pimiento" met, but the resulting marriage—bound together with mayonnaise and called "pimento cheese" by any self-respecting Southerner—has been put into sandwiches, stuffed into celery sticks, and slathered on crackers for almost one hundred years. "I've been caught eating a pound in two days (though it keeps well)," wrote the novelist Reynolds Price, "especially when life is hard." It's also unclear when cheese straws, often given a little kick by cayenne, became the go-to cocktail nibble for Southern hostesses, but by the 1950s, there was a recipe in almost every Junior League cookbook from Baltimore on down. A cookie tin of them, layered between sheets of waxed paper, makes a great gift, but be warned: The lucky recipients will expect the same year after year. You'll need a cookie press to form the cheese straws in their most traditional shape; otherwise you can roll out the dough as instructed in the recipe.

CHEESE STRAWS

1½ cups all-purpose flour, plus more for dusting

1 teaspoon dry mustard powder

1 teaspoon salt

⅛ teaspoon cayenne

½ cup (1 stick) unsalted butter, cut into small pieces, softened

6 ounces sharp cheddar, grated (about 2¼ cups)

1 Preheat oven to 375°F. Whisk together flour, mustard powder, salt, and cayenne. In a food processor, pulse butter, cheese, and flour mixture just until a dough forms.

2 Divide dough into four equal pieces. Fit a cookie press with the ribbon disk and fill with one portion of dough. (Alternatively, wrap each piece in plastic and chill 30 minutes; roll out dough with a rolling pin ½ inch thick, then cut into strips with a pastry wheel or sharp knife, using a ruler as a guide.) Press dough in a continuous line onto a baking sheet (the line should be about 12 inches long; it's okay if dough breaks during pressing since it will be cut into shorter pieces). Then repeat, pressing out remaining dough in separate lines, side by side. Cut into 3-inch lengths; if desired, cut each piece in half lengthwise, creating 3-by-½-inch strips. Arrange strips 1 to 2 inches apart on baking sheet. Repeat with remaining dough. Chill until firm, about 15 minutes.

3 Bake until golden and firm to the touch, rotating sheets halfway through, 10 to 12 minutes. Transfer to a wire rack to cool completely. (Cheese straws can be stored in an airtight container up to 2 weeks.)

MAKES ABOUT 24

REGIONAL FLAVOR

OKRA

The unripe fruit of a species of hibiscus, okra has been eaten in India, Asia, and the Middle East for centuries. Its texture and flavor have been described as something like a cross between eggplant and asparagus. It offers a welcome variety to summer's tidal wave of tomatoes, zucchini, and yellow squash. Southerners eat okra sliced and fried, crisply pickled, sautéed or stewed with tomatoes, and reduced to utter silkiness in gumbos and other stews.

A sun-loving plant, okra thrives on every continent except Antarctica. But one reason it hasn't become a more popular ingredient across the United States may be its unfortunate reputation for having a slimy consistency. Blame the cooks, not the vegetable. When okra is cooked slowly, it releases complex sugars and moisture. Those qualities thicken soups and stews beautifully, but can prove troublesome when you want to serve okra on its own. Sidestep the slippery factor by buying the freshest okra you can find (avoid pods with telltale dark age spots) and by cooking it quickly over high heat. Whole pods are easy to manage; try sautéing them in a hot, bacon-greased skillet for a few minutes or grill over glowing coals, which adds a hint of smokiness.

To really go for broke, slice okra and panfry it. Although fried chicken joints in the South turn out okra nuggets like french fries, they really are best when homemade—battered in coarse cornmeal and flour and cooked to a golden crisp. Serve fried okra fresh and hot, right out of the pan, with a little hot sauce or pepper-infused vinegar on the side to focus the sweet, green flavor of the vegetable and to cut the richness of the crust.

FRIED OKRA Using egg whites instead of whole eggs results in a lighter, crispier coating. Trim 1 pound okra; slice crosswise ½ inch thick. Whisk together 2 large egg whites and 2 tablespoons cold water. In another bowl, whisk to combine 1¼ cups yellow cornmeal, ¼ cup all-purpose flour, and ½ teaspoon cayenne; season with coarse salt and freshly ground pepper. In a deep 12-inch cast-iron skillet, heat 1 quart neutral-tasting oil, such as safflower, to 375°F on a deep-fry thermometer. Add half the okra to egg mixture; lift and let excess drain back into the bowl. Dredge in flour mixture, coating completely. Working in batches, add okra to hot oil; cook, gently stirring (without disturbing crust), until golden brown, 3 to 6 minutes; adjust heat as needed to keep oil between 300°F and 350°F. Use a mesh skimmer or slotted spoon to transfer okra to a paper towel–lined baking sheet. Return oil to 375°F between batches. Season with salt.

DILLY BEANS

PICKLED OKRA

PICKLED WATERMELON RIND

PICKLED WATERMELON RIND

1 large watermelon (about 25 pounds)
2 tablespoons coarse salt
1 gallon cold water
3 cups sugar
2 cups cider vinegar
1 piece (½ inch) fresh ginger, peeled
½ teaspoon mace
2 small cinnamon sticks
1 lemon, thinly sliced

1 Cut watermelon in half; remove flesh (reserve for another use). Using a metal spoon, scrape rind to remove all traces of pink. Cut rind crosswise into 1-inch-wide strips. Using a vegetable peeler or a small sharp knife, peel the green skin from the rind. Cut away any bruises or bad spots. Cut rind into 2-inch lengths.

2 In a large nonreactive bowl, combine salt and the cold water. Add rind; let soak in brine overnight. Rinse rind two or three times in fresh cold water; drain well.

3 In a large nonreactive pot, combine sugar and vinegar and heat, stirring, until sugar is dissolved. Fold an 8-by-16-inch piece of cheesecloth in half to make a square; rinse and squeeze dry. Place ginger, spices, and lemon on the cheesecloth; tie closed with one end of a 12-inch-long piece of cotton string. Tie a loop in the other end and slip it over the handle of a wooden spoon. Suspend spice bag in the vinegar syrup by placing the spoon across the top of the pot. Add the rind and return to a boil. Reduce heat and simmer 30 minutes, then remove from heat and let sit overnight at room temperature. Discard spice sachet.

4 With a slotted spoon, transfer rind to sterilized jars, dividing evenly and leaving ¾ inch of space beneath the rim. Pour hot syrup over rind, covering it by ¼ inch and leaving at least ¾ inch of space beneath the rim. Slide a clean plastic chopstick or wooden skewer along the inside of each jar to release any air bubbles. Wipe mouth of jar with a clean, damp cloth. Place hot lid on jar; turn screw band firmly without forcing.

5 Place a wire rack in the bottom of a large pot and fill partway with hot water. Using a jar lifter or tongs, place jars upright on rack. Add enough hot water to cover by 2 inches, and bring to a boil. Boil 10 minutes. Remove jars from water bath; let stand on clean dish towels 24 hours. Check cool jars for the slight indentation in the lids that indicates a vacuum seal. Jars that do not seal properly or that leak during processing should be refrigerated and pickles consumed within a week. Allow sealed pickles to stand in a cool, dry place 2 to 3 weeks before serving. Refrigerate after opening.

MAKES 7 PINTS

THE SOUTH

BACKSTORY

What started as necessity—settlers would put up excess produce in the hope that the jars would carry them through the winter—has now become a legacy, as American families in every region hand down pickling recipes from one generation to another. Pickles and preserves became and remain prevalent in the South, perhaps owing to an abundance of crops in the summer months. This trio of pickles, made with three of the region's staple ingredients— watermelon, okra, and green beans—is quintessential. Instructions for sterilizing jars for canning are on page 409. If you'd rather not can the pickles, simply pour the brining mixture over the items to be pickled in a heatproof bowl, then let cool completely before refrigerating. They're good for up to one month in an airtight container.

PICKLED OKRA

2 pounds tender small okra
1 quart distilled white vinegar
3 cups water
¼ cup plus 2 tablespoons coarse salt
16 small garlic cloves (peeled)
8 small fresh hot red chile peppers, such as New Mexican or Mirasol
1 bunch fresh dill (about 24 sprigs)
½ cup yellow mustard seeds

1 Rinse okra and cut away any bruises or bad spots. Trim stem ends of okra, but do not remove caps.

2 In a large pot, bring vinegar, the water, and salt to a boil. Evenly divide garlic, peppers, dill sprigs, and mustard seeds among sterilized jars (see page 409). Pack tightly with okra, alternating direction of okra. Leave at least ¾ inch of space beneath the rim of the jar. Pour hot liquid over okra, covering it by ¼ inch and leaving ½ inch of space beneath the rim. Slide a clean plastic chopstick or wooden skewer along the inside of each jar to release any air bubbles. Wipe mouth of jar with a clean, damp cloth. Place hot lid on jar; turn screw band firmly without forcing.

3 Seal jars as instructed in step 5 of recipe on page 161. Jars that do not seal properly or that leak during processing should be refrigerated and pickles consumed within a week. Allow sealed pickles to stand in a cool, dry place 6 to 8 weeks before serving. Refrigerate after opening.

MAKES 8 PINTS

DILLY BEANS

Coarse salt
1 pound green beans, stem ends trimmed
1 cup water
1 cup distilled white vinegar
8 sprigs dill
4 garlic cloves
¼ teaspoon cayenne
2 teaspoons mustard seeds

1 Wash two pint-size jars and lids in hot, soapy water, and rinse well. Dry thoroughly.

2 Prepare an ice-water bath. In a large pot of salted boiling water, cook beans 2 minutes; remove from heat with a mesh spider or slotted spoon and immediately transfer to the ice bath to stop the cooking. Once cool, drain beans.

3 In a small saucepan, bring 1 cup water, the vinegar, and 2 tablespoons salt to a boil.

4 Evenly divide dill, garlic, cayenne, mustard seeds, and beans among clean jars, leaving at least ¾ inch of space beneath the rim. Pour hot liquid over beans, covering them by ¼ inch and leaving at least ¾ inch of space beneath the rim. Place lids on jars and let stand until cool completely. Refrigerate at least 1 day and up to 1 month before serving.

MAKES 2 PINTS

DEVILED EGGS

8   medium eggs
1   tablespoon Dijon mustard
¼   cup mayonnaise
1   tablespoon finely chopped fresh chives
    Coarse salt and freshly ground pepper
    Paprika, for garnish

1 Place eggs in a saucepan; fill with enough cold water to cover by 1 inch. Bring to a boil; turn off heat. Cover; let stand 11 minutes. Transfer to a bowl and cover with cold water until cool. Peel eggs and slice in half lengthwise; separate the yolks from the whites. Trim curve off whites so they will stand upright.

2 Place yolks in a coarse sieve set over a medium bowl; press through with the back of a spoon. Mix in mustard, mayonnaise, and chives; season with salt and pepper. Fill egg-white halves with yolk mixture and refrigerate in a covered container up to 4 hours. Before serving, garnish with paprika.

SERVES 8

THE SOUTH

BACKSTORY

Deviled eggs are found all over the United States, but they are particularly popular in the South, where you might expect a platter—perhaps several—to appear at almost any gathering or get-together. Their popularity has yielded scores of variations, including mixing the egg yolks with pickle relish, blue cheese, or even caviar. Yet mayonnaise spiked with a little Dijon mustard and a dash of paprika remains the gold standard. Use medium eggs so they will be small enough to serve as hors d'oeuvres.

ZESTY CRAB CAKES

¼ cup yellow cornmeal

2 tablespoons unsalted butter, melted and cooled

2 large eggs

3 tablespoons sour cream

2 tablespoons coarsely chopped fresh flat-leaf parsley

2 tablespoons fresh lemon juice, plus wedges for serving

½ teaspoon Worcestershire sauce

½ teaspoon paprika

¼ teaspoon cayenne

½ teaspoon coarse salt

1 pound lump crabmeat, picked over

3 hot pickled peppers, such as Peppadew, coarsely chopped

¾ cup plain fresh breadcrumbs

¼ cup neutral-tasting oil, such as safflower

1 Line a baking sheet with parchment; sprinkle with 2 tablespoons cornmeal. Whisk together butter, eggs, sour cream, parsley, lemon juice, Worcestershire, paprika, cayenne, and salt in a large bowl. Gently mix in crabmeat, peppers, and breadcrumbs.

2 For each crab cake, shape ⅔ cup crab mixture into a patty; place on prepared sheet. Sprinkle patties with remaining 2 tablespoons cornmeal, dividing evenly. Cover with plastic wrap; refrigerate 15 minutes.

3 Heat oil in a large skillet over medium-high. Working in batches, cook crab cakes until golden brown and crisp, 4 to 5 minutes per side. Serve immediately, with lemon wedges.

SERVES 4

SOFT-SHELL CRABS

A visit to North Carolina's Roanoke Island, located west of the Outer Banks, promises many things—close encounters with aquatic wildlife, the lingering mystery of the Lost Colony (a group of settlers who came from England in 1587 and disappeared with barely a trace shortly thereafter), and, if your timing is right, one of the freshest soft-shell crab dinners you'll find anywhere.

Soft-shell crabs are simply blue crabs that have shed their hard exteriors—a phenomenon many crabbers attribute to the full moon—and are caught in the short amount of time before their shells have hardened again. These seasonal delicacies can be found along much of the Atlantic seaboard, but they thrive in the cool, clear waters off Roanoke Island, especially in May and June. This is when blue crabs come here to spawn, protected from tides and human traffic by the island's marshes and swamps.

Although the pickings are generous, the job of a professional crabber in search of soft-shells (known to the pros as "peelers") is anything but easy. First, the traps are baited, marked with colorful buoys, and set; then they are checked every few hours and emptied of their catch. Crabs that show no signs of being ready to shed are thrown back, and others (the ones whose swimmer fins show a thin red or green line, rather than the usual black) are held in tanks, and watched carefully around the clock until they discard their shells, usually within a few days.

As soon as that happens the vigil ends and the crabs are quickly sold, mostly to local seafood markets and restaurants. A soft-shell crab this fresh and tender should be enjoyed at its simple best—very lightly seasoned and grilled or sautéed, or dredged in flour and panfried for a sandwich like no other.

SOFT-SHELL CRAB SANDWICH The key to this beachside shack favorite is the sauce, which is quick to prepare and will taste much better than anything from a bottle. Stir together 1 cup mayonnaise, 3 tablespoons sweet pickle relish, 1 tablespoon fresh lemon juice, 1 teaspoon Old Bay seasoning, and a pinch of freshly ground pepper. (Sauce can be refrigerated in an airtight container up to 1 week before serving.) Follow steps 1 and 2 in the recipe on page 168 to clean and panfry soft-shell crabs. Serve each fried crab on a split roll topped with sauce, lettuce, and tomato, with additional sauce on the side.

PANFRIED SOFT-SHELL CRABS

THE SOUTH

BACKSTORY

From Maryland to the Gulf of Mexico, summer brings with it an abundance of soft-shell crabs. Frying the crabs whole makes the most of their incomparable texture; serve them with coleslaw or other regional sides, or sandwich them between slices of white bread. Buy live crabs only on the day you plan to cook them. They should be kept in the coldest part of the refrigerator, wrapped in plastic or wet newspaper, until ready to be cleaned and cooked. If you prefer, you can ask your fishmonger to clean the crabs for you.

- 12 soft-shell crabs
- 1½ cups all-purpose flour
- 2 teaspoons coarse salt
- 1 teaspoon freshly ground pepper
- ¾ cup neutral-tasting oil, such as safflower
- 6 tablespoons unsalted butter
- ¼ cup loosely packed fresh flat-leaf parsley, chopped
- 3 lemons, cut in half

1 Preheat oven to 200°F. To clean crabs, hold each crab with one hand and use kitchen shears to snip off the eyes and mouth, cutting about ¼ inch behind the eyes. Scoop out soft matter just behind this cut. Lift up the apron (flap of shell on the belly) and cut or twist off. Lift the shell on each side of the body and scrape off the gray gills; discard. Rinse crab lightly and pat dry with paper towels. Whisk together flour, salt, and pepper; place on a plate.

2 Heat 2 tablespoons oil in a medium skillet over medium-high until hot but not smoking. While oil is heating, dredge 2 crabs in flour mixture to coat completely, shaking off excess. Place flour-coated crabs, back side down, in pan; reduce heat to medium if oil starts to smoke. Sauté crabs until golden and crisp on the first side, about 3 minutes (do not stand too close to pan; crabs tend to spatter during cooking). Use tongs to turn crabs over and cook until other side is golden, about 2 minutes more.

3 Add 1 tablespoon butter and a large pinch of parsley to skillet. Squeeze the juice of half a lemon over crabs. Transfer crabs to a parchment-lined baking sheet and keep warm in the oven.

4 Repeat steps 2 and 3 until all the crabs are cooked. Serve warm.

SERVES 6

OYSTER PO'BOYS

½ cup (1 stick) unsalted butter
2 tablespoons minced garlic
4 ciabatta rolls, split
⅔ cup whole-wheat flour
½ cup powdered milk
½ teaspoon cayenne
1½ teaspoons coarse salt
2 tablespoons finely chopped fresh flat-leaf parsley
2 tablespoons finely chopped fresh chives
   Freshly ground pepper
32 fresh large oysters, shucked and drained
   Neutral-tasting oil, such as safflower, for frying
2 ounces arugula, tough stems trimmed, washed well and drained
4 anchovy fillets, rinsed (optional)
2 lemons, cut into wedges

1 Preheat oven to 400°F. Melt butter in a small saucepan with garlic; let cool slightly, then purée in a food processor. Remove some of the bread from inside rolls. Place rolls on a baking sheet, cut sides up.

2 Whisk together whole-wheat flour, powdered milk, cayenne, salt, and herbs in a bowl; season with pepper. Dredge oysters in mixture, coating completely; shake off excess.

3 Heat 1 inch oil in a large skillet over medium-high. Meanwhile, spread 2 teaspoons garlic butter over each split roll. Bake until golden brown, about 5 minutes.

4 Fry oysters in batches until golden brown, 30 to 45 seconds per side. Using a mesh skimmer or slotted spoon, transfer oysters to paper towels and let drain. Layer rolls with oysters, arugula, and anchovies. Serve with lemon wedges.

SERVES 4

THE SOUTH

BACKSTORY

Perhaps the second-best way to eat oysters, after on the half-shell, is deep-fried and piled high in a po'boy, the signature sandwich of New Orleans. Although po'boys are made by stuffing crusty French bread with all sorts of fillings, including shrimp, catfish, or roast beef, fried oysters are a perennial favorite among locals and tourists alike. The sandwich is said to be the invention of Bennie and Clovis Martin of Martin Brothers Grocery, who wanted to offer a cheap meal for striking streetcar workers in 1929 (the Martins themselves were former streetcar workers). Whenever they saw one of the struggling men coming to their shop, they would say "Here comes another poor boy," and over time the sandwich became known as such, with due abbreviation. With their crisp, hot battered shells and juicy interiors, fried oysters produce sandwiches that are nothing short of spectacular. Arugula, garlic butter, optional anchovies, and ciabatta rolls combine in this modern representation.

CHICKEN AND ANDOUILLE GUMBO

THE SOUTH

BACKSTORY

The signature stew of New Orleans, gumbo truly bears the imprint of nearly every ethnic group to have settled in the Crescent City. The name derives from the African gombo, meaning "okra," a key ingredient. The French contributed roux (a paste made of flour and cooking fat), here cooked until it's "brown," much darker than in any French dish. Spain is the source of the dish's rice, and the seasonings are borrowed from the Caribbean. And some versions, including the familiar shrimp-and-andouille one, are thickened with filé powder, made from ground sassafras leaves, which comes from the Choktaw tribe of Native Americans. You will also find ample examples of gumbo made with chicken and okra, including the one here, which also features the "holy trinity" of Cajun and Creole cooking: celery, onion, and bell pepper. No matter the type of gumbo, it is always served over rice.

10 bone-in chicken thighs (about 2½ pounds), skin removed
    Coarse salt and freshly ground pepper
 1 pound andouille sausage (about 6 links), cut into ½-inch pieces
 ½ cup plus 1 tablespoon neutral-tasting oil, such as safflower
 1 cup all-purpose flour
 3 celery stalks, cut into ½-inch dice
 1 medium onion, cut into ½-inch dice
 1 green bell pepper, cut into ½-inch dice
 3 garlic cloves, finely chopped
12 ounces okra, trimmed and sliced crosswise ½ inch thick
 1 teaspoon dried thyme
 2 dried bay leaves
 5 cups chicken stock, preferably homemade (page 410)
 1 can (28 ounces) whole peeled tomatoes, chopped, juice reserved
 1 tablespoon plus 1 teaspoon filé powder

1 Season chicken with salt and pepper. Cook andouille in a large, heavy pot or Dutch oven over medium heat until lightly browned, stirring occasionally, about 10 minutes. Remove from heat. Transfer sausage to a plate with a slotted spoon. Add ½ cup oil to pot; swirl to collect any loose browned bits, strain mixture through a fine sieve, and discard solids.

2 Wipe pot clean; pour in strained oil and heat over medium until shimmering. Gradually sprinkle in flour, stirring until incorporated. Cook, stirring often, until roux is deep brown, about 30 minutes, reducing heat if necessary. If roux begins to smoke, remove pot from heat for a few minutes, then resume cooking.

3 Add celery, onion, bell pepper, and garlic to pot with roux. Raise heat to medium-high and cook, stirring frequently, and reducing heat if roux is smoking, until vegetables have softened, 5 to 8 minutes. Stir in okra; cook until bright green, 2 to 3 minutes Add thyme and bay leaf, and season with salt.

4 Gradually stir the stock into vegetable mixture, stirring and scraping bottom of pot until thoroughly combined. Stir in tomatoes and their juice, and add the chicken; raise heat and bring to a boil. Add andouille, and reduce heat to a steady simmer; cook, stirring occasionally, until chicken is tender when pierced with a fork and sauce is thickened, about 40 minutes.

5 Transfer chicken to a plate; when cool enough to handle, remove meat from bones, and return to pot; discard bones. Remove bay leaves from pot and discard; stir in filé powder. Serve gumbo hot over rice.

SERVES 8

SHRIMP

Along the coasts of the Gulf of Mexico and southeastern Atlantic, shrimpers have been trawling the waters for generations. For them, it's more than just a business—it's a gratifying way of life. Despite declining profits, most shrimpers can't imagine doing anything else.

These days, the average American eats four pounds of shrimp a year. That doesn't seem like much in the grand scheme of things, but it's twice what was consumed in the 1990s. That's largely due to cheap imports—shrimp raised in crowded, murky aquaculture ponds in countries that include Guyana, Mexico, China, and Thailand. Although the market share of American shrimp is tiny in comparison, any shrimper from Louisiana, say, or Florida can explain the superiority of the wild-caught shellfish. They know there is nothing like its sweet taste and firm texture.

When trawlers go out for long periods of time, the shrimp are sorted by size, bagged, and frozen at sea—ready to be sold upon return. But the boats that work inshore waters—where the best-flavored, highest-quality shrimp are caught—process their catch in a simpler, more low-tech enterprise. The shrimp, which have already been separated by size on the boat, are vacuumed from the vast ice holds onto a conveyor belt. They move to a scale, which then dumps them into large plastic vats. There may be a bit of haggling over whether the size has been marked correctly (the bigger the shrimp, the more money the shrimper makes). And then, if the buyer wants the heads off, the shrimp are spread out on large tables and workers head them just as home cooks would—by pinching the heads between the forefinger and thumb. Many of these shrimp are shipped to top seafood markets and restaurants throughout the country, where they fetch a premium price, but most of them are consumed locally— in a gumbo or piled onto buttery grits, perhaps, or "barbecued" in a sizzling cast-iron skillet the Cajun way, as in the recipe at right.

MR. JIM'S LOUISIANA BARBECUED SHRIMP This dish, now an integral part of the Southern canon, debuted at Pascal's Manale restaurant in New Orleans in 1954, when a frequent customer known as Mr. Jim taught his recipe to the kitchen staff. Squeeze the juice from 2 lemons and reserve; slice 1 lemon crosswise into four or five rounds. Heat a 12-inch cast-iron skillet over medium-high. Heat 1/2 cup (1 stick) unsalted butter, cut into small pieces, until foamy. Add 3 minced garlic cloves, 1 tablespoon finely chopped fresh rosemary, and the reserved lemon juice and slices. Stir in 1/4 cup Worcestershire sauce and 1 1/2 teaspoons hot sauce and bring to a simmer. Peel 1 pound medium to large shrimp, leaving heads (optional) and tails intact; pat dry. Season with coarse salt and freshly ground pepper. Add to skillet; cook until seared on both sides, 3 to 4 minutes. Adjust seasoning and serve hot, with a baguette.

SHRIMP AND GRITS

FOR THE GRITS

- 3 cups water
- 3 cups milk
  - Coarse salt and freshly ground pepper
- 1 cup white grits, preferably stone-ground
- ⅔ cup grated mild cheddar (2½ ounces)
- 1 tablespoon unsalted butter

FOR THE SHRIMP

- 2 slices thick-cut bacon, cut into ¼-inch pieces
- 1 garlic clove, minced
- ¼ onion, finely chopped
- ¼ green bell pepper, ribs and seeds removed, finely chopped
- 1 pound medium shrimp, peeled and deveined
  - Coarse salt and freshly ground pepper
- 1 tablespoon neutral-tasting oil, such as safflower
- 1 tablespoon all-purpose flour
- ¾ cup chicken stock, preferably homemade (page 410)
- 1 tablespoon fresh lemon juice

1 Make the grits: Combine the water, milk, and 1 teaspoon salt in a medium saucepan; bring to a boil. Gradually whisk in grits, then cook, stirring constantly, until thickened and bubbling, about 10 minutes. Reduce heat to low. Cook, stirring frequently and scraping across bottom of pan, until tender and creamy throughout, 1¼ to 1½ hours. Remove from heat. Stir in cheese and butter, and season with salt and pepper.

2 Make the shrimp: Cook bacon in a large skillet over medium heat until beginning to crisp, about 5 minutes; transfer to a paper towel–lined plate using a slotted spoon. Cook garlic, onion, and bell pepper in rendered bacon fat, stirring occasionally, until just tender but not browned, 2 to 3 minutes.

3 Season shrimp on both sides with salt and pepper. Raise heat to medium-high; push vegetables to edge of skillet. Add oil and heat until shimmering. Add shrimp in a single layer; cook until seared on the first side, about 2 minutes. Flip and sear the other side 1 minute. Push shrimp to edge of skillet with vegetables; sprinkle flour into center. Cook, stirring flour into shrimp-vegetable mixture, 2 minutes. Add stock. Simmer, stirring, until sauce thickens, about 2 minutes. Add lemon juice and stir in reserved bacon. Season with salt and pepper.

4 To serve, divide grits among warmed shallow bowls and top with shrimp and vegetable mixture.

SERVES 4

BACKSTORY

This Lowcountry classic has long been enjoyed at breakfast, especially in the fall, when the shrimp season is at its peak. These days, you'll find it at lunch and dinner as well. At its simplest, shrimp and grits is nothing more than that: a buttery heap of sautéed shrimp on steaming hot grits. There are countless variations, however; here, for instance, it's robustly sauced with bacon, onion, and bell pepper, and cheese is added to the grits. No matter what, buy the freshest shrimp you can find and search out stone-ground grits. When the dried corn kernels have been ground slowly between cool millstones, they retain the flavor and nutrition that is processed right out of mass-produced supermarket brands. And even though stone-ground grits take longer to cook (and usually longer than indicated on the package instructions), you will be rewarded with their deep, sweet, authentic flavor.

GRILLED CHICKEN WITH SPICY PEACH GLAZE

BACKSTORY

A true Southern barbecue does not only involve slow-cooked smoked meats; sometimes it's as simple as slathering chicken with a spicy, sweet sauce and grilling it. No self-respecting cook would dare use a sauce from a bottle, and it's easy to prepare your own without much effort. Here, peach preserves are combined with garlic, soy sauce, olive oil, and spices for a quick no-cook sauce that caramelizes to a burnished glaze on the grill. Grilled peaches served alongside seal the deal on regional flavor.

1 cup peach preserves or jam
1 large garlic clove, minced
2 tablespoons extra-virgin olive oil
1 tablespoon plus 1 teaspoon soy sauce
1 tablespoon dry mustard powder
½ teaspoon cayenne
  Coarse salt and freshly ground pepper
  Vegetable oil, for grill
4 skin-on bone-in chicken breasts (about 5 pounds), split into halves
4 ripe but firm peaches, halved and pitted

1 Heat grill to medium. (If you are using a charcoal grill, the coals are ready when you can hold your hand 4 inches above the grates for just 4 to 5 seconds.) In a medium bowl, combine peach preserves, garlic, olive oil, soy sauce, dry mustard, and cayenne; season with salt and pepper and mix well to combine.

2 When grill is hot, brush grates with vegetable oil. Rinse chicken breasts and pat dry with paper towels. Season with salt and pepper and place, skin side down, on the grill. Cook about 10 minutes on each side before brushing top with some glaze. Continue cooking another 10 to 12 minutes, turning chicken every 3 to 5 minutes and brushing top with glaze, until chicken is cooked through. (Move the chicken to a cooler part of grill if it gets too dark before it is cooked through.) Transfer chicken to a platter.

3 While chicken is cooking, place peach halves on the grill, cut side down, and cook 2 minutes. Turn, and brush the tops with glaze. Grill 3 to 4 minutes more, until the peaches are soft and the cavities fill with juices. Transfer peaches to platter and serve.

SERVES 8

NORTH CAROLINA–STYLE PULLED-PORK SANDWICHES

1 boneless pork butt (about 5 pounds)
Coarse salt and freshly ground pepper
Apple Cider Barbecue Sauce (recipe follows)
Cornmeal Rolls (recipe follows)

1 Heat a charcoal grill to between 200°F and 210°F (place an oven thermometer on grates in covered grill). When grill is hot, scatter presoaked wood chips over charcoal briquettes that have burned to white; push to one side. Fill a disposable aluminum pan or baking pan with water and set next to the charcoal briquettes. Place a rack over the pan.

2 Cut four pieces of kitchen twine long enough to fit around the pork. Securely tie two pieces lengthwise and two crosswise at even intervals. Generously season with salt and pepper. Place pork on center of the rack, fat side down; cover grill and cook 1 hour. Generously brush pork with barbecue sauce on all exposed sides. Continue to cook (covered), brushing with sauce every hour, another 3 hours. About 30 minutes before end of cooking, preheat oven to 275°F.

3 Transfer pork to a shallow roasting pan fitted with a wire rack and place in the oven. Cook, basting every hour, until an instant-read thermometer inserted in middle registers 180°F, about 3 hours.

4 Remove pork from oven. When cool enough to handle, remove twine; pull apart meat and place on a cutting board. Chop the meat coarsely into 1-inch pieces. (Pork can be prepared up to this point 1 to 2 days in advance; let cool completely, then refrigerate in an airtight container. When ready to serve, warm in a 300°F oven before proceeding.) Transfer pork to a medium bowl and toss with 1½ cups barbecue sauce.

5 To serve, divide the pork mixture among 12 buns and pass the remaining barbecue sauce on the side.

Alternate Oven Method Preheat oven to 275°F. Tie pork with twine as directed above, then place on a wire rack set in a shallow roasting pan; place in oven and cook 1 hour. Generously brush with barbecue sauce on all sides, and continue to cook, brushing every hour, 5 to 5½ hours more, or until a meat thermometer registers 180°F.

SERVES 10 TO 12

(Continued on next page)

(Continued on next page)

THE SOUTH

BACKSTORY

Order "barbecue" in North Carolina and you'll be presented with a delectable heap of tender, smoky-sweet, charred bits of pork. There are two schools of barbecue here: eastern, where whole hogs are cooked and served with a hot-pepper vinegar-based sauce, and western, also referred to as Lexington-style, which involves only the pork shoulder (the top portion of which is called the butt), resulting in richer-tasting meat. This recipe falls into the second category, with a tomato sauce that gets a hint of sweetness from molasses and plenty of bite from cider vinegar, which cuts the richness and provides the signature zing of the region's barbecue. Before getting started, read the instructions on page 409 for setting up the grill to use a smoker. You don't have to eat the pork in a sandwich, but pillowy cornmeal buns are just right for holding the well-smoked meat along with the optional—though entirely authentic—coleslaw topping. Green tomatoes baked with a crisp breadcrumb topping are another regional touch.

APPLE CIDER BARBECUE SAUCE

2 teaspoons black peppercorns

6 garlic cloves, smashed and peeled

4 fresh or dried bay leaves

12 cinnamon sticks

8 dried hot chiles or 2 teaspoons crushed red-pepper flakes

¾ cup packed light-brown sugar

2 cups unsweetened apple cider

3 cups cider vinegar

1 can (28 ounces) tomato purée

½ cup unsulfured molasses

In a small stockpot, bring all the ingredients to a boil over medium-high heat. Reduce to a simmer and cook, stirring occasionally, until sauce has thickened, about 1½ hours. Pass sauce through a fine sieve into a bowl, pressing to extract as much liquid as possible; discard solids. Sauce can be refrigerated up to 2 weeks; let cool completely before transferring to airtight containers, and reheat over low before serving.

MAKES 5 CUPS

GREEN TOMATO GRATIN

2 tablespoons unsalted butter, melted, plus more for baking dish

5 green tomatoes, halved crosswise

5 slices white sandwich bread, trimmed of crusts

1½ tablespoons chopped fresh flat-leaf parsley
    Coarse salt and freshly ground pepper

2 tablespoons honey

1 Preheat oven to 350°F. Generously butter a gratin or baking dish large enough to accommodate the tomato halves in one layer. Place the bread in a food processor, and pulse until crumbled with no large pieces. Transfer to a small bowl. Add the parsley, and salt and pepper to taste, and drizzle with the melted butter. Toss to combine, and set aside.

2 Place tomato halves in the prepared baking dish, cut side up. Season with salt and pepper; drizzle with honey and sprinkle crumb mixture on top, dividing evenly. Bake until tomatoes have softened, 35 to 40 minutes. Increase oven heat to broil. Place tomatoes under broiler until crumbs are golden brown, about 2 minutes. Serve immediately.

SERVES 8 TO 10

CORNMEAL ROLLS

- ½ cup warm milk (about 110°F)
- ½ cup warm water (about 110°F)
- 1½ tablespoons sugar
- 1 package active dry yeast (1 scant tablespoon)
- 4 large egg yolks
- 1½ teaspoons salt
- 3 tablespoons unsalted butter, melted and cooled
- 1 cup yellow cornmeal, plus more for sprinkling
- 2 cups bread flour
  Olive oil, for bowl and plastic wrap
- 1 tablespoon milk

1 In the bowl of an electric mixer, combine the warm milk and water with the sugar; sprinkle with yeast. Let stand until foamy, about 10 minutes. Attach bowl to mixer fitted with the paddle attachment. Add 3 egg yolks, the salt, butter, cornmeal, and flour; beat on low speed 2 minutes. Switch to the dough hook; beat until dough is smooth, soft, and does not stick to your fingers when squeezed, about 5 minutes.

2 Turn out dough onto a clean surface. Knead lightly into a ball; place in a bowl brushed with olive oil. Cover securely with plastic wrap; let rise in a warm spot until dough is doubled in bulk, about 45 minutes. Meanwhile, preheat oven to 400°F.

3 Punch down the dough, turn out onto work surface, and divide evenly into 12 pieces with a bench scraper or sharp knife. Using the palm of your hand, roll each piece gently, pressing down while rolling to shape into a smooth 2¼-inch ball. Place on a parchment-lined baking sheet. Repeat rolling until all the dough is used. Loosely cover with oiled plastic wrap. Let rise in a warm spot 10 minutes.

4 In a small bowl, combine remaining egg yolk and 1 tablespoon milk. Brush tops of rolls with egg wash and sprinkle with cornmeal. Bake until deep golden brown, rotating sheet halfway through, about 15 minutes. Transfer rolls to a wire rack to cool. Rolls are best served the same day they are baked.

MAKES 12

FRIED CATFISH SANDWICHES

Neutral-tasting oil, such as safflower, for frying

4 cups yellow cornmeal

1 teaspoon crushed red-pepper flakes

½ teaspoon cayenne

Coarse salt and freshly ground pepper

12 catfish fillets (about 8 ounces each), cut in half crosswise

24 slices white sandwich bread

Mayonnaise, for serving (optional)

Pickle relish, for serving (optional)

1 Vidalia or other sweet onion, sliced into ¼-inch rounds

1 Fill a deep, heavy-bottomed skillet with about 2½ inches oil. Heat over medium until oil registers 365°F on a deep-fry thermometer. Meanwhile, whisk together cornmeal, red-pepper flakes, and cayenne in a shallow dish; season with salt and pepper.

2 Rinse catfish and pat dry with paper towels. Season with salt and pepper. Dredge fillets in cornmeal mixture, turning to coat both sides. Working in batches, carefully submerge fillets in oil and fry until crust is crisp and golden and fish is cooked through, about 3 minutes. With a slotted spatula, transfer to a large plate.

3 To serve, spread bread slices with mayonnaise and/or relish, as desired. Layer with catfish and onion slices. Serve immediately.

SERVES 12

TURNIP GREENS

2 tablespoons unsalted butter

2 small onions, finely chopped

2 cups chicken stock, preferably homemade (page 410)

Coarse salt and freshly ground pepper

4 large bunches turnip greens, tough stems discarded and leaves coarsely chopped

Hot sauce, such as Tabasco, for serving (optional)

1 Melt butter in a small stockpot over medium heat. Add onions; cook, stirring occasionally, until soft and translucent, about 6 minutes. Add stock and season with salt and pepper. Bring to a boil.

2 Add turnip greens in batches, letting first batch wilt before adding the next; cover and cook until greens are tender, 3 to 4 minutes. Transfer to a platter with a slotted spoon. Serve immediately, with hot sauce, if desired.

SERVES 12

THE SOUTH

BACKSTORY

You don't have to visit Belzoni, Mississippi—the "Catfish Capital of the World"—to appreciate the important role catfish plays in the Southern diet. Because the fish can be raised successfully in ponds and brooks, even those in a landlocked state can usually get their hands on some fresh catch, long prized for its delicate flavor. While it is often blackened in Louisiana, in other parts of the South the fish is floured and deep-fried, then served between slices of white bread at fish fries, restaurants, and family dinners. Stewed turnip greens are a traditional side; here, the sandwich is also served with a salad made with sliced fresh tomatoes and sliced scallions.

BUTTERMILK FRIED CHICKEN

1   whole fryer chicken (2½ to 3 pounds), cut into 10 parts
1   quart buttermilk, well shaken
1½ tablespoons dry mustard powder
1¼ teaspoons cayenne
    Coarse salt and freshly ground pepper
1½ cups all-purpose flour
2   tablespoons yellow cornmeal
    Neutral-tasting oil, such as safflower, for frying

1 Place chicken parts in one or two shallow dishes, just large enough to hold them snugly. In a medium bowl, whisk together the buttermilk, mustard powder, and 1 teaspoon cayenne; season with salt and pepper. Pour marinade over the chicken, making sure the parts are completely submerged. (Alternatively, divide the chicken and marinade evenly among large resealable bags; rest the bags on a rimmed baking sheet to catch any leaks.) Cover tightly and refrigerate at least 4 hours or up to overnight.

2 Remove chicken from the marinade and allow to drain on a wire rack set over a rimmed baking sheet for 1 hour before cooking (discard marinade). Meanwhile, whisk together the flour, cornmeal, and remaining ¼ teaspoon cayenne; season with salt and pepper. Spread mixture in a shallow dish.

3 When you are ready to begin frying, pour a scant ½ inch oil into a large cast-iron skillet and heat over medium until oil registers 375°F on a deep-fry thermometer. (Alternatively, test by dropping a cube of white crustless bread into the oil; it should turn golden brown within 1 minute.)

4 While the oil is heating, and working with a few parts at a time, dredge chicken in the flour mixture, turning to completely coat. Shake off excess flour and set chicken on a parchment-lined baking sheet as you work.

5 Preheat oven to 200°F. Set a clean wire rack on a rimmed baking sheet with several layers of paper towels on top of rack. Working in batches (skillet should be filled but without pieces touching each other), arrange chicken, skin side down, in a single layer. Adjust heat so temperature of oil remains between 330°F and 340°F during frying. Cover and cook until chicken is crisp and golden on bottom and parts remove easily from pan, 4 to 5 minutes. Carefully turn chicken and continue frying (covered) until crisp and cooked through (breasts should register 160°F and thighs 165°F on an instant-read thermometer), 4 to 5 minutes more. Remove each part as soon as it is ready (wings, drumsticks, and thinner breast pieces cook faster than thighs). Transfer to prepared rack on baking sheet and keep warm in the oven while cooking remaining chicken, returning oil to 375°F before adding each batch. Serve chicken hot.

SERVES 4

THE SOUTH

BACKSTORY

Fried chicken is among the most emblematic foods of the South, and you can hardly find a Southerner who doesn't have an opinion on what's best— battered or floured, panfried or deep-fried, served hot with waffles for breakfast or eaten cold on a picnic. The crowning glory of fried chicken is its crisp, subtly spiced crust, and this recipe, which calls for the meat to be simply dredged in seasoned flour before panfrying, will not disappoint. If you prefer a thicker crust, double dredge: coat the chicken in the flour mixture and let sit for fifteen minutes, then dredge in flour again, tapping off excess. Buttermilk makes the chicken incomparably moist, so don't skip the important step of marinating (preferably overnight). Allowing the chicken to drain for a good hour before you dredge in flour will help ensure an evenly coated, lump-free crust.

RED BEANS AND RICE

THE SOUTH

BACKSTORY

In New Orleans, Creole red beans and rice was created as a "Monday" dinner—the bone from the ham that would be served on Sunday would go into the pot to simmer all day along with the red beans, lending deep flavor to this humble dish. Don't worry if you're missing a ham bone: in this updated version, andouille sausage—a typical ingredient in Creole (and Cajun) cooking—provides all the necessary depth.

2 pounds dried red beans, picked over and rinsed

4 tablespoons unsalted butter

1 pound andouille or other smoked sausage, thinly sliced

4 garlic cloves, finely chopped

4 celery stalks, finely chopped

1 large onion, finely chopped

2 red bell peppers, ribs and seeds removed, finely chopped

1 to 2 tablespoons chili powder

2 dried bay leaves

3 to 4 tablespoons Louisiana hot sauce, or to taste

3 tablespoons Worcestershire sauce

Coarse salt and freshly ground pepper

½ coarsely chopped fresh flat-leaf parsley (optional)

Cooked white rice, for serving

1 Place beans in a large pot and cover with cold water by 2 inches. Let soak overnight. (Alternatively, bring beans and water to a boil and continue to boil 2 minutes; remove from heat and let stand, covered, 1 hour.) Drain beans, rinse in several changes of cold water, and drain again.

2 Melt butter in a Dutch oven, or large heavy-bottomed pot over medium heat. Add sausage and cook, stirring occasionally, until browned, 7 to 10 minutes. Transfer sausage to a plate. Add garlic to pot and cook until fragrant, stirring frequently, 1 to 2 minutes. Add celery, onion, bell pepper, and chili powder to taste; cook, stirring occasionally, until vegetables are softened, 8 to 10 minutes.

3 Return sausage and accumulated juices to pot. Add bay leaves, beans, hot sauce to taste, Worcestershire, and enough water to cover. Bring to a boil; reduce to a simmer. Cook (uncovered) until the beans are tender, about 1½ hours. Season with salt and pepper. Remove and discard the bay leaves. Add parsley, if using, and stir to combine. Serve immediately over rice.

SERVES 8 TO 10

CHICKEN AND DUMPLINGS

FOR THE CHICKEN

- 1 pound boneless, skinless chicken thighs (5 to 6 thighs)
- 1 pound boneless, skinless chicken breast halves (about 3 pieces)
- Coarse salt and freshly ground pepper
- 1 tablespoon neutral-tasting oil, such as safflower
- 1 tablespoon unsalted butter
- 1 large onion, finely chopped
- 1¾ cups chicken stock, preferably homemade (page 410)
- 1½ teaspoons finely chopped fresh thyme
- 2 tablespoons cornstarch
- 2 tablespoons all-purpose flour
- 2 cups milk
- 3 carrots, peeled and sliced diagonally ¼ inch thick
- ½ pound green beans, trimmed and cut into 1-inch pieces

FOR THE DUMPLINGS

- 1 cup all-purpose flour
- ½ cup yellow cornmeal
- 2 teaspoons baking powder
- ¼ teaspoon coarse salt
- 2 tablespoons cold unsalted butter, cut into small pieces
- 1 cup milk

1 Prepare the chicken: Rinse chicken and pat dry with paper towels; season with salt and pepper. Heat oil in a Dutch oven or heavy 6-quart pot over medium; cook thighs, turning once, until browned and cooked through (juices should run clear when pierced), 8 to 10 minutes. Transfer to a platter. Cook breast pieces until browned and cooked through, 5 to 8 minutes. Transfer to a cutting board; cut breasts crosswise into thirds.

2 Add butter to pot and heat until melted. Add onion; cover and cook, stirring occasionally, until softened, about 6 minutes. Stir in chicken stock and thyme; bring to a boil. Combine cornstarch and flour in a bowl; gradually whisk in milk, then whisk mixture into pot. Boil, whisking constantly, until thickened, about 5 minutes. Return chicken to pot and stir to combine. Remove from heat. (Stew can be prepared up to this point a day ahead; let cool completely, then refrigerate, covered. Reheat over low before proceeding.)

3 Bring a medium saucepan of water to a boil; add salt. Blanch carrots and green beans until crisp-tender, about 5 minutes. Drain in a colander, then rinse with cold water to stop the cooking; stir into chicken mixture.

4 Prepare the dumplings: Whisk together flour, cornmeal, baking powder, and salt. Using your fingertips, work butter into flour mixture until texture of coarse meal. Pour in milk; stir with a fork until dough just comes together. Return chicken mixture to a simmer and drop dough by tablespoons on top. Cover; cook 15 minutes without lifting lid (the dumplings will puff up). Serve hot.

SERVES 6

THE SOUTH

BACKSTORY

A big pot of chicken and dumplings is a common—and entirely welcome—meal in the South, where there are as many ways to prepare it as there are home cooks. This version is aromatic with thyme and includes green beans and carrots; the chicken is browned first in the pot, then the flavorful browned bits are incorporated into the stew. Originally, the dumpling dough was rolled out and cut into thick strips for draping on top; the dough for these dumplings is simply dropped into the pot by the spoonful.

HOPPIN' JOHN

Come New Year's Day, superstitious Southerners in search of good luck dine on Hoppin' John, the South Carolina Lowcountry dish of black-eyed or field peas with rice. Explanations abound for the curious name, some more colorful than others (including what hosts would say when offering up a bowlful: "hop in, John"), but the most likely is that it is a loose translation of the names of similar dishes brought from Africa. More accepted is the belief behind the New Year's tradition: Eat frugally on the first day of the year and you'll be sure to prosper for the rest (small sacrifice indeed).

1 pound dried black-eyed peas, picked over and rinsed

3 ham hocks (about 12 ounces each)

2 tablespoons neutral-tasting oil, such as safflower

3 cups coarsely chopped onion (about 3 medium onions)

4 garlic cloves, minced

3 celery stalks, coarsely chopped

1 teaspoon dried thyme

1 dried bay leaf

½ teaspoon crushed red-pepper flakes
  Coarse salt and freshly ground pepper

¾ cup loosely packed fresh parsley leaves, coarsely chopped
  Cooked white rice, for serving

1 Place beans in a large pot with the ham hocks and cover with cold water by 2 inches. Bring to a boil, skimming foam from the surface. Reduce heat to a gentle simmer; cook, partially covered, until beans are tender but not mushy, 30 to 40 minutes. Drain in a colander, reserving cooking liquid. Pull meat from ham hocks and cut into bite-size pieces.

2 Heat oil in a large Dutch oven or heavy-bottomed pot over medium-high. Cook onion, garlic, celery, and thyme, stirring frequently, until tender, about 8 minutes (reduce heat to medium if onion begins to brown). Add ham hock meat, the beans, 4 cups reserved cooking liquid (or more as needed to cover), bay leaf, and red-pepper flakes; season with salt and pepper. Bring to a boil, then reduce to a simmer. Cook (uncovered), stirring occasionally, until broth thickens slightly, about 30 minutes (add more reserved liquid as needed to keep beans submerged). Stir in parsley and serve immediately over rice.

SERVES 8

MASHED TURNIPS

2　large turnips (about 1 pound), peeled and cut into ½-inch dice

2　Yukon Gold potatoes (about 1 pound), peeled and cut into ½-inch dice

1　dried bay leaf

　　Coarse salt and freshly ground pepper

1　tablespoon unsalted butter

3　tablespoons sour cream

1 Combine turnips, potatoes, and bay leaf in a large saucepan, and cover with water by 2 inches. Bring to a boil; add 1 tablespoon salt. Cook until vegetables are very tender and can be easily mashed with a fork, 20 to 25 minutes. Drain and discard bay leaf.

2 Return vegetables to pot; place over low heat just until dry, about 1 minute. Add butter and sour cream and mash with a potato masher or a whisk until mostly smooth. Season with salt and pepper and serve hot.

SERVES 4

THE SOUTH

BACKSTORY

Say what you will about the rich diet of the region, but Southerners love vegetables. Of course, the vegetables are often flavored with bacon or ham hocks to make sides with a richness of their own. Many such dishes are considered an essential component of "meat and three" plates at Southern restaurants (known in local parlance as "meat and threes"). Besides the threesome presented here, other favorites include stewed turnip greens (page 184), fried okra (page 159), creamed corn (page 262), and even macaroni and cheese (page 46; it's considered a "vegetable" south of the Mason-Dixon). Or you can forgo the meat entirely and feast on these hearty sides with a wedge of cornbread and a glass of cold buttermilk.

STEWED COLLARD GREENS

2　bunches (about 2 pounds) collard greens, stems removed

3　tablespoons neutral-tasting oil, such as safflower

½　red onion, thinly sliced

3　slices bacon (3 ounces), cut crosswise into ¼-inch strips

2　tablespoons cider vinegar

1　cup chicken stock, preferably homemade (page 410)

1 Working in batches, stack greens on a cutting board; cut crosswise into 2-inch-thick strips. Gather strips; cut crosswise into 2-inch pieces. Transfer to a large bowl of cold water; swish to remove grit. Repeat with several changes of water until free of grit. Lift greens from water and let drain on kitchen towels (or paper towels).

2 Heat oil in a large skillet over medium-high. Add onion and bacon; cook, stirring, until onion is translucent and bacon fat has rendered, about 4 minutes. Add greens; cook, tossing, until greens begin to wilt. Raise heat to high; add vinegar. Cook, scraping up browned bits from bottom of skillet with a wooden spoon, until vinegar has evaporated, about 1 minute. Add stock; reduce heat. Simmer, covered, until greens are just tender, 12 to 14 minutes. Serve hot.

SERVES 8

FRIED GREEN TOMATOES

4 large, firm green tomatoes, cut crosswise into ½-inch-thick slices

Coarse salt and freshly ground pepper

1 cup yellow cornmeal, preferably stone-ground

½ teaspoon cayenne

2 large eggs

½ cup neutral-tasting oil, for frying

1 Pat dry tomato slices with paper towels and season both sides with salt and pepper. Mix cornmeal and cayenne in a shallow dish. Lightly beat eggs in another dish.

2 Heat oil in a large cast-iron skillet over medium until hot but not smoking. Dip tomatoes in egg, coating completely, then allow excess to drip back into the bowl. Dredge in cornmeal, turning to coat. Working in batches, arrange tomatoes in pan in a single layer and fry until golden brown, about 3 minutes per side. Using a slotted spatula, transfer to a paper towel–lined plate to drain. Serve hot.

MAKES ABOUT 20

THE SOUTH

BACKSTORY

Green tomatoes are inevitable in fall, when the late-season fruit must be picked before ripening to avoid getting damaged by the oncoming frost. In parts of the South, green tomatoes are gathered all summer long, as Creole tomatoes would otherwise grow so large they would break their own branches. Green tomatoes are too firm and acrid to eat raw, and so into chutneys and pickle brine they often go— or into a cast-iron skillet for this mouthwatering Southern specialty. Frying mellows the flavor and texture of the tomatoes, leaving behind a tender juiciness beneath a crisp cornmeal crust.

HUSH PUPPIES

1 cup yellow cornmeal

½ cup all-purpose flour

1 teaspoon sugar

1 teaspoon baking powder

1 teaspoon baking soda

Coarse salt

¼ teaspoon cayenne

1 medium onion

1 large egg

1 cup buttermilk

Vegetable or peanut oil, for frying (about 2 quarts)

1 Preheat oven to 200°F. Whisk together cornmeal, flour, sugar, baking powder, baking soda, 1 teaspoon salt, and the cayenne. Grate onion on the large holes of a box grater into another bowl to yield 3 tablespoons, reserving juice. Add egg and buttermilk and whisk to combine, then stir into cornmeal mixture just until combined, with some lumps remaining. Batter will be as thick as a heavy pancake batter.

2 Heat 4 inches oil in a large, heavy pot or Dutch oven over high until a deep-fry thermometer reaches 360°F. Working in batches, drop batter by the tablespoon into oil. Fry, turning occasionally, until cooked through and deep golden brown, 4 to 5 minutes. Transfer hush puppies to a paper towel–lined baking sheet in the oven while finishing the batches. Return oil to 360°F between batches. Serve warm.

SERVES 4

THE SOUTH

BACKSTORY

Southerners adore a tall tale, so it's no surprise that these balls of deep-fried cornmeal batter come with a doozy: the term originated with the cooks at fish camps on the Florida Gulf, who would quiet their dogs with fried-batter scraps flung straight from the skillet. Whether the tale holds true doesn't really matter. The important thing to remember is that when dollops of cornmeal batter are perked up with a little cayenne pepper and onion, deep-fried until crunchy on the outside and fluffy within, and served straight out of the pan, they are absolutely irresistible. Who wouldn't hush right up?

SPOON BREAD

THE SOUTH

BACKSTORY

"Americans might well try polenta," read a 1955 headline from the New York Times, *"a dish like spoon bread." Today, with polenta served all over the country and spoon bread rare outside the South, the opposite recommendation may be in order. Light as a soufflé but with a more modest soul, this side dish deserves to reclaim nationwide fame. Here, the traditional cornmeal pudding is flavored with onion and spicy sausage (which can be omitted, if desired), but the creamy texture recalls its Southern roots.*

3 tablespoons unsalted butter, plus more for baking dish
1 onion, cut into ½-inch dice
5 ounces chorizo, cut into ½-inch dice
2 cups water
1 cup white cornmeal
1½ cups fresh (from 2 large ears) or frozen corn kernels (do not thaw)
1½ teaspoons coarse salt
5 large eggs
1½ cups heavy cream

1 Heat 2 tablespoons butter in a medium skillet over medium. Add onion and cook, stirring occasionally, until softened, about 4 minutes. Add chorizo and sauté until onion is soft and chorizo is lightly browned, about 4 minutes more. Drain excess fat and transfer mixture to a medium bowl and let cool.

2 Preheat oven to 350°F. Bring the water to a boil in a small saucepan. Slowly pour in cornmeal, stirring constantly. Reduce heat to medium-low and cook, stirring, until thickened, about 2 minutes. Add to sausage mixture. Stir in corn kernels, salt, and the remaining tablespoon butter, and combine well.

3 Whisk together eggs and cream. Stir into sausage mixture until incorporated. Pour into a buttered 2-quart soufflé dish or deep-pie plate. Bake until set and top is golden brown, about 1 hour. Serve hot or at room temperature.

SERVES 8

BUTTERMILK BISCUITS

2¼ cups all-purpose flour, plus more for dusting

2¼ teaspoons baking powder

1 teaspoon sugar

¾ teaspoon salt

½ teaspoon baking soda

6 tablespoons cold unsalted butter, cut into small pieces

1 cup buttermilk

1 Preheat oven to 450°F. Sift together flour, baking powder, sugar, salt, and baking soda into a medium bowl. Work in butter with your fingertips or a pastry blender until mixture resembles coarse meal. Mix in buttermilk with your hands until just combined.

2 Turn out dough onto a lightly floured surface and pat into a 7-inch disk about 1 inch thick. Cut out 12 rounds with a floured 2-inch biscuit cutter, gathering and patting out scraps as necessary.

3 Arrange rounds on a parchment-lined baking sheet. Bake until cooked through and golden brown, rotating sheet halfway through, 10 to 15 minutes. Serve warm.

MAKES 1 DOZEN

THE SOUTH

BACKSTORY

Every day at breakfast. Communal chicken suppers on Sunday, after church. Any time, filled with country ham and smothered with gravy. For generations of Southern folks, the common denominator would be biscuits, hot and fragrant from the oven. Every experienced home cook could turn out a tender, light-as-air batch without thinking twice or even having to measure. To this day, biscuits remain a powerful symbol of the region, its traditions, and family memories—as well as the quickest, easiest bread to make. In this classic biscuit recipe, buttermilk tenderizes and adds flavor, and although some purists will tell you that a low-gluten flour such as White Lily will give you the lightest texture, we found that all-purpose flour also gives equally excellent results. So there is really no reason not to start creating some family memories of your own, even if you do have to measure—at least at first.

CARAMEL CAKE

THE SOUTH

BACKSTORY

A nationwide love affair with layer cakes originated in the South, with the first published recipes for them appearing after the Civil War. Whether for a special occasion or a ladies' tea, these confections were—and still are—presented with pride, atop the finest footed cake pedestals, then sliced and served with the family silver. White mountain cake—named because of the height of the layers and the blanket of snowy white frosting—was one of the first examples of well-known Southern cakes. Another is this rich caramel-frosted cake, sometimes referred to as brown mountain cake, which can still be found in roadside diners, barbecue joints, and home kitchens throughout Dixieland. The key to this icing is to cook the caramel to a dark amber for maximum flavor and to allow the mixture to cool completely before beating in the butter.

1¼   cups (2½ sticks) unsalted butter, softened, plus more for pan and rack

4½   cups sifted cake flour (not self-rising), plus more for pan

2   tablespoons baking powder

¾   teaspoon salt

1½   tablespoons pure vanilla extract

1½   cups milk

2¼   cups sugar

7   large egg whites
    Caramel Frosting (page 413)

1 Preheat oven to 350°F. Butter two 9-by-2-inch round cake pans. Line bottoms with parchment. Butter parchment and dust with flour; tap out excess. Into a medium bowl, sift together cake flour, baking powder, and salt. Stir vanilla into milk.

2 With an electric mixer on medium speed, beat butter until creamy. With mixer running, add sugar in a steady stream; continue beating until mixture is light and fluffy. Reduce speed to low. Add flour mixture in three batches, alternating with the milk mixture and starting and ending with the flour; beat just until combined. (Do not overbeat.)

3 Using the mixer, whisk egg whites until stiff peaks form. Fold one-third of whites into the batter to lighten; fold in remaining whites in two batches.

4 Divide batter between prepared pans and smooth tops with an offset spatula. Bake until a cake tester inserted in the centers comes out clean and the cake layers spring back when pressed lightly in the center, about 40 minutes. Transfer pans to a wire rack; let cool 15 minutes. Brush rack with butter. Run a sharp knife around edges of cakes; invert onto buttered rack. Reinvert onto another rack and let cool completely, top side up.

5 Using a serrated knife, level tops of cake layers. Place one layer, cut side up, on a serving platter; spread a layer of caramel frosting on top. Stack second layer, cut side down, on top; generously spread top and sides of both cakes with frosting.

MAKES ONE 9-INCH LAYER CAKE

SWEET POTATO PIE

All-purpose flour, for dusting

Basic Pie Dough (page 412; 1 disk reserved for another use)

2 sweet potatoes (about 1½ pounds), cooked and peeled

2 tablespoons unsalted butter

½ cup packed plus 3 tablespoons light-brown sugar

2 tablespoons pure maple syrup

1 tablespoon bourbon (optional)

1 teaspoon pure vanilla extract

½ teaspoon ground cinnamon

½ teaspoon salt

Pinch of freshly grated nutmeg

1 cup half-and-half

2 large whole eggs plus 1 large egg yolk

½ cup plus 1 tablespoon pecans, toasted (page 408) and coarsely chopped

1 tablespoon heavy cream

Whipped cream, for serving

THE SOUTH

BACKSTORY

Many Southerners might take or leave a pumpkin pie come Thanksgiving, but sweet potato pie for dessert is as essential to the meal as the turkey itself. In this version, toasted pecans and brown sugar are sprinkled over the crust before the filling is added. The pie's robust depth and earthy sweetness are unbeatable when topped with whipped cream, especially when it is spiked with bourbon and vanilla.

1 On a lightly floured surface, roll out dough to a 13-inch round about ⅛ inch thick. Brush off excess flour. Fit dough into a 9-inch pie plate. Trim edge to ½ inch, then fold under flush with rim, pinching to seal. Crimp edge with a fork. Cover with plastic wrap and chill at least 30 minutes or up to 1 day.

2 Preheat oven to 375°F, with a rack in the middle. Prick bottom of dough all over with a fork. Line with parchment, and fill with pie weights or dried beans. Bake until edges begin to turn brown, about 15 minutes. Remove parchment and pie weights and bake 8 minutes more. Transfer pie plate to a wire rack and let cool.

3 With an electric mixer on medium speed, beat sweet potatoes and butter until smooth. Add ½ cup brown sugar along with the maple syrup, bourbon (if using), vanilla, cinnamon, salt, and nutmeg. Mix until well combined. Add half-and-half, 1 whole egg, and the yolk; mix until smooth.

4 Sprinkle remaining 3 tablespoons brown sugar and the chopped pecans evenly over bottom of prepared crust. Pour in filling. Lightly beat remaining egg with the cream; using a pastry brush, gently coat edge of crust evenly with egg wash. Return the pie to oven; bake until filling is set, 30 to 40 minutes. Transfer to a wire rack to cool. Serve warm or at room temperature, topped with whipped cream.

MAKES ONE SINGLE-CRUST 9-INCH PIE

KEY LIME PIE

THE SOUTH

BACKSTORY

The official state pie of Florida is both sweet and tart, and exceptionally creamy. Connoisseurs claim not only that the juice must be from real key limes for the pie to be authentic, but also that they can tell the difference in just one bite. Luckily, although the golf ball–size limes can be hard to come by even in the Florida Keys, the juice is available in large supermarkets and specialty food stores all over the United States. The pie can also be frozen overnight and served partially thawed.

Graham-Cracker Crust (page 413)

1 can (14.5 ounces) sweetened condensed milk

4 large eggs, separated

¾ cup key lime juice, preferably fresh (from about 20 key limes)

½ cup plus 1 tablespoon sugar

¾ cup cold heavy cream

1 Preheat oven to 375°F. Butter a 9-inch pie plate. Press graham-cracker crust evenly into bottom and up sides of pie plate. Refrigerate until firm, about 30 minutes. Bake until crust is set and lightly browned, about 12 minutes. Transfer pie plate to a wire rack and let cool completely. Reduce oven temperature to 325°F.

2 Combine condensed milk, yolks, and lime juice in a large liquid measuring cup or a bowl and pour into crust. Return pie to oven, and bake until center is just set, 15 to 17 minutes. Transfer to a wire rack to cool completely.

3 In a heatproof mixing bowl set over (not in) a pan of simmering water, whisk sugar and egg whites until warm to the touch and sugar is dissolved. Remove from heat. Using an electric mixer on medium-high speed, whisk until stiff peaks form and meringue is glossy, about 5 minutes.

4 Using a clean whisk attachment, whip cream until soft peaks form. Gently whisk one-third of the cream into meringue. Fold in remaining cream with a flexible spatula. Spread meringue mixture over top of pie; freeze until topping is firm enough to slice, about 2 hours or up to 1 day.

MAKES ONE SINGLE-CRUST 9-INCH PIE

BLACK-BOTTOM PIE

FOR THE CRUST AND FILLING

Graham-Cracker Crust (page 413)

- 1 cup sugar
- 1 cup unsweetened Dutch-process cocoa powder
- 2 tablespoons cornstarch
- ⅛ teaspoon salt
- 1½ cups milk
- 3 ounces bittersweet chocolate, finely chopped
- 2 tablespoons unsalted butter, cut into small pieces
- ½ teaspoon pure vanilla extract

FOR THE TOPPING

- 1½ teaspoons unflavored powdered gelatin
- 5 tablespoons cold water
- ¾ cup sugar
- 1 tablespoon cornstarch
- ⅛ teaspoon salt
- 1 cup milk
- 1 teaspoon pure vanilla extract
- 2 tablespoons light rum
- 4 large egg whites, room temperature

1 Preheat oven to 350°F. Press graham-cracker crust evenly into bottom and up sides of a 9-inch pie plate. Refrigerate until firm, about 30 minutes. Bake until crust is set and begins to turn golden brown, about 12 minutes. Transfer pie plate to a wire rack and let cool completely.

2 Make the filling: Sift together sugar, cocoa, cornstarch, and salt into a medium saucepan. Gradually whisk in milk. Cook over medium-high heat, stirring constantly, until almost boiling. Reduce heat to medium; add chocolate. Cook, stirring constantly, until chocolate has melted and mixture is thick, about 2 minutes. Remove from heat; whisk in butter and vanilla until smooth. Spread chocolate mixture over crust. Refrigerate until cold and firm, about 1 hour.

3 Make the topping: Prepare an ice-water bath. In a small bowl, sprinkle gelatin over 2 tablespoons cold water. Let soften, about 5 minutes. In a medium saucepan, whisk together ¼ cup sugar, the cornstarch, and salt. Gradually whisk in milk. Cook over medium-high heat, stirring constantly, until mixture is thick and boiling, about 5 minutes. Remove from heat; stir in gelatin mixture and let cool completely. Stir in vanilla and rum. Briefly place pan in the ice bath to thicken slightly; do not let it set completely.

4 With an electric mixer on medium-low speed, whisk egg whites until soft peaks form. Reduce speed to low; continue beating while you make the syrup.

5 In a small saucepan, bring remaining ½ cup sugar and 3 tablespoons water to a boil, stirring to dissolve sugar. Brush down sides of pan with a wet pastry brush to prevent crystals from forming. Cook, without stirring, until syrup registers 240°F on a candy thermometer.

6 Raise mixer speed to high and beat egg whites just until stiff peaks begin to form. Immediately pour syrup down side of bowl in a slow, steady stream. Beat until meringue is glossy and cooled, about 7 minutes.

7 Fold meringue into gelatin mixture in three batches until just combined. Spread mixture in chocolate-filled crust. Refrigerate at least 3 hours or up to overnight (covered), before serving.

MAKES ONE SINGLE CRUST 9-INCH PIE

THE SOUTH

BACKSTORY

Black-bottom pie, another cherished Southern tradition, consists of a cookie-crumb crust lavishly layered with a rich dark-chocolate custard topped by an airy meringue. When the first recipes for this (and other icebox pies) appeared around the turn of the twentieth century, the dessert was reserved for only the most special occasions because of one very expensive—and crucial—ingredient: the ice necessary to "refrigerate" it. Today, black-bottom pie continues to make a delicious impression, retaining its nostalgic appeal despite being updated with a few delightful touches, such as the rum-spiked meringue in this version.

PEACHES

Cradling a peach in your palm is like wrapping your fingers around a little sphere of sunlight. The tawny-gold fruit, flushed crimson in places, is gorgeous to behold—and, as anyone who has sampled a late-summer specimen will tell you, heavenly to taste.

Whether you're making cobbler, pie, or preserves, you'll discover that peaches go well with a host of nuts, fruits, and herbs. Almonds and peaches are a classic pairing. In fact, the two are botanical cousins, which helps explain why peach pits look a bit like unshelled almonds. Peaches are also related to plums, apricots, cherries, and nectarines—all of which are considered stone fruits because of their pits—and they all complement one another. (The nectarine is a smooth-skinned type of peach—some peach trees even produce the occasional nectarine.) Acidic ingredients, such as lemon, lime, and orange, are a good match because they balance the sweetness of peaches and slow the browning of the cut flesh.

First cultivated in China and brought to America by European settlers, peaches are classified as clingstone or freestone based on how easy it is to dislodge the pit from the flesh. The former type is widely used for commercial canning; most fresh peaches that you see at roadside stands or farmers' markets are freestones. The fruits also come in two main colors: white peaches are more prone to bruising than their yellow peers, but connoisseurs tout them as especially aromatic, juicy, and sweet.

The only time of year to eat a fresh peach is in late summer and early fall. Unlike an apple or pear, a peach accumulates all its sugar on the tree; once picked, it will stop sweetening altogether. This is why timing is so essential and why peaches sold in the supermarket never taste nearly as good as those eaten straight from a tree (or from a roadside farmstand). When shopping for peaches, don't use the blush on their cheeks to judge ripeness; look instead at the background color, which should be yellow or cream, depending on the variety. Fruit with a green cast was picked prematurely and will not be sweet. Select larger peaches, which are generally more flavorful. They should have a deep fruity fragrance and feel slightly soft. Ripen firm peaches at room temperature; once they begin to soften along the suture line that runs from stem to blossom end, they are ready. Once ripe, store peaches in the refrigerator and eat them as quickly as possible. Their flavor will hit your mouth and immediately dissolve, leaving behind a fleeting but unforgettable taste.

POACHED PEACHES Bring 2 cups water, $1\frac{1}{2}$ cups sugar, $\frac{3}{4}$ cup dry white wine, $\frac{1}{4}$ teaspoon coarse salt, 1 piece (1 inch) cinnamon stick, 4 strips (3 inches each) lemon zest, and $\frac{1}{4}$ teaspoon whole black peppercorns, if desired, to a boil in a medium stockpot, stirring to dissolve sugar. Add 6 ripe peaches (about $2\frac{1}{2}$ pounds), halved and pitted. Cover with cheesecloth or parchment to keep submerged. Reduce heat; simmer, turning peaches once, until tender and skins are loose, 7 to 9 minutes. Remove from heat; discard cinnamon. Stir in 1 tablespoon fresh lemon juice, and add $\frac{1}{2}$ cup (3 ounces) raspberries. Let cool, covered with cheesecloth to keep moist, 30 minutes. Refrigerate at least 2 hours (or up to 3 days). Remove peaches; slip off and discard skins. Strain poaching liquid; discard solids. Divide peaches and liquid among bowls, top each with more raspberries, and serve. You can also serve the peaches on top of ice cream, drizzled with poaching liquid or doused with Champagne.

PEACH AND BERRY COBBLER

THE SOUTH

BACKSTORY

Although they are particularly beloved in Georgia, where they are the official state fruit (as they are in South Carolina), peaches have a special place in the hearts of everyone down South, and not only because the fruit ripens to such perfection under the hot summer sun. Large-scale orchards were planted after the Civil War, and peaches became one of the key crops in helping the South rebound during Reconstruction. Tucked under a sweet dough that soaks up the juices, the fruit here yields a dessert just as delightful as an afternoon spent lounging under a canopy of peach trees. Sweet-tart berries are a good match for the peaches; a bit of grated fresh ginger adds even more flavor to the filling. Serve the cobbler on its own or topped with whipped cream or ice cream.

2¾ pounds ripe peaches, halved lengthwise, pitted, and cut into ¾-inch-thick wedges (about 8 cups)

1 cup fresh blueberries, blackberries, or raspberries

⅔ cup granulated sugar

3 tablespoons cornstarch

2 tablespoons light-brown sugar

1 tablespoon fresh lemon juice

1 teaspoon finely grated peeled fresh ginger

½ teaspoon salt, plus a pinch

2 cups all-purpose flour

2 teaspoons baking powder

½ cup (1 stick) cold unsalted butter, cut into small pieces

1 vanilla bean, split lengthwise and seeds scraped (reserve pod for another use)

1 cup plus 2 tablespoons heavy cream, plus more for brushing
Sanding sugar, for sprinkling

1 Preheat oven to 375°F, with racks in upper and lower thirds. Stir together peaches, berries, ⅓ cup granulated sugar, the cornstarch, brown sugar, lemon juice, ginger, and a pinch of salt in a large bowl. Transfer to a 2-quart baking dish.

2 Whisk together flour, baking powder, and remaining ½ teaspoon of salt and ⅓ cup granulated sugar in a medium bowl. Cut butter into flour mixture using a pastry blender or two knives until only pea-size clumps remain.

3 Stir vanilla seeds into the cream to combine; add to flour mixture and stir with a fork just until a soft, sticky dough forms. Use a bench scraper or knife to divide dough into 10 equal pieces; arrange on top of filling. Brush dough with cream and sprinkle evenly with sanding sugar.

4 Place a parchment-lined baking sheet on lower rack of oven to catch juices. Bake cobbler on top rack until topping is golden brown and juices are bubbling, 55 to 70 minutes. If topping is browning too quickly, tent with foil. Let cool on a wire rack 1 hour before serving.

SERVES 8 TO 10

LOUISIANA BREAD PUDDING

¼ cup (2 fluid ounces) bourbon

½ cup raisins

4 cups bread cubes (¼ inch), from ½ day-old baguette

1½ cups milk

½ cup heavy cream

2 large eggs

½ cup sugar

1 tablespoon pure vanilla extract

½ teaspoon salt

½ teaspoon ground allspice

2 tablespoons unsalted butter

Bourbon Sauce (recipe follows)

1 Heat bourbon in a medium saucepan over medium-low, then pour over raisins in a small bowl; let soak at least 1 hour or up to overnight.

2 Preheat oven to 350°F. In a large bowl, stir together bread, milk, and cream. In another bowl, whisk together eggs, sugar, vanilla, salt, and allspice; pour over bread mixture. Stir in raisins and bourbon.

3 Melt butter in an 8-inch square baking dish in oven. Remove from oven and swirl to coat bottom of dish. Pour in bread mixture, distributing raisins evenly. Bake until bread cubes are browned around edges and custard is set, about 35 minutes. Transfer to a wire rack to cool completely. Serve with bourbon sauce.

SERVES 4 TO 6

BOURBON SAUCE

1½ cups heavy cream

2 teaspoons cornstarch

1 cup sugar

1 cup (8 fluid ounces) bourbon

Bring cream to a simmer over medium heat in a small saucepan. Whisk together cornstarch and 2 tablespoons cold water; slowly whisk into cream. Bring to a boil, whisking constantly. Reduce heat to low; simmer, whisking, 1 minute. Remove from heat; stir in sugar and bourbon. Let cool completely. (Sauce can be refrigerated up to 2 days in an airtight container. Bring to room temperature before serving.)

MAKES ABOUT 2 CUPS

THE SOUTH

BACKSTORY

It's no secret that the citizens of New Orleans love their food rich and their spirits flowing freely, so it should come as no surprise that one of that city's more famous desserts (along with bananas Foster, another boozy concoction) combines these two qualities to indulgent effect. Louisiana's French roots make for a singularly scrumptious bread pudding, which traces its lineage back to the pain perdu *of France. Day-old baguettes and a velvety egg custard benefit from the faint perfume of allspice, a Caribbean addition. Bourbon hard sauce is essential on the side.*

CHOCOLATE-BOURBON PECAN PIE

3 tablespoons all-purpose flour, plus more for dusting

Basic Pie Dough (page 412; 1 disk reserved for another use)

½ cup (1 stick) unsalted butter, melted

½ cup sugar

½ cup dark corn syrup

2 large eggs

2 tablespoons (1 fluid ounce) aged bourbon

¼ teaspoon coarse salt

1½ cups pecans: 1 cup coarsely chopped, the rest left whole

1 cup coarsely chopped semisweet chocolate (about 6 ounces)

1 tablespoon heavy cream

1 large egg yolk

1 Preheat oven to 375°F. On a lightly floured surface, roll out dough to an 11-inch round about ⅛ inch thick. Wrap dough around rolling pin and drape into a 9-inch pie plate. Fit dough into pan, pressing into edges. Trim edge to 1 inch, then fold under flush with rim and crimp as desired. Prick bottom of crust a few times with a fork. Freeze 15 minutes.

2 Line pie shell with parchment, pressing into sides of pan; fill with pie weights or dried beans. Bake 20 minutes. Remove parchment and weights. Bake until crust is dry but not turning brown, about 5 minutes more. Transfer pie plate to a wire rack and let cool at least 15 minutes. Reduce oven temperature to 350°F.

3 In a medium bowl, stir together butter, sugar, flour, corn syrup, eggs, bourbon, and salt. Stir in chopped pecans and chocolate. Pour into crust. Arrange whole pecans on top of filling. In a small bowl, whisk together cream and egg yolk and brush over edges of pie. Bake until just set in center and crust is golden, about 40 minutes. Tent with foil if browning too quickly. Transfer to a wire rack to cool completely before serving.

MAKES ONE SINGLE-CRUST 9-INCH PIE

THE SOUTH

BACKSTORY

People down south are experts when it comes to hospitality, and nothing makes guests feel as welcome as a freshly baked pie—except maybe two. Pecan pie is decidedly rich; this one gets an extra kick from aged bourbon and semisweet chocolate. It's joined by a double-crust rhubarb pie—the well-loved filling aptly demonstrates why rhubarb is nicknamed the "pie plant."

RHUBARB PIE

2 pounds rhubarb, trimmed and
   cut into ½-inch pieces (6 to 7 cups)

1⅓ cups granulated sugar

¼ cup cornstarch

   Pinch of coarse salt

1 teaspoon finely grated lemon zest, plus
   1 tablespoon fresh lemon juice

   All-purpose flour, for dusting

   Basic Pie Dough (page 412)

2 tablespoons unsalted butter,
   cut into small pieces

1 tablespoon heavy cream

1 large egg yolk

   Fine sanding sugar (or granulated sugar),
   for sprinkling

1 Preheat oven to 375°F, with rack in lower third. In a large bowl, stir together rhubarb, granulated sugar, cornstarch, salt, and lemon zest and juice.

2 On a lightly floured surface, roll out 1 disk of dough to a 13-inch round, about ⅛ inch thick. Fit dough into a 9-inch deep-dish glass pie plate. Trim edge to 1 inch, then fold under flush with rim and crimp as desired. Fill with rhubarb mixture and dot with butter. Place in refrigerator to chill while rolling out dough for top.

3 On a lightly floured surface, roll out remaining dough disk to a 13-inch round. Drape over filling. Trim edge to 1 inch, then fold under and crimp as desired. Make five 2½- to 3-inch slits in crust to vent. Refrigerate 15 minutes.

4 In a small bowl, whisk together cream and egg yolk. Using a pastry brush, gently coat pie shell with egg wash. Sprinkle with sanding sugar. Bake until bottom crust is golden and filling is bubbling vigorously, 1 hour 10 minutes to 1 hour 25 minutes. Tent with foil if top is browning too quickly. Transfer to a wire rack and let cool at least 4 hours before serving.

MAKES ONE DOUBLE-CRUST 9-INCH DEEP-DISH PIE

POUND CAKE

1 pound (4 sticks) unsalted butter, softened, plus more for pans
3¼ cups all-purpose flour
1 tablespoon coarse salt
2 cups sugar
1 teaspoon pure vanilla extract
9 large eggs, room temperature, lightly beaten

Like other British customs, pound cake has been adopted by the Southern states as one of their own. There you'll find the cake plain, dusted, glazed, iced, or even cut up and used in trifles (another English transplant). The cake owes its name to the traditional ingredients—one pound each of flour, butter, sugar, and eggs—which remain more or less the same today. The recipe isn't difficult, but it tends to be a bit finicky, so follow the instructions carefully for cakes that turn out tender and airy, not tough and dense. In particular, always leave the butter and eggs out at room temperature for sufficient time before mixing (if they're too cold, the batter will look curdled and won't bake properly), and cream the butter and sugar thoroughly for better volume before adding the other ingredients. No matter how pure and wholly satisfying the original, tinkering with the recipe is too hard to resist, so you'll probably want to try your hand at one (or all) of the easy variations that follow.

1 Preheat oven to 325°F. Butter two 5-by-9-inch loaf pans. In a medium bowl, whisk together flour and salt.

2 With an electric mixer on high speed, cream butter and sugar until light and fluffy. Scrape down sides of bowl. Reduce speed to medium and add vanilla. Add eggs in four batches, mixing thoroughly after each and scraping down sides of bowl. Reduce speed to low and add flour mixture in four batches, mixing until just incorporated.

3 Divide batter between pans. Tap on counter to distribute evenly, then smooth tops with an offset spatula. Bake until a cake tester inserted into center of each cake comes out clean, about 1 hour. Transfer pans to a wire rack and let cool 30 minutes. Run a sharp knife around edges of cakes, then turn out cakes onto racks to cool completely.

MAKES 2 LOAVES

VARIATIONS

Vanilla Bean Fold in seeds of 1 vanilla bean (split lengthwise and scraped) in place of vanilla extract.

Poppy Seed Fold 1 tablespoon poppy seeds into finished batter.

Toasted Coconut Fold 2 cups sweetened shredded coconut into finished batter. Before baking, sprinkle ⅓ cup additional coconut over each cake; tent with foil to bake.

Jam Fold 1 cup cherry, peach, or other jam into the finished batter.

Blueberry–Sour Cream Use ½ cup sour cream in place of ½ cup (1 stick) butter. Toss 2 cups fresh blueberries with 2 tablespoons flour; fold into finished batter. Before baking, sprinkle 2 tablespoons sanding sugar over each cake.

Chocolate Use 1 cup best-quality unsweetened cocoa powder in place of 1 cup of the flour.

Chocolate Chip Fold 2 cups semisweet or bittersweet chocolate chips into finished batter.

Brown Sugar–Walnut Use 2 cups packed dark-brown sugar in place of the granulated sugar. Fold 2 cups toasted (page 408) walnuts, finely chopped, into finished batter.

Created to be more filling than a cookie, the original Moon Pie—which was introduced in 1917 and is still being produced by the same family-owned business in Chattanooga—featured two graham crackers around a marshmallow-cream filling, all dipped in chocolate. Today you can find them in other flavors, including vanilla, strawberry, and banana (and there are also "double deckers" with three cookies and two layers of filling). Yet the classic flavor combination remains the standard-bearer. And it is the best place to start for anyone wanting to replicate them at home. This version is embellished with chopped salted peanuts, which could just as easily be omitted. Making your own marshmallow filling is what sets these cookies apart from the rest. It does require accuracy when cooking the sugar syrup to the right temperature, but your mixer will do most of the heavy lifting (and the addition of gelatin helps ensure you achieve the right texture, even on the first try). Whether you also choose to use homemade graham crackers is entirely up to you, but the press-in-the-pan dough is simple enough to prepare, and the cookies' flavor and texture can't be beat. Make a batch of these for your Southern pals and they'll think you're out of this world.

TENNESSEE-STYLE MARSHMALLOW COOKIES

2   envelopes unflavored gelatin (about 2 tablespoons)
⅔   cup cold water
1½ cups granulated sugar
⅔   cup light corn syrup
⅛   teaspoon coarse salt
1   teaspoon pure vanilla extract
    Confectioners' sugar, for cutting
9   store-bought graham-cracker sheets, split in half, or 18 homemade graham-cracker squares (page 413)
8   ounces semisweet chocolate, melted
1   cup salted, roasted peanuts, chopped
    Vegetable oil cooking spray

1 Coat a 9-inch square baking pan with cooking spray; line with parchment. Sprinkle gelatin over ⅓ cup cold water in a mixing bowl; let stand 5 minutes.

2 Heat granulated sugar, corn syrup, remaining ⅓ cup water, and the salt in a medium saucepan over medium-high, stirring occasionally, until syrup reaches 238°F on a candy thermometer, about 5 minutes.

3 Whisk gelatin in mixer on low speed, adding syrup in a slow, steady stream down side of bowl. Gradually increase speed to high, until mixture is almost tripled in volume, about 8 minutes. Whisk in vanilla. Transfer to prepared baking pan. Smooth top with an offset spatula. Let stand until set, at least 3 hours or up to overnight, covered with plastic wrap.

4 Dip surface of crackers into chocolate to coat, and transfer to parchment-lined baking sheets. Refrigerate until set, about 10 minutes. Cut out nine 2½-inch square marshmallows using a cookie cutter or a knife dipped in confectioners' sugar.

5 Sandwich marshmallows between crackers, chocolate sides in. Dip half of each sandwich into chocolate, on the diagonal; sprinkle with peanuts, and transfer to a parchment-lined baking sheet. Refrigerate until set, about 10 minutes.

MAKES 9

MIDWEST

T

here is something grand and mythical about the heart of the United States. The pastoral tradition that began in the small family farms of New England, the mid-Atlantic, and the South surged west into Ohio, on through Indiana and Illinois to the rich soils of Iowa, before turning into a near-constant battle against the harsh conditions of the Great Plains.

Evolving agricultural practices helped shape the region's food as well as the economy. Back in the eighteenth century, Connecticut dairymen and cheese makers took advantage of cheap farmland and proximity to the shipping lanes of the Great Lakes and moved their industry into western New York State and then, by the early nineteenth century, into Ohio, where milk became a common ingredient in both sweet and savory dishes, and eventually to Wisconsin, which came to be known as America's dairyland.

Stuffed pork chops, creamed corn, seven-layer salad—Midwestern cooking is the kind of cooking you learn by doing every day. There is an abiding sense of community throughout this region. Talk to natives of Minnesota, Wisconsin, or the Dakotas about the foods of home, for example, and odds are they will get misty-eyed over their mom's own version of "hotdish," any one of a number of thrifty, filling casseroles.

Uncomplicated desserts abound as well. This is the region where the legendary Johnny Appleseed lives on in cider mills and pick-your-own orchards. You'll see one beautiful apple pie after another neatly arrayed at county fairs and roadside stands. Persimmon pudding, Indiana's signature Hoosier (sugar cream) pie, and cherry pie—made from the fruit of orchards planted by Michigan's early settlers—are other evocative sweets that have stood the test of time. And don't forget the radiant simplicity of Shaker lemon tarts, which, despite the name, predate the utopian settlements that spread from New Hampshire to Indiana. Under various other monikers, the recipe was commonly found in the kitchens of earlier cooks; it's known as Ohio lemon pie in an early edition of *The Joy of Cooking*.

Notwithstanding the native foods of the region, such as wild rice and freshwater whitefish and trout (fish fries and fish boils are a favorite community activity around the Great Lakes), the Midwestern culinary personality is rooted in the foods of immigrants from central, northern, and eastern Europe, and it perhaps finds its highest expression in Chicago. A major rail hub since the nineteenth century (thus having access to ingredients from around the country) and site of the world-famous Union Stock Yard (from 1865 to 1971), Chicago is where the big city meets big appetites. The metropolis has even taken the humble hot dog to a whole new level: a skinless all-beef Chicago "red hot" comes in a steamed poppy-seed bun and is loaded with half a dozen condiments, including mustard, relish, pickles, celery salt, onions, peppers, and tomatoes—everything, in fact, but (heaven forbid) ketchup.

Another long-held favorite of Midwestern cities, particularly St. Louis and Kansas City, is a tender, meaty slab of barbecued pork ribs served with a sweet, tomato-based sauce. All you need to make that meal perfect are some easy sides and some hard-driving rhythm and blues.

Sheboygan, Wisconsin, reinvented the bratwurst as another grab-and-go classic. Back in the 1920s, local German butchers would make the coarse-ground pork sausages fresh each day for an eager clientele. Served on a buttered hard roll with onions—and a cold brew on the side—they were introduced to the concessions stands at the Milwaukee County Stadium in 1953, where they took Major League Baseball by storm. A trip to the ballpark might well be polished off with an ice-cream cone made with malted milk, another Wisconsin invention that changed the nation. Malt shops, after all, are as much a part of midcentury Americana as saddle shoes and sockhops.

RECIPES

LINGONBERRY PUNCH

TOM AND JERRY

CHICAGO FIZZ

SOUR CHERRY LEMONADE

DRINKS

LINGONBERRY PUNCH

In northern Europe, lingonberries grow wild on low evergreen scrubs, free for the taking by anyone with a basket. The tart red berries are distant smaller cousins of American cranberries. This drink, similar to a Cape Codder, is a staple of Midsummer Night celebrations in Scandinavia and where many of that region's emigrants settled in the United States—Minnesota and other parts of the upper Midwest. Lingonberry juice and frozen berries are available from Scandinavian specialty retailers and online; you can also find the juice at IKEA.

Place 3 cups of fresh **lingonberries** in a resealable plastic bag and freeze until solid, at least 2 hours or up to 1 month. Combine 1 cup (8 fluid ounces) good-quality **vodka** and 2 quarts **lingonberry juice** in a large punch bowl or divide between two large pitchers; add frozen lingonberries. Serve immediately. **SERVES 5 TO 8**

TOM AND JERRY

This creamy version of a hot toddy is ladled from monikered punch bowls straight into matching ceramic mugs. The drink has its roots in the nineteenth century but peaked during the Eisenhower administration. It's still popular in the upper Midwest, though, where its potent rum-brandy mix is just what you need when the below-zero temperatures reach double digits. Like a perfectly laid fire, the egg mixture takes a little effort to pull off, but rest assured: Make a batch for a bunch of friends and you will give the party of the year.

Whisk 3 large **egg yolks** with 1 tablespoon (½ fluid ounce) **dark rum** and 3 tablespoons **sugar**. Stir in ¼ teaspoon ground **cinnamon** and a pinch each of ground **allspice** and **cloves**. With an electric mixer, whisk 3 large **egg whites** until stiff peaks form, then gently but thoroughly fold whites into yolk mixture. Gently heat 1½ cups **milk** in a small saucepan until steaming. Stir egg mixture until smooth, and divide among six mugs (about ¼ cup each). Slowly pour 1 tablespoon (½ fluid ounce) dark rum into each mug, stirring constantly to avoid curdling, until blended, then stir in 2 tablespoons (1 fluid ounce) **brandy**. Pour ¼ cup hot milk into each mug and grate **nutmeg** over top. (If serving in larger mugs, top off with more hot milk.) Serve immediately. **SERVES 6**

SOUR CHERRY LEMONADE

Lemonade and summer are made for one another, especially when a screened-in porch and a lazy afternoon are involved. Make a good thing even better by adding fresh or frozen sour cherries.

In a large saucepan, bring 1 pound **sour cherries**, 1 cup **granulated sugar**, 1 tablespoon fresh **lemon juice**, and 1 cup **water** to a simmer over medium heat. Cook until cherries are juicy and have broken down, stirring occasionally, about 20 minutes. With a slotted spoon, remove cherries (and pits) from pot and discard. Reduce remaining juices until thickened and reduced to 1 cup. Let cool completely. (Cherry syrup can be refrigerated in an airtight container up to 3 days.)

Fill a large pitcher with **ice**, then add 1½ cups fresh lemon juice (from about 9 lemons), ½ cup **superfine sugar**, ½ cup cooled cherry syrup, and 4 cups **club soda**, stirring to combine. Serve immediately, garnished with more sour cherries. **SERVES 6**

CHICAGO FIZZ

Frothy fizz cocktails (which always include lemon or lime juice and carbonated water), always seem to go together with nightclubs and lively music—perhaps because the most famous example, the Ramos Gin Fizz, originated in New Orleans. No surprise, then, that Chicago, another city with a rich music tradition straight from the Mississippi Delta, should come up with its own riff; this drink gets its rolling, satiny bass notes from dark rum and ruby port.

Combine ¼ cup (2 fluid ounces) each **dark rum** and **ruby port**, 1 teaspoon **superfine sugar**, 2 tablespoons fresh **lemon juice**, and 1 large **egg white** in a cocktail shaker. Shake briefly, then add **ice** to fill shaker and shake vigorously for about 8 seconds. Strain into a collins glass and top off with **club soda**. Serve immediately. **MAKES 1**

PECAN CHEESE BALLS

2 packages (8 ounces each) cream
   cheese, softened

8 ounces sharp cheddar, finely grated
   (2½ cups)

1 tablespoon Dijon mustard

1 teaspoon Worcestershire sauce
   Pinch of freshly ground pepper

1 cup finely chopped toasted (page 408)
   pecans (about 5 ounces)
   Assorted crackers, for serving

1 With an electric mixer on medium speed, beat cream
cheese, cheddar, mustard, Worcestershire, and pepper
until well combined. Mix in ¼ cup chopped pecans. Cover
with plastic wrap and chill at least 3 hours or up to 1 day.

2 Divide the cheese mixture in half and shape each portion
into a ball. Spread remaining ¾ cup chopped pecans on
a plate and roll cheese balls in pecans to coat completely,
pressing nuts to adhere. Cover and refrigerate until ready
to serve, up to 2 hours, with crackers.

SERVES 12 TO 16

THE MIDWEST

BACKSTORY

*Cheese balls are alive and well in the Midwest, particularly
in Wisconsin, the dairy capital, but you need not be
Midwestern to understand their widespread appeal.
There's simply no substitute for a cheese ball at a holiday
open house or a cocktail party—not a store-bought version,
but one put together from scratch, with sharp cheddar,
tangy cream cheese, a few seasonings such as mustard and
Worcestershire sauce, and a coating of chopped toasted
nuts. This recipe makes enough for two generously sized
cheese balls, but you can easily halve the ingredients to
make just one.*

VARIATIONS

Cheddar and Cranberry With an electric mixer, beat ⅓ stick
softened butter, 1 package (8 ounces) softened cream cheese,
2 teaspoons fresh lemon juice, ⅛ teaspoon Worcestershire
sauce, 1 to 2 dashes hot-pepper sauce, ⅛ teaspoon coarse
salt, and a pinch of freshly ground pepper until combined.
Stir in 8 ounces finely shredded cheddar cheese and 2
tablespoons store-bought cranberry chutney, then form
mixture into a ball. Chill as directed in above recipe. Roll
in ¾ cup dried cranberries, finely chopped.

Roquefort and Walnut With an electric mixer, beat ⅓ stick
softened butter, 1 package (8 ounces) softened cream cheese,
2 teaspoons fresh lemon juice, ⅛ teaspoon Worcestershire
sauce, 1 to 2 dashes hot-pepper sauce, ⅛ teaspoon coarse
salt, and a pinch of freshly ground pepper until combined.
Stir in 6 ounces Roquefort cheese and 1 minced shallot, then
form mixture into a ball. Chill as directed in above recipe.
Roll cheese ball in 1 cup toasted walnuts, coarsely chopped.

SMOKED TROUT AND HORSERADISH ON PUMPERNICKEL

8   small slices (¼ inch thick) pumpernickel bread

2   tablespoons unsalted butter, softened

2   tablespoons prepared horseradish with beets

4   ounces fillets of smoked trout, pin bones and skin removed, fillets flaked into large pieces

16 small sprigs dill

1   lemon

Spread one side of each pumpernickel slice with butter, then cut bread in half. Top each triangle with horseradish, a piece of trout, and a sprig of dill. Cover with plastic wrap and keep at room temperature until ready to serve, up to 2 hours. Before serving, halve lemon and squeeze juice over tops.

SERVES 4

THE MIDWEST

BACKSTORY

The harsh winters of Minnesota and Wisconsin deterred many a settler, but the Scandinavians who arrived in the late nineteenth century found a familiar bit of home in the region's snowy landscape. With them they brought their love for smoked fish, often complementing its taste with horseradish—here, the kind that's mixed with grated beets—and dill. Trout, a local catch, is especially good smoked, and makes a fitting appetizer for a Midsummer Night celebration, another longstanding Scandinavian tradition that's become a Midwestern tradition in its own right.

STUFFED MUSHROOMS

    1   tablespoon olive oil, plus more for baking dish and drizzling
   24   large button mushrooms
    6   ounces sweet Italian sausage (about 2 links),
        removed from casing
    2   garlic cloves, minced
    1   large shallot, minced
        Coarse salt and freshly ground pepper
    1   tablespoon finely chopped fresh flat-leaf parsley
    2   teaspoons finely chopped fresh oregano,
        plus whole leaves for garnish (optional)
    1   large egg, lightly beaten
    2   tablespoons plain dry breadcrumbs
    2   tablespoons finely grated parmesan

1 Preheat oven to 375°F. Lightly oil a 9-by-13-inch baking dish. Clean the
mushrooms, then remove stems and finely chop (to yield about 1 cup);
reserve caps. In a large skillet, heat olive oil over medium-high. Cook sausage,
breaking it up with a fork, until no longer pink, about 5 minutes. Add garlic,
shallot, and chopped mushroom stems; season with salt and pepper. Reduce
heat to medium and cook until vegetables are tender, stirring occasionally,
4 to 6 minutes. Transfer to a bowl, stir in parsley and oregano, and let cool.

2 Add egg, breadcrumbs, and cheese to cooled sausage mixture; stir to combine.
Place mushroom caps in prepared baking dish and season cavities with salt
and pepper. Stuff caps with sausage mixture, packing tightly. Drizzle lightly
with olive oil.

3 Bake mushrooms until tender and tops are browned, 25 to 30 minutes. Serve
hot, garnished with additional oregano leaves, if desired.

MAKES 24

VARIATIONS

Vegetable-and-Walnut-Stuffed Mushrooms Follow recipe, omitting sausage
and oregano, and starting with 32 button mushrooms. In step 1, remove
stems from mushrooms and finely chop (to yield about 1 cup). Finely chop
8 mushroom caps; reserve remaining 24 caps. In a large skillet, heat olive
oil over medium-high. Add 1 small onion and 1 celery stalk, both finely chopped,
along with the garlic and chopped mushroom stems and caps; season with
salt and pepper. Reduce heat to medium and cook until vegetables are tender,
stirring occasionally, 6 to 8 minutes. Transfer to a bowl and stir in ⅔ cup
finely chopped walnuts, 1 teaspoon dried thyme, 1 teaspoon finely chopped
fresh rosemary, and the parsley; let cool. Proceed with steps 2 and 3, adding
2 tablespoons grated provolone along with the parmesan. Garnish with
additional rosemary, if desired.

BACKSTORY

*There are times in life when
nothing will do but hearty,
homey food—and plenty of it.
Take these stuffed mushrooms.
Serve them as an hors d'oeuvre
at any party, no matter
the occasion, and they will
disappear instantly. And there
is no end to what you can
put in them. The two versions
here include one with sweet
Italian sausage, garlic, and
parmesan, and a vegetarian
filling that is rich with
walnuts. No matter which
one you try, you can make the
mushrooms ahead through
step 2, then cover them
and refrigerate for up to a
day. You'll just need to
increase the baking time
by about five minutes.*

PIGS IN A BLANKET

THE MIDWEST

BACKSTORY

If little cocktail franks wrapped in pastry remind you of your childhood (close your eyes and you're back in the family room), then you will be happy to know that retro rules. Perhaps, though, in some places—the Midwest and Great Plains, for instance—the savory bites never fell out of favor. Why else would the American Farm Bureau Foundation's "Dates to Celebrate Agriculture" calendar include a National Pigs in a Blanket Day? Mark your own so you don't forget to celebrate on April 24.

1 sheet frozen puff pastry, thawed
1 package (12 ounces) cocktail franks, patted dry
1 large egg, lightly beaten
2 to 3 teaspoons poppy seeds
   Ketchup or mustard, for serving

1 Preheat oven to 400°F. Unfold pastry on a work surface. Using a pizza cutter or sharp knife (and a ruler or other straight edge), cut pastry into 10 equal strips; cut each strip crosswise into thirds (to yield thirty 1-by-3-inch pieces). Wrap a strip of pastry around each frank, and place, seam side down, 2 inches apart on a rimmed baking sheet.

2 Using a pastry brush, coat top of pastries with beaten egg, then sprinkle evenly with poppy seeds. Bake until golden, rotating sheet halfway through, 25 to 30 minutes. Serve hot with ketchup or mustard, as desired.

MAKES 30

DIG-DEEP LAYER SALAD

  2 cups hard wheat berries (pearl barley can be substituted)
  2 quarts water
  ¼ cup plus 2 tablespoons fresh lemon juice (from about 2 lemons)
  ¼ cup white-wine vinegar
  1 tablespoon plus 1 teaspoon Dijon mustard
  1 tablespoon sugar
  ½ teaspoon celery seeds
     Coarse salt and freshly ground pepper
  1 cup extra-virgin olive oil
  ¾ bunch celery, stalks sliced thinly on the diagonal (about 2¼ cups)
1½ cups dried cherries, preferably tart
  8 ounces Maytag blue cheese, crumbled (2 cups)
  1 small head green cabbage (1 pound), thinly shredded
     (about 5 cups)
  5 large carrots, peeled and grated (about 5 cups)

1 Place wheat berries in a small pot and add the water. Cover and bring to a boil over high heat. Reduce heat to low and simmer until berries are tender, about 40 minutes. Drain in a colander and transfer to a large glass serving bowl.

2 In a medium bowl, whisk together lemon juice, vinegar, mustard, sugar, and celery seeds; season with salt and pepper. Whisk in the olive oil in a slow, steady stream until completely combined and dressing is emulsified. Drizzle 2 tablespoons dressing over the wheat berries.

3 Arrange celery slices over wheat berries and drizzle with 2 tablespoons dressing. Cover the celery with cherries and drizzle with 2 tablespoons dressing. Crumble half the blue cheese over the top of the cherries and drizzle with 2 tablespoons dressing.

4 Layer the carrots over the blue cheese and drizzle with 2 tablespoons dressing. Crumble the remaining blue cheese over the carrots and drizzle with 2 tablespoons dressing. In another bowl, toss together the shredded cabbage and 3 tablespoons dressing; layer the cabbage over the blue cheese. Cover salad and refrigerate 24 hours to allow flavors to meld. Serve at room temperature.

SERVES 8 TO 10

THE MIDWEST

BACKSTORY

Layered salads are a boon to anyone looking for an easy, portable dish to bring to a cookout or family reunion. They look pretty in their transparent serving vessels, and they offer a veritable symphony of textures and flavors. What make this particular version Midwestern are the ingredients. Maytag blue cheese, prized for its robust taste, has been produced on a family-owned Iowa farm since 1941; dried tart cherries are from Michigan. Wheat berries, or whole wheat kernels, are a product of the so-called wheat belt that spans the Midwest, and whose center is Kansas; when boiled the same way as rice or other grains, they are nutty and chewy, and a wholesome addition to salads, including this one.

FARMHOUSE CHOWDER

BACKSTORY

There is no law dictating that the thick, well-seasoned stews called chowders need a New England provenance. Take this one: Like its relatives in the Northeast, it has a strong sense of place but it takes inspiration from the farmyard and kitchen garden rather than the coast. This stunner is rich with chicken and earthy carrots, rutabaga, and turnip, all bathed in a creamy, full-flavored stock and sprinkled with dill. A chilled glass of lager makes a great accompaniment to chowder, no matter where it hails from.

1 whole chicken (3½ to 4 pounds)
1 large onion, halved, one half left whole, the other half chopped
2 carrots, 1 halved lengthwise, 1 cut into ½-inch dice
4 sprigs flat-leaf parsley, plus more for garnish
10 black peppercorns
2 tablespoons unsalted butter
2 tablespoons flour, preferably instant (like Wondra)
1 small turnip, cut into ½-inch dice
4 ounces rutabaga or parsnip, cut into ½-inch dice
Coarse salt and freshly ground pepper
½ cup heavy cream
1 tablespoon fresh dill, finely chopped, for garnish

1 Place chicken, breast side down, in a large pot. Add enough water to just cover chicken (8 to 10 cups). Add onion half, the carrot halves, parsley, and peppercorns. Bring to a boil, partially covered. Reduce heat and simmer gently 1 hour. Remove chicken and let cool, then shred into bite-size pieces; discard bones and skin.

2 Strain broth through a fine sieve lined with cheesecloth into another pot (discard solids) and bring to a simmer. Cook 20 minutes.

3 Melt butter in a large pot over medium heat. Cook chopped onion and diced carrot, stirring occasionally, until onion is translucent, about 5 minutes. Stir in flour and cook, stirring, 1 minute. Whisk in broth and bring to a boil. Add turnip and rutabaga; season with salt and pepper. Reduce heat and simmer until root vegetables are tender, 6 to 8 minutes.

4 Stir in shredded chicken and cream and heat until warmed through, about 1 minute. Season with salt and pepper and garnish with dill. Serve immediately.

SERVES 8 TO 10

SLOPPY JOES

1¼ pounds ground beef chuck
    Coarse salt and freshly ground pepper
1   onion, finely chopped
2   garlic cloves, minced
1   can (14.5 ounces) puréed tomatoes
2   tablespoons light-brown sugar
1   tablespoon cider vinegar
1   tablespoon tomato paste
1   teaspoon Worcestershire sauce
1½ cups water
4   hamburger buns

1 Cook beef in a large skillet over medium-high heat, breaking apart pieces with a spoon, until lightly browned, 5 to 6 minutes. Season with salt and pepper. Add onion and garlic; cook, stirring occasionally, until translucent, about 5 minutes.

2 Add puréed tomatoes, brown sugar, vinegar, tomato paste, Worcestershire, and the water. Reduce heat to medium-low; simmer until thickened, stirring occasionally, about 20 minutes. Dividing evenly, spoon over bottom halves of buns, top with top halves, and serve immediately.

SERVES 4

THE MIDWEST

BACKSTORY

The origin of this well-loved sandwich is lost in the mists of time, but its top-ranking status as a quick and satisfying family meal has never been in question. Think of it as the other way to enjoy ground beef in a bun, except with this dish the meat is browned with chopped onion and garlic, then made into more than the sum of its parts by way of a tangy-sweet tomato sauce and seasonings. There's no reason to reach for store-bought powdered mixes (or canned versions of the finished product) when making Sloppy Joes from scratch is so easy to do—and so clearly worth the extra effort.

GRILLED KIELBASA RING WITH SAUERKRAUT

THE MIDWEST

BACKSTORY

Spend just a day in blustery Wisconsin during the cold-weather months and you'll understand the lasting appeal of the hardy dishes that German and Polish settlers brought to the state. This example is a salute to that heritage, specifically the local fondness for sausages and smoked meats, customarily accompanied by sauerkraut. Kielbasa—garlicky pork Polish sausage, sometimes made with beef or veal—is a particular favorite in the Midwest. This recipe calls for kielbasa in a ring, available from specialty food shops, Polish butcher shops, or online retailers. Other authentic options include bratwurst (beef sausage flavored with nutmeg, ginger, and other spices); knockwurst (smoked pork and beef sausage flavored with garlic); and weisswurst (mild veal sausage flavored with cardamom and lemon). Here, the grilled kielbasa and sauerkraut fit neatly into a hollowed-out round of bread that has been toasted until crisp. The combination is just right for a late-summer meal enjoyed outdoors, before the chill sets in, but can certainly be enjoyed any time of the year.

1 loaf round rustic bread, split crosswise

2 tablespoons olive oil, plus more for grill

1 ring kielbasa (about 1 pound), top scored in 1-inch increments

3 tablespoons hot, spicy Bavarian-style or horseradish mustard

2 cups sauerkraut, preferably homemade (recipe follows)

1 Heat grill to medium-high. (If you are using a charcoal grill, coals are ready when you can hold your hand 5 inches above grates for just 3 to 4 seconds.) Using your hands, remove about ½ cup bread from each side of the loaf (discard). Brush hollowed-out sides of bread with the olive oil.

2 Lightly oil hot grates. Grill kielbasa, flipping once, until browned and heated through, 8 to 10 minutes. Grill bread, flipping once, until toasted, about 3 minutes. Transfer kielbasa and bread to a cutting board. Halve kielbasa crosswise. Spread hollowed-out sides of bread with mustard; top each side with half of the sauerkraut and a halved kielbasa ring. Cut each into wedges; serve.

SERVES 4 TO 6

SAUERKRAUT

1 large head green cabbage (3 pounds), shredded (14 cups), 3 whole small leaves reserved

1 tablespoon caraway seeds

Coarse sea salt

1 Combine shredded cabbage, caraway seeds, and 1 tablespoon salt in a large bowl. Let stand 20 minutes. Rub mixture to release liquid (forming a brine), about 5 minutes.

2 Pack cabbage mixture into 3 pint-size canning jars, making sure brine covers cabbage by at least 1 inch and leaving 1 to 2 inches of space at the top. Fold and push 1 reserved cabbage leaf into each, filling the top space. Close jars tightly, and transfer to a 2-inch-deep nonreactive container. Let stand in a cool (64°F to 70°F), dark place for 5 days.

3 Slowly open and quickly close each jar to release pressure, being careful not to let the liquid bubble out. Let stand 5 more days. Reopen jars to release pressure. Let stand 5 more days. Taste to determine if kraut is sour enough. Let stand until kraut is to your liking, continuing to open jars every few days to release pressure. Sauerkraut can be refrigerated, submerged in brine, up to 6 months.

MAKES 3 PINTS

GRILLED BACON-WRAPPED WHITEFISH

    Extra-virgin olive oil, for brushing

2   whole whitefish (about 3 pounds each), cleaned

    Coarse salt and freshly ground pepper

4   lemons, 3 cut into ¼-inch-thick rounds
    and 1 cut into 1-inch pieces

1   bunch fresh thyme, plus more sprigs for garnish

20 strips bacon (about 1¼ pounds)

1 Heat grill to high. (If you are using a charcoal grill, the coals are ready when you can hold your hand 4 inches above the grates for just 1 to 2 seconds.) Brush two large fish-grilling baskets with olive oil. Using a sharp knife, make diagonal slits (in serving-size portions) along both sides of fish. Season both sides with salt and pepper. Reserve 6 to 8 lemon rounds and a few sprigs of thyme; place the remaining lemon rounds and thyme inside the fish cavities, dividing evenly.

2 On a large cutting board, lay 2 bacon slices end to end, slightly overlapping; repeat with 6 more slices laying so pairs are parallel to one another and 1 inch apart. Center and place a bacon slice at end, 1 inch apart from and parallel to overlapping slices. Arrange a fish over bacon, placing head and tail on single slices. Wrap bacon around fish and secure with toothpicks. Tuck a few reserved thyme sprigs under bacon. Place fish in a prepared basket. Repeat with remaining bacon, fish, and reserved thyme.

3 Place baskets on grill; cover and cook until fish are opaque throughout, about 10 minutes per side. Transfer fish to a platter. Grill reserved lemon rounds until lightly charred. Garnish fish with additional thyme, and the lemon pieces and grilled lemon slices.

SERVES 12

THE MIDWEST

BACKSTORY

Its firm white flesh and year-round availability—it is caught commercially and by sport fishermen in both summer and (from their icehouses) winter—have made whitefish a big part of the Midwestern diet. An essential component of a "fish boil," where diners watch an elaborate show of huge, bubbling cauldrons, fresh catch is also fried and served in a "shore lunch," or simply grilled. Here, the fish is stuffed with lemon slices and fresh thyme before being wrapped in bacon and grilled whole. The bacon lends richness to the lean fish. You could use other types of fish, such as striped bass, cod, or halibut, depending on what's available at your local market. Serve with a wild rice salad (see page 259) or boiled potatoes tossed with butter and chopped parsley.

BARBECUED RIBS

2 racks (2 to 2½ pounds each) St. Louis–style pork ribs

2 tablespoons packed light-brown sugar

2 tablespoons coarse salt

2 teaspoons freshly ground pepper

2 teaspoons hot paprika

2 teaspoons dry mustard powder

1 teaspoon celery seeds

Vegetable oil, for grill

Kansas City Barbecue Sauce (page 411)

1 Place one rib rack, meat side down, on a work surface. With a knife, cut a small slit through the silvery membrane at one end of the rack. Using a paper towel, grip the cut portion of the membrane, gently peel it from the rack, and discard. Repeat with remaining rack.

2 Combine brown sugar, salt, pepper, paprika, mustard powder, and celery seeds in a bowl. (If mixture is clumpy, pass through a medium sieve.) Rub mixture on both sides of each rib rack, dividing equally. Place ribs on a rimmed baking sheet, cover, and refrigerate at least 2 hours or up to overnight. Let stand at room temperature 30 minutes before cooking.

3 Prepare charcoal grill as instructed (see page 409). Lightly oil grates. Place rib racks, bone side down, on top grill rack directly over aluminum pan. Cover and cook ribs, without turning, until the meat is tender but not falling off the bone and has shrunk about ½ inch from ends, 3 to 3½ hours, adding 8 briquettes to each charcoal pile every hour.

4 Reserve 1 cup barbecue sauce in a small serving dish. Brush both sides of ribs with remaining sauce, dividing evenly. Cover and grill until ribs are glistening and deep mahogany, about 15 minutes. Remove from grill; let stand 10 minutes before cutting into servings of about 3 ribs each. Serve reserved sauce alongside.

Alternate Oven Method You can also achieve great ribs indoors. This oven version lacks the smoky complexity that grilling imparts, but the flavor and texture remain otherwise uncompromised. Preheat oven to 350°F, with a rack in the middle. Fit a rimmed baking sheet with a wire rack. Place ribs, bone side down, on rack. Roast, rotating halfway through, until meat is tender but not falling off the bone, about 2 hours. Reserve 1 cup barbecue sauce in a serving dish. Brush both sides of ribs with remaining sauce. Return ribs to oven until glistening and deep mahogany, about 15 minutes. Let stand 10 minutes before cutting and serving, with reserved sauce.

SERVES 6

THE MIDWEST

BACKSTORY

While much of the country associates regional barbecue with the states located south of the Mason-Dixon line, Missouri holds its own among barbecue meccas. Like all authentic "barbecued" meats, Kansas City ribs are cooked "low and slow." You don't need a pit or a backyard smoker to make them, however; a charcoal grill will do (see page 409). St. Louis–style pork ribs—cut from spare ribs for a more uniform appearance and even cooking— are meaty and very flavorful; the ribs are enhanced, though not overwhelmed, by a spice rub. But the real secret to making good Kansas City barbecue is the sauce; this one is ultra-thick, sweet, and smoky with spices. Coleslaw (see page 50), sliced white onion, and white sandwich bread are must-have accompaniments; grilled jalapeños offer another spicy kick.

STUFFED PORK CHOPS

  1 cup cubed (½ inch) rustic bread (trimmed of crusts)

  1 tablespoon unsalted butter

  ¼ cup extra-virgin olive oil

  ½ onion, finely chopped

  4 celery stalks, finely chopped

  ¼ cup plus 1 tablespoon mixed chopped fresh
     flat-leaf parsley and fresh thyme

 2¼ teaspoons ground coriander

  ½ cup plus 3 tablespoons chicken stock,
     preferably homemade (page 410)

     Coarse salt and freshly ground pepper

  4 bone-in pork chops (each 1 inch thick and about 9 ounces)

  2 garlic cloves, minced

  ¼ cup dry sherry

1 Preheat oven to 350°F. Toast bread cubes on a baking sheet until golden, tossing halfway through, about 7 minutes. In a large ovenproof skillet over medium, heat butter and 1 tablespoon olive oil. Cook onion, stirring frequently, until soft, about 3 minutes. Add celery; cook, stirring, 1 minute. Transfer to a medium bowl. Reserve skillet. Toss bread, herbs, ¼ teaspoon coriander, and 3 tablespoons stock with onion mixture; season with salt and pepper.

2 With a sharp paring knife, make a deep slit in each pork chop, cutting horizontally to the bone. Dividing evenly, fill with bread mixture, spreading it with your fingers. Using a fork, mix garlic, remaining 2 teaspoons coriander, ½ teaspoon salt, and 1 tablespoon olive oil to make a paste; rub over pork.

3 In same skillet, heat remaining 2 tablespoons olive oil over medium-high. Cook pork until golden brown on bottom, 2 to 3 minutes; turn over pork and transfer skillet to oven. Cook until an instant-read thermometer inserted into pork (avoiding bone) registers 155°F, about 15 minutes. Transfer to a plate.

4 Add sherry and remaining ½ cup stock to skillet. Cook over medium-high heat, stirring, until reduced by half. Serve with pork.

SERVES 4

SKILLET-FRIED TROUT WITH HERBS AND POTATOES

4   whole brook trout (1½ to 2 pounds each),
    scaled, gutted, and gills removed

    Coarse salt and freshly ground pepper

¼   cup extra-virgin olive oil, plus more for fish

1   bunch fresh herbs, such as thyme, rosemary, or oregano

1   pint cherry tomatoes (1½ cups), halved

1 Heat grill to medium-high. (If using a charcoal grill, coals are ready when you can hold your hand 5 inches above grates for just 2 to 3 seconds.) Open fish like a book. Season cavity of each with salt and pepper, and drizzle with some oil. Stuff with herbs. Close fish, and tie each with kitchen twine at intervals to enclose. Rub both sides of fish with oil.

2 Toss tomatoes with ¼ cup oil in a bowl; season with salt and pepper. Working in batches, transfer fish and some tomatoes to a large cast-iron skillet and place on hot grill. Cook until fish is browned and crisp, flipping fish and tomatoes halfway through, and removing the tomatoes as they blacken in spots, about 14 minutes. Serve hot.

SERVES 4

THE MIDWEST

BACKSTORY

One of the largest and deepest freshwater lakes in the world, Lake Superior, in Michigan, has given the region a bounty of lake trout (and whitefish, lake herring, and ciscoes) for centuries. American Indians smoked their catch to preserve it; Scandinavian immigrants, who arrived in the 19th century to work in the timber and mineral industries, started the area's commercial fishing efforts. This lake is but one of many that populate the upper Midwest states and the Dakotas, and that means that no matter which part of the region you find yourself in, a meal of just-caught trout is always within arm's reach— a mere cast of the line away. But whether or not you reel in the fish yourself, cooking whole trout over a hot grill (or, even better, a campfire) is an enjoyable and highly recommended ritual. Here the fish are first stuffed with fresh herbs and tied; cherry tomatoes cooked alongside make a flavorful accompaniment.

SAUERBRATEN

THE MIDWEST

BACKSTORY

In Wisconsin and other parts of the Midwest, sauerbraten is very much a part of the German-American culture and cuisine. Although I grew up in New Jersey, sauerbraten was also a fixture of my childhood. My mother learned to cook it (and other German specialties) from Mr. Maus, our next-door neighbor on Elm Place in Nutley. Once he parted with his secret recipes for sauerbraten and Kartoffelklösse, or potato dumplings, these two dishes became family favorites at our house. For many Sunday dinners, the bottom round of beef was purchased from the co-op on Thursday; marinated in a concoction of spices, herbs, and wine; and cooked on Saturday. The potatoes were boiled on Saturday, riced and dried, and then mixed with eggs and nutmeg and flour and salt and formed into dumplings as large as snowballs, to be boiled in a big pot of steaming water. Mr. Maus served these with the slightly sour sauerbraten; he finished his sauce with a little bit of homemade cider vinegar. We loved the entire meal, especially the robust tanginess of the meat, and of course, enjoyed hot gravy-soaked sandwiches made the next day from the leftovers.

1 bottom round of beef (4 to 5 pounds)
  Coarse salt and freshly ground pepper
¼ cup neutral-tasting oil, such as safflower
4 garlic cloves, coarsely chopped
2 large onions, thinly sliced
2 dried bay leaves
¼ cup tomato paste
¼ cup ketchup
1 cup red-wine vinegar
2 cups dry red wine
2 cups water
¼ cup sour cream

1 Rub beef dry with paper towels, and then season with salt and pepper. Tie kitchen twine around beef at 2-inch intervals and once from end to end. Heat 2 tablespoons oil in a large (8-quart) heavy-bottomed pot over medium until hot but not smoking. Brown meat all over, including ends, about 3 minutes per side; transfer to a plate.

2 Reduce heat to medium-low and add remaining 2 tablespoons oil and the garlic and onions to pot. Cook, stirring often, until onions are softened, 5 to 7 minutes. Add bay leaves, tomato paste, ketchup, vinegar, and wine. Raise heat to medium-high; bring mixture to a boil.

3 Return beef to pot; add the water. Cover pot with a tight-fitting lid. Reduce heat to medium-low; simmer 2 hours. Turn beef; continue to simmer until tender, 1½ to 2 hours more. Let cool slightly. (The dish can be refrigerated up to 2 days; let cool completely before storing and reheat over medium-low before proceeding.)

4 Transfer beef to a cutting board. Remove twine; let beef stand 15 minutes. Skim fat from sauce in pot. Bring sauce to a simmer over medium heat; cook until reduced by one-fourth, about 7 minutes. Season with salt and pepper. Remove from heat; whisk in sour cream.

5 Cut beef across the grain into ¼-inch-thick slices. Return slices to pot and turn to immerse in sauce, then transfer to a large serving platter. Ladle more sauce on top and serve.

SERVES 10 TO 12

CHICKEN AND MUSHROOM HOTDISH

1⅓ pounds boneless, skinless chicken breast halves (about 2 large)
 Coarse salt and freshly ground pepper

¼ cup plus 1 tablespoon extra-virgin olive oil

1 leek, white and pale green parts only, coarsely chopped, washed well and drained (page 408)

1 celery stalk, cut into ½-inch dice

10 ounces cremini mushrooms, halved if large

3 tablespoons all-purpose flour

3 tablespoons dry sherry

2¼ cups chicken stock, preferably homemade (page 410)

¾ cup milk

1 dried bay leaf

8 slices dense multigrain bread, trimmed of crusts and cut into triangles

2 tablespoons coarsely chopped fresh flat-leaf parsley

⅓ cup finely grated parmesan (about 1 ounce)

1 Preheat oven to 350°F. Pat dry chicken with paper towels, and then season on both sides with salt and pepper. In a medium sauté pan, heat 2 tablespoons olive oil over medium-high until shimmering. Add chicken and sauté until golden brown on bottom, 3 to 4 minutes. Turn over chicken, reduce heat to medium, and cook until opaque throughout, about 10 minutes more. Use tongs to transfer chicken to a plate.

2 Heat remaining 3 tablespoons olive oil in pan. Add leek, celery, mushrooms, and a pinch of salt. Cook, stirring occasionally, until vegetables are golden brown and tender, 8 to 10 minutes. (Reduce heat if vegetables brown too quickly.) Stir in flour and cook, stirring often, 2 minutes. Add sherry, stock, milk, and bay leaf; cook, scraping up browned bits from bottom with a wooden spoon, until sauce is thickened, about 5 minutes. Season with salt and pepper. Discard the bay leaf.

3 Arrange bread on bottom of a shallow 2-quart baking dish, overlapping slices slightly. Spoon half of the vegetables and sauce over bread. Slice chicken crosswise, ½ inch thick, and arrange on bread. Top with any accumulated juices from chicken. Spread remaining vegetables and sauce over chicken, sprinkle evenly with parsley and parmesan, and bake until golden brown and bubbling, 25 to 30 minutes. Let stand 15 minutes before serving.

SERVES 6

THE MIDWEST

BACKSTORY

A "hotdish," the colloquial term for a casserole in Minnesota and some parts of Wisconsin and the Dakotas, is the ideal comfort food: warm, nourishing, and designed to feed a crowd. The casseroles many of us grew up on emerged during the heyday of canned condensed soups, when convenience foods were a shortcut for making sauces. For anyone who has only tasted one of the ever-popular casseroles made with canned cream of mushroom or celery soup, this version will be a revelation. To develop layers of flavor, the chicken is browned first, then removed and the drippings left in the pan. Fresh mushrooms and other vegetables are then sautéed until golden before the sauce ingredients (a little flour, sherry, chicken stock, and milk) are added and simmered until properly thickened. But here's the real secret to this dish's success: the chicken pieces and mushroom sauce are layered in the baking dish with pieces of chewy whole-grain bread, which absorb some of the wonderful sauce during baking and lend the dish heft. A topping of crisp, golden parmesan is the crowning touch.

WILD RICE

To shove off in a canoe onto Big Rice Lake, in northern Minnesota, is to launch back into time. No mechanized boats break the silence; no houses line the shore. The only sign of human existence is a footpath vanishing into the tall plants crowding the shallow water. Birds tilt on the high reeds but do not take flight as the boat pushes past, perhaps sensing that little will be disturbed. And that's true, because although this is a harvest, it is quiet work, done by two sets of hands: one poling the boat from behind, the other bending armfuls of stalwart shafts downward and knocking ripened rice into the boat.

Upon the return home, the rice is spread out in the sun to dry and then parched in an enormous iron kettle over a roaring fire. The rice must be stirred constantly with a paddle to keep it from burning and must be removed at just the right moment: If it gets too hot, it pops like popcorn, and if it doesn't parch long enough, it will spoil. The grains of rice are then separated from the hulls and winnowed, a few pounds at a time, in a green-willow and birch-bark basket, and gently tossed in the air with a circular motion so that the chaff is carried away by the wind. Like buffalo for the Lakota and corn for the Hopi, manoomin, or wild lake rice, is part of the heritage of the Anishinaabe tribe (also known as the Ojibwa).

While all wild rice varieties are tall annual grasses, manoomin is not the "wild rice" found at the average grocery store. Most of what is sold under that name is actually cultivated in diked paddies. By contrast, the wild rice grown according to the methods of this tribe is found in shallow lakes and moving streams.

Offering a culinary connection to America's roots, wild lake rice has quietly traveled across time, delivered by the slow progress of a boat through the water, sound emanating only from the parting of the rice plants and the steady tempo of the poler's hands. As its forked end heaves the bearer's energy into the mud, the tall reeds reflexively swish back into place with ancient elegance, leaving everything but history behind.

WILD RICE WITH MUSHROOMS AND PARSLEY Fill a saucepan with cold water; add 1 cup wild rice and 1 teaspoon coarse salt. Bring to a boil, then reduce heat and simmer until grains are tender, about 45 minutes. Drain before using. Meanwhile, heat 2 tablespoons extra-virgin olive oil in a large skillet over medium-high. Add 1 pound button mushrooms, trimmed and sliced, and season with coarse salt and freshly ground pepper. Cook, stirring occasionally, until mushrooms are browned, about 13 minutes. Add 2 minced garlic cloves; cook, stirring, until fragrant, about 30 seconds. Stir in cooked rice and remove from heat. Add 3 tablespoons chopped fresh flat-leaf parsley and 1 tablespoon fresh lemon juice; season with salt and pepper. Toss to combine, and serve as a flavorful side for chicken, pork, or fish.

TWICE-BAKED POTATOES WITH SOUR CREAM AND CHIVES

8 small russet potatoes
   (about 2½ pounds), scrubbed

1 tablespoon neutral-tasting oil,
   such as safflower

1 cup sour cream

¼ cup milk

3 tablespoons unsalted butter

¼ cup snipped fresh chives,
   plus more for garnish

   Coarse salt and freshly ground pepper

1 Preheat oven to 400°F. Rub potatoes with the oil, dividing evenly. Place on a baking sheet; bake until potatoes are easily pierced with the tip of a sharp paring knife, about 45 minutes. Let cool slightly.

2 Cut a thin slice lengthwise off the top of each potato and discard. Using a small spoon, scoop out flesh from each potato into a bowl, leaving ½ inch intact around edge. Add sour cream, milk, butter, and chives; mash with a potato masher or fork until combined. Season with salt and pepper. Spoon mixture into potato skins. Bake until heated through and lightly browned on top, about 20 minutes. Serve hot, garnished with more chives.

SERVES 8

THE MIDWEST

BACKSTORY

Chicago has had a long, proud steakhouse tradition ever since the days the city's stockyards were immortalized by such diverse voices as Carl Sandburg and Frank Sinatra. One of the all-time great steakhouse sides—twice-baked potatoes—is unbelievably easy to make (the oven does most of the work), yet they bestow a sense of occasion on even the most everyday meals. Here, tangy sour cream contrasts nicely with the fluffy richness of the potatoes.

WILD RICE SALAD

2 cups wild rice

6½ cups water

Coarse salt

2 tablespoons sugar

2 tablespoons fresh lemon juice

2 tablespoons white-wine vinegar

¼ cup plus 2 tablespoons olive oil

2 large shallots, thinly sliced (about 1 cup)

1 tablespoon minced garlic

1 piece (4 inches) fresh ginger, peeled and very thinly sliced into rounds

2 cups dried sour cherries

1 cup fresh flat-leaf parsley, some coarsely chopped, some left whole

1 Bring rice, 6 cups water, and 1 teaspoon salt to a boil in a medium saucepan. Reduce heat to a simmer; cover and cook until grains are tender and beginning to burst, about 45 minutes. Drain.

2 Stir together sugar, lemon juice, and vinegar in a small bowl. Heat olive oil in a medium saucepan over medium-high. Add shallots, garlic, and ginger; season with salt. Cook, stirring constantly, until shallots are translucent, about 3 minutes. Stir in dried cherries and remaining ½ cup water. Cook until cherries are plump, about 10 minutes. Remove from heat and stir in sugar mixture.

3 Stir together cherry mixture and rice in a large dish. Cover and let stand at least 1 hour at room temperature or up to 1 day in the refrigerator (and let come to room temperature). Just before serving, stir in parsley.

SERVES 12

THE MIDWEST

BACKSTORY

A rare delicacy for the rest of the United States, wild rice is common in Minnesota, where it grows truly wild and is often still harvested in the Native American way—by canoe. Its name is misleading, however: Wild rice is not an actual rice but a marsh grass native to the areas surrounding the Great Lakes. While it's delicious simply boiled and tossed with a little melted butter, wild rice is prepared in multiple ways in Minnesota—even for breakfast, legend has it, by lumberjacks. One of the most popular ways to enjoy it is in salads, such as this one; its earthy taste mixes very well with the tartness of dried sour cherries (another native Midwestern ingredient).

CORN

By midsummer, corn stalks shoot up so quickly that farmers claim to hear them creaking in the field. Soon, the first ears of sweet corn arrive at the market, manna for those who await the season with a growl in the pit of their stomachs.

Perhaps more than any other crop, corn is wedded to the New World, where it's been cultivated for more than seven thousand years. Both a grain and a vegetable, it can be eaten at every stage of development, from when the ear is a few inches long to when the kernels are old and dry. But it cannot grow without human help. Its seeds are so tightly clustered and wrapped that if an ear falls to the ground, it will rot instead of germinate.

The Aztecs and Mayans understood that corn was as dependent on them for life as they were on it, and their respect for it is reflected in the painstaking ways in which they prepared it. They scraped milk from young ears for puddings, roasted mature corn on the cob, and dried kernels like beans or ground them into flour. They popped corn, parched it, and soaked off the hulls with ash lye to make hominy.

Although tens of thousands of varieties once grew in the Americas, the United States has become an ocean of what is called field corn. Pigs, cows, and chickens consume several billion bushels of it a year. So do people, but only after it's been processed into cereal and chips, candy and soda sweetened with corn syrup, and gravies and pies thickened with cornstarch.

Unlike field corn, sweet corn is a delicate crop, and one that accounts for a tiny percent of the corn grown in the United States. Its kernels frequently fail to germinate, its ears are susceptible to disease, and its season passes in the wink of an eye. Corn lovers, sated for another year, will begin counting the days until next July. Without these long months of anticipation, would corn still taste as sweet?

GRILLED CORN DISKS Enjoy peak-of-season summer corn in a new way—as an hors d'oeuvre for a casual party. Remove husks and silk from corn and cut ears into rounds about 1 inch thick. Brush with olive oil, and season with salt and pepper. Cook on a medium-hot grill (it's ready when you can hold your hand 5 inches above grates for just 4 to 5 seconds), cut side down, about 2 minutes per side.

CREAMED CORN

9 ears of corn, husked

4 tablespoons unsalted butter

1 garlic clove, minced

1 teaspoon finely chopped fresh thyme

Coarse salt

1 Grate 6 ears of corn on the large holes of a box grater into a bowl. Carefully slice off kernels from remaining 3 cobs using a sharp knife; transfer to bowl. Working over the bowl, scrape the cobs with the back of the blade to extract the creamy liquid.

2 Melt 1 tablespoon butter in a medium saucepan over medium heat. Cook garlic until fragrant, stirring, about 30 seconds. Stir in corn along with liquid and the thyme; season with salt. Cover and reduce heat to medium-low; cook, stirring often, until corn is tender but still has a slight bite, 25 to 30 minutes. Stir in remaining 3 tablespoons butter until melted. Serve immediately.

SERVES 6

THE MIDWEST

BACKSTORY

The arrival of the sweet corn harvest in the Midwest quickens the pulse. In Iowa, the country's biggest corn producer, bowls of creamed corn show up on nearly every table. The liquid that oozes from the kernels when an ear of corn is scraped over a grater is called milk. Thickened with butter, it makes a rich, velvety, and (best of all) corny broth. That's two corn textures in one dish. Garlic and fresh thyme add to the flavor. Indianans share a love of corn and are particularly known for their version of succotash, made with green beans instead of lima beans. This old American Indian dish gets its name from the Narragansett word misickquatash, *meaning "fragments." In other words, succotash is a jumble. Eighteenth-century Americans added salt pork, but today the emphasis is on freshness, accentuated here by cooking the beans very briefly to retain some of their snap.*

INDIANA SUCCOTASH

6 ears of corn, husked

Coarse salt and freshly ground pepper

1 pound green beans, trimmed and cut into 1-inch pieces

3 tablespoons unsalted butter

1 bunch scallions, trimmed and cut into ¼-inch pieces

½ teaspoon celery seeds

¾ teaspoon paprika

1 Carefully slice kernels from corn using a sharp knife. Bring a large pot of water to a boil, and add salt. Blanch green beans until crisp-tender, about 3 minutes; remove using a mesh skimmer or slotted spoon and spread out on a baking sheet or plate to cool.

2 Melt butter in a medium skillet over medium heat. Add scallions and celery seeds and cook, stirring frequently, until scallions begin to soften, about 5 minutes. Add corn and season with salt; cook, stirring, until heated through, 3 to 5 minutes. Stir in green beans and paprika. Season with salt and pepper and cook until heated through, about 2 minutes. Serve warm.

SERVES 6

INDIANA SUCCOTASH

CREAMED CORN

HOOSIER PIE

Basic Pie Dough (page 412; 1 disk reserved for another use)
½ cup all-purpose flour, plus more for dusting
1 cup sugar
½ teaspoon salt
2 cups heavy cream
2 teaspoons pure vanilla extract
2 tablespoons unsalted butter, cut into small pieces
¼ teaspoon freshly grated nutmeg
Fresh raspberries, for serving
Raspberry Whipped Cream, for serving (optional; recipe follows)

1 Roll out dough on a lightly floured surface to an 11-inch round, about ⅛ inch thick. Fit into a 9-inch pie plate; crimp edges. Refrigerate until firm, at least 30 minutes or up to 1 day (covered with plastic wrap).

2 Preheat oven to 425°F. Prepare a large ice-water bath. Sift together sugar, flour, and salt into a nonreactive bowl. In a small saucepan, heat cream over medium-high until hot but not boiling. Whisk into sugar mixture; continue to whisk until sugar is dissolved. Stir in vanilla. Set bowl in the ice bath and let cool completely, stirring occasionally.

3 Pour filling into pie shell. Dot with butter and sprinkle with nutmeg. Bake 15 minutes. Reduce oven to 350°F. Cover edges of crust with a ring of foil. Bake until the tip of a sharp knife inserted in center of filling comes out clean, 50 to 55 minutes more. Let cool slightly on a wire rack. Serve warm with berries and raspberry whipped cream, if desired.

MAKES ONE 9-INCH PIE

RASPBERRY WHIPPED CREAM

2 teaspoons sugar
1 cup fresh raspberries
1½ cups cold heavy cream

1 In a small bowl, sprinkle sugar over raspberries. Let stand until juices are released, about 30 minutes. Mash gently with a fork until saucy but still chunky.

2 With an electric mixer on medium speed, whisk cream until medium-stiff peaks form. Fold the raspberry mixture into the whipped cream, leaving it slightly swirled.

MAKES 1 QUART

BACKSTORY
Variations on this empty-larder sweet, also known as sugar cream pie, are found throughout the Midwest, as well as in Pennsylvania Dutch country (and even up into Canada, with maple syrup replacing the sugar); this one, which uses no eggs, has become synonymous with the name for native Indianans. It's especially popular with the local Amish communities, who have been preparing it since the 1800s. In this recipe, raspberries add nice touches of color and tartness to the dessert (as a garnish and to flavor the whipped cream), but if you prefer to hew to tradition, you can certainly leave them out.

SHAKER LEMON TARTLETS

THE MIDWEST

BACKSTORY

The sweet-and-sour filling in these tarts is composed of only three ingredients—paper-thin slices of lemon (rind and all), sugar, and eggs—a fitting expression of the Shakers' loathing of wastefulness. Baked in a pie shell, the dessert is commonly known as Ohio lemon pie, so named for the Shakers who eventually made their home in the state.

2 large lemons, preferably organic, washed well
2 cups sugar
   Basic Pie Dough (page 412)
   All-purpose flour, for dusting
4 large eggs, lightly beaten

1 Cut lemons crosswise into paper-thin rounds using a mandoline or a very sharp knife; discard ends and seeds. Place lemon slices in a medium nonreactive bowl, and add sugar; toss to coat. Cover with plastic wrap and let stand at room temperature overnight.

2 Roll out dough on a lightly floured work surface to ⅛ inch thick. Cut dough into seven 6-inch rounds. Fit rounds into 4½-inch round tartlet pans with removable bottoms. Trim edges flush with tops. Place pans on a rimmed baking sheet; freeze dough until firm, at least 30 minutes or up to 1 day (covered with plastic wrap).

3 Preheat oven to 450°F, with rack in lower third. Add eggs to lemon mixture and stir to combine. Pass through a fine sieve into a medium bowl. Dividing evenly, pour filling into tart shells, then arrange lemon slices on top.

4 Place tart pans on a rimmed baking sheet and bake 15 minutes. Reduce heat to 350°F; bake until filling is set and beginning to brown on top, about 15 minutes more. Let cool on sheet on a wire rack 10 minutes, then transfer to a rack and let cool completely.

MAKES SEVEN 4½-INCH TARTLETS

PERSIMMON PUDDING

4½ tablespoons unsalted butter, softened, plus more for pudding mold

¼ cup (2 fluid ounces) brandy

¼ cup golden raisins

¼ cup dried currants

3 to 4 very ripe persimmons

1 cup half-and-half

2 cups all-purpose flour

2¼ teaspoons ground cinnamon

¾ teaspoon freshly grated nutmeg

¼ teaspoon salt

1½ cups sugar

3 large eggs

1½ teaspoons pure vanilla extract

1 tablespoon fresh lemon juice

1½ teaspoons baking soda

1½ tablespoons hot water

1 cup pecans (4 ounces), toasted (page 408) and coarsely chopped

Fresh bay leaves, for garnish (optional)

Sugared pecans, for garnish (optional; see note)

1 Brush a 2-quart pudding mold with butter. In a small saucepan over low heat, bring brandy, raisins, and currants to a simmer. Remove pan from heat; let stand 15 minutes. Drain in a sieve, discarding liquid.

2 Meanwhile, slice tops off persimmons. Scoop out flesh, and pass through a fine sieve into a bowl, discarding seeds and skins. (You should have about 1½ cups purée.) Whisk in half-and-half until combined.

3 Into a medium bowl, sift together flour, spices, and salt. With an electric mixer on medium speed, cream butter and sugar until light and fluffy. Beat in eggs, vanilla, and lemon juice. Add persimmon mixture in two batches, scraping down sides of bowl after each. Dissolve baking soda in the hot water; beat into persimmon mixture. Add flour mixture and beat just until combined. Stir in chopped pecans and the reserved raisins and currants by hand.

4 Pour batter into prepared mold. Cut a round of parchment 4 inches larger in diameter than mold. Place on mold, and secure just under the rim with kitchen twine or a heavy-duty rubber band. Cover with foil, crimping edge to seal.

5 Place a wire rack or folded kitchen towel in the bottom of a pot large enough to hold the mold, with about 2 inches clearance on all sides. Fill with enough water to reach halfway up sides of mold and then remove mold. Cover pot and bring water to a boil; reduce heat to a gentle simmer. Place mold in pot; cover and steam until a cake tester inserted in middle of pudding comes out clean, about 2 hours 20 minutes, checking frequently to keep water at a low, steady simmer and adding boiling water as needed to maintain water level.

6 Carefully remove the mold from the pot; discard foil and parchment. Let cool 15 minutes; unmold onto a platter. Garnish with bay leaves and sugared pecans, if desired.

SERVES 8 TO 10

Note To make sugared pecans, whisk ¼ cup sugar into a beaten egg white; stir in 2 cups pecans. Spread evenly on a baking sheet; bake at 250°F, tossing occasionally, until golden brown, about 30 minutes. Let cool; store in an airtight container up to 2 weeks.

THE MIDWEST

BACKSTORY

It might have a British pedigree, but persimmon pudding has been adopted by Indiana and surrounding states, where persimmons are grown in abundance, as one of their own. Vivid orange persimmons reach their peak in autumn as the leaves begin to fall, their late harvest a harbinger of holiday festivities. Indeed, in some parts of the Midwest, no Thanksgiving feast or Christmas dinner is complete without the steamed pudding served as the last course. This is not an American-style creamy pudding, but a super-moist cake studded with dried fruit and toasted nuts. Fresh bay leaves and sugared pecans are optional garnishes.

CHERRIES

If April and May are the months when cherry orchards explode in white tufts of fragrant blossoms, June is when the ruddy-barked, low-crotched trees are swollen with pendants of bright, shining cherries. There are basically two types: Sweet cherries are the relatives of *Prunus avium*, "bird's cherry," a reminder that one of the chief woes of the cherry grower is to harvest his fruit before birds do it for him. The sour cherry, *Prunus cerasus*, is considered by almost everyone to be best for baking. But some people prefer their acidic bite even for eating fresh. Because the bulk of the U.S. sour-cherry crop is, upon harvest, immediately canned, frozen, or made into that familiar red gel known as cherry pie filling, fresh sour cherries are difficult to find outside of prime sour-cherry country, which is centered around Traverse City, Michigan, although farmers' markets in other regions offer them for a few fleeting weeks in late June and early July. Sweet cherries prefer life in the Pacific Northwest, where it is warmer and drier; in fact, in as early as 1847, seven hundred cherry seedlings, the ancestors of today's best-selling Bing cherry, traveled west to Oregon in an ox cart.

Whatever the variety, cherry orchards are almost always planted well above the Mason–Dixon line in pleasing, ruler-straight rows, often spanning the slope of some gentle, postcard-quality mountain. These trees are also fond of rich volcanic soil and fine lake breezes. In fact, cherries seem to thrive only in physically wondrous settings.

It would be enough just to look at the fruit, as certain seventeenth-century Dutch still-life painters were keenly aware. It might be even enough just to ponder them, as cherry-struck poets from Shakespeare to D. H. Lawrence have insinuated. But ultimately cherries are too delicious to be strictly ornamental or metaphoric. They're for eating—in pies and tarts, soups and jams, ades and ices—or, better yet, in a cherry orchard straight from a laden tree.

SWEET CHERRIES WITH ROBIOLA CHEESE The delicate texture of Robiola, a mild and creamy Italian cheese, is a great partner for sweet cherries. You could also use ricotta or a soft goat cheese. Place cheese on a serving platter. Top with 8 ounces (1½ cups) fresh sweet cherries, 3 tablespoons sliced almonds (toasted), and 1 teaspoon fresh thyme. Drizzle with extra-virgin olive oil. Serve with a baguette, ripped into pieces. **SERVES 4**

CHERRY PIE

Traverse City, Michigan—home of the annual cherry festival every July—advertises itself as the Cherry Capital of the World. This prideful moniker is by no means undeserved: America is the leading producer of sour cherries, and Michigan produces close to 75 percent of the country's tart cherries. So it should come as no surprise that cherry pie has been described as the "true taste of Michigan." There, cherry pie is taken so seriously that restaurants don't hesitate to brag about serving the second- or third-best one in the country. Good thing most of us don't face such stiff competition, although this double-crust version could very well make you a winner in your hometown.

All-purpose flour, for dusting

Basic Pie Dough (page 412)

6 cups fresh or frozen (thawed) sour cherries

¼ cup cornstarch

1 cup sugar, or to taste

1 teaspoon pure vanilla extract

½ teaspoon pure almond extract

2 tablespoons unsalted butter, cut into small pieces

1 large egg, lightly beaten

1 tablespoon heavy cream

1 Preheat oven to 375°F. Place a large sheet of foil on bottom oven rack to catch any juices. On a lightly floured work surface, roll out one disk of dough to ⅛ inch thick. Fit into a 9-inch pie plate, and trim edges to a 1-inch overhang. Roll out remaining disk of dough into a 12-inch round about ⅛ inch thick. With a 1-inch cookie cutter (or bottom of a 1-inch pastry tip), cut out four or five holes from center of dough round.

2 If using fresh cherries, remove pits. In a large bowl, toss together cherries, cornstarch, sugar, and both extracts. Transfer mixture to prepared pie plate, spreading evenly. Dot with butter. Place remaining dough round on top, tuck overhang under edge of bottom dough, and crimp to seal. Refrigerate 30 minutes.

3 Whisk together egg and cream, then brush dough with egg wash. Bake on a parchment-lined baking sheet until crust is golden brown and juices are bubbling in center, about 1 hour if using fresh cherries, 1 hour and 35 minutes if using frozen. (Tent with foil if top crust is browning too quickly.) Transfer to a wire rack and let cool completely before serving.

MAKES ONE DOUBLE-CRUST 9-INCH PIE

CARAMEL CORN

12 cups popped popcorn (from ½ cup kernels)

1½ cups Beer Nuts or shelled salted peanuts

½ cup plus 2 tablespoons (1¼ sticks) unsalted butter

1¼ cups packed light-brown sugar

⅓ cup light corn syrup

1½ teaspoons coarse salt

¼ teaspoon baking soda

1 Preheat oven to 250°F. Place popcorn and nuts in a large heatproof bowl. Melt butter in a large heavy saucepan over medium heat. Stir in brown sugar, corn syrup, and ½ teaspoon salt; cook, stirring occasionally, until sugar dissolves. Raise heat to high; bring to a boil without stirring. Cook until a candy thermometer registers 248°F, 2 to 4 minutes. Remove from heat; stir in baking soda.

2 Pour caramel over popcorn mixture and stir to coat. Transfer to a rimmed baking sheet and spread in an even layer. Bake 45 minutes, stirring twice. Remove from oven and immediately sprinkle with remaining teaspoon salt. Let cool, then break into clusters. (Caramel corn can be stored at room temperature in an airtight container up to 1 week.)

MAKES 12 CUPS

THE MIDWEST

BACKSTORY

Popcorn vendors Frederick William Rueckheim and his brother Louis pulled out the stops for the 1893 World's Columbian Exposition in Chicago. They unveiled their snack-food experiment: popcorn and peanuts coated in molasses. An instant hit, it quickly evolved into Cracker Jack. Over time, the molasses was replaced with corn syrup and/or brown sugar. Our riff on the original recipe ups the salty-sweet ante with the addition of Beer Nuts, another curious invention of the American Midwest.

MALTED MILK BALL ICE CREAM

1 recipe Vanilla Ice Cream (page 75, modified as instructed below)

1¼ cups malted milk powder

4 ounces milk chocolate, melted and cooled slightly

1 cup chopped malted milk balls

1 Follow basic recipe for vanilla ice cream, omitting vanilla. Stir malted milk powder and melted chocolate into mixture at end of step 2.

2 Freeze mixture as directed in step 3, folding malted milk balls into ice cream after churning. If not serving immediately, transfer to an airtight container and freeze up to 3 months. Let ice cream stand at room temperature 15 to 20 minutes before serving.

MAKES 1½ QUARTS

THE MIDWEST

BACKSTORY

It's a simple matter to make ice cream at home: start with a basic vanilla recipe, such as the one on page 75, then add desired flavorings. Here, two Midwest originals—malted milk powder, a Wisconsin invention based on an English formula, and caramel corn (see page 275)—put regional stamps on an all-American favorite.

CARAMEL CORN ICE CREAM

¾ cup sugar

¼ cup water

½ cup heavy cream

½ teaspoon pure vanilla extract

½ teaspoon salt

1½ tablespoons unsalted butter, cut into small pieces

1 recipe Vanilla Ice Cream (page 75, modified as instructed below)

6 ears corn, kernels shaved off, cobs cut into pieces

½ cup sugar-coated peanuts

1 cup Caramel Corn (page 275; omit peanuts)

Sugar cones, for serving

1 Bring sugar and the water to a boil in a medium saucepan over medium-high heat, stirring constantly. When sugar has dissolved, raise heat to high. Cook, without stirring, until mixture is medium amber, 7 to 8 minutes. Remove from heat. Carefully stir in cream (mixture will spatter), then the vanilla and salt. Let cool 5 minutes. Whisk in butter until combined. Let cool completely. (Sauce can be refrigerated, covered, up to 5 days. Bring to room temperature before serving.)

2 Follow basic recipe for vanilla ice cream, adding kernels and cob pieces along with vanilla to cream mixture in step 1; once mixture is removed from heat, cover, and let steep 30 minutes. Strain and discard solids before proceeding with step 2.

3 Freeze mixture as directed in step 3, folding cooled caramel sauce, sugar-coated peanuts, and caramel corn into ice cream after churning. If not serving immediately, transfer to an airtight container and freeze up to 3 months. Let ice cream stand at room temperature 15 to 20 minutes before serving.

MAKES 1½ QUARTS

MALTED MILK BALL ICE CREAM

CARAMEL CORN ICE CREAM

BUCKEYE CANDIES

1½ cups creamy peanut butter (not the natural variety)

1 cup (2 sticks) unsalted butter, softened

6 cups (1½ pounds) confectioners' sugar

12 ounces semisweet chocolate, finely chopped (1½ cups)

½ teaspoon pure vanilla extract

1 Line a baking sheet with waxed paper or parchment. In a medium bowl, beat peanut butter and butter with a wooden spoon until thoroughly combined, about 2 minutes. Gradually mix in confectioners' sugar in batches, kneading with your hands to form a smooth dough, about 10 minutes.

2 Using the palms of your hands, roll mixture into 1-inch balls and place on prepared baking sheet. Cover and chill in refrigerator, about 2 hours or up to overnight.

3 Melt chocolate in a heatproof bowl set over (not in) a pan of simmering water, stirring until smooth; stir in vanilla. Working with one at a time, insert a toothpick into chilled peanut-butter balls and dip into melted chocolate, leaving the top bare. Return to lined baking sheet until set, about 15 minutes. Smooth tops to cover holes from toothpicks. (Buckeyes can be refrigerated in a single layer in an airtight container, up to 1 week.)

MAKES 68

BACKSTORY

It's hard to resist the salty-nutty-sweet combination of peanut butter and chocolate, especially in the form of bite-size candies. This classic confection is one of the simplest recipes in the world to follow. The peanut butter mixture is quickly mixed by hand, rolled into balls, then chilled and partially dipped in melted milk chocolate, with just enough filling left exposed that the candy resembles the nut of the mighty buckeye, the state tree of Ohio.

SOUTHWEST

The remote reaches of the Southwest, from the starkly beautiful mountains of northern New Mexico to the brush country of South Texas, are the cradle of a unique cuisine that has thrived in America for five centuries. It is, at its heart, rustic food based on simple ingredients. The deep, earthy savor of pinto beans (frijoles) and tortillas cannot be discounted, but perhaps the most emblematic flavor of the Southwest is the chile; by the end of the sixteenth century, red and green varieties had been planted by Spanish colonists and Mexican Indians.

When you taste the chiles in a bowl of just-made salsa, you are experiencing something ancient and alluring in their fresh, spicy complexity. And if you have ever been to New Mexico (where both the chile and the pinto bean are honored as state vegetables) in August, when farmers bring their roasters to market along with their harvest of fresh green and red chiles, then you can attest to the fact that there is nothing like the aroma that fills the air. You can buy the freshly roasted chiles by the pound—or by the bushel. Aficionados slip the charred skins off their bounty while it's still warm, then freeze the chiles to use all winter long in posole and other stews.

One of the oldest threads running through the cooking of the Southwest is Tex-Mex, which has become wildly popular all over the United States in recent decades. Loosely defined as a blend of Texan and Mexican traditions, it stretches from eighteenth-century Spanish missions to the nineteenth-century Republic of Texas; from tiny border towns to the largest city in the state, Houston, where Tex-Mex food is woven into the fabric of everyday life. This is big-flavored, stick-to-your-ribs fare: tamale pie, chicken enchiladas, Texas red chili (the concept of stewing meat and chiles together is as old as the Aztecs), and fajitas, the dish that turned humble skirt steak into a most sought-after cut of beef. This food cries out for a classic margarita (which was probably created in Mexican bars that catered to American tourists) or an agua fresca made with juicy prickly pear, which tastes like watermelon, strawberry, and kiwifruit all rolled into one.

One border-state favorite that deserves wider recognition is the *biscochito*, a crisp, lard-based cookie flavored with Mexican cinnamon and anise seed. Usually made to celebrate weddings, baptisms, and other happy occasions, biscochitos also signal the beginning of the Christmas season. Texas sheet cake is another regional classic that merits a place on more American tables. This ever-popular dessert—a one-bowl chocolate cake covered with warm chocolate icing and sprinkled with chopped pecans—may just become your signature birthday cake.

There are vast parts of Texas that are historically closer to the South than they are to Mexico, which explains, in large part, a devotion to pecans, barbecue (although beef, rather than pork, is the meat of choice), and dishes like Texas caviar, which features black-eyed peas, a legume native to Africa and brought over with slaves.

Cowboy cooking is yet another Southwestern subgenre. The men (and some women) who drove Longhorn cattle across Texas to market in the decades after the Civil War were a resilient, resourceful bunch. One of them, a man named Charles Goodnight, jury-rigged a cook box to a wagon, and this "chuckwagon" dispensed sourdough biscuits, black coffee, long-simmered pinto beans, chicken-fried steak, and barbecued beef brisket, which by virtue of its layer of fat literally bastes itself. Barbecued brisket remains popular with modern-day cowboys, who will ask for a side of onion rings, often made with sweet onions like Texas 1015s. This kind of food speaks to the spirit of the Wild West, and it lives on in every American who has ever dreamed of a home on the range.

RECIPES

TEQUILA BLOODY MARY

CLASSIC MARGARITAS

MICHELADA

PRICKLY PEAR AGUAS FRESCAS

DRINKS

TEQUILA BLOODY MARY

How to make a Southwestern-style Bloody Mary? Swap out the vodka for tequila and the celery stalks for a sprig of cilantro. It's a surefire eye-opener at brunch.

Stir together 3 cups **tomato juice**, 3 tablespoons prepared **horseradish** (or more to taste), ½ cup (4 fluid ounces) best-quality **tequila**, 2 teaspoons **Worcestershire sauce**, juice of 1 **lime**, 1 teaspoon freshly ground **pepper**, and a dash of **hot sauce** in a pitcher. Pour into ice-filled glasses; garnish with **cilantro leaves**. Serve immediately. **MAKES 6**

CLASSIC MARGARITAS

Made with fresh, not bottled, lime juice and a premium tequila, this zesty drink is instant refreshment in a (salt-rimmed) glass. Some believe margaritas should be served only over ice, but frozen versions have been around since the invention of the blender in the 1930s (and lest you doubt its mark on the history of the cocktail, the world's first frozen-margarita machine, invented in 1971 by a Dallas restaurateur, is now part of the Smithsonian museum). It's easy to alter the basic formula today: Grand Marnier is often substituted for Triple Sec, and other fruits, such as watermelon, cactus pear, mango, strawberry, or pomegranate, are exchanged for the lime.

Pour **coarse salt** onto a saucer. Rub rims of six glasses with a **lime wedge**; dip each rim in salt. Fill glasses with **ice**. In a large pitcher, combine ¾ cup fresh **lime juice** (from 6 to 8 limes), ¾ cup (6 fluid ounces) best-quality **tequila** (preferably silver), and a ¼ cup plus 2 tablespoons (3 fluid ounces) **Triple Sec** or other citrus-flavored liqueur. Strain into glasses and serve. **MAKES 6**

MICHELADA

Down Mexico way, the cocktails can get quirky. None more so than the Michelada, a sort of cross between a margarita and a Bloody Mary made with beer instead of tequila or vodka. It's a longtime favorite in Mexico, where "prepared beers" are popular. In the United States, it's the next big leap for those just getting used to putting a lime wedge in their cerveza. The drink's name may be a slightly twisted version of mi chela helada, "my cold one" in Mexico City slang. Actually, it's cold and hot at the same time, and shockingly refreshing. Maggi seasoning is a flavor-enhancing sauce available at supermarkets and Latin grocers or from online sources. Soy sauce may be used in its place.

Pour **coarse salt** onto a saucer. Rub a **lime wedge** around the rim of a glass; dip in salt to coat. Add ¼ cup fresh **lime juice** (from 2 to 3 limes), 2 dashes **Worcestershire sauce**, ¼ teaspoon **maggi seasoning**, and ¼ teaspoon **hot sauce**, such as Tabasco; stir. Fill with **ice**, and top with **Mexican lager**, such as Corona, Pacífico, or Tecate; stir. Garnish with a lime wedge. **MAKES 1**

PRICKLY PEAR AGUAS FRESCAS

The fruit of the nopal cactus, which grows throughout the deserts of the Southwest, are called prickly pears and have been a staple of the Native American diet for centuries. They are often sliced and tossed into salads, added to stews, and juiced and used in cocktails and other refreshments. Here, red prickly pears (the fruit is also yellow or white) make a vibrant base for the Mexican specialty called agua fresca ("fresh water"), combining fresh fruit juice with water, sugar, lime juice, and ground canela (Mexican cinnamon). Look for prickly pears and canela at Mexican food markets and from online retailers.

Peel 4 **prickly pears**: Slice off both ends of each pear and discard. Make a slit down length of pear, cutting only through the skin, then use your fingers to peel off skin (wear protective gloves). Cut pears into pieces. Purée in a blender, then strain through a fine sieve into a bowl, pressing on solids with a flexible spatula to extract as much liquid as possible. Return pear liquid to blender and add ¼ cup **sugar**, juice of 2 **limes**, ¼ teaspoon ground **canela** or regular cinnamon, and 2 cups **ice**; purée until smooth, about 1 minute. Pour into glasses; serve, garnished with **lime slices**. Serve immediately. **MAKES 6**

CHILES

The rustic cuisines of New Mexico, Arizona, and Texas are transformed from simple to sublime by red and green chiles. Brought from Mexico by Spanish settlers in the sixteenth century, the peppers have flourished ever since in the harsh desert climate.

The promise of spice wealth was, of course, what beckoned the Europeans who first crossed the Atlantic. In search of India and its black peppercorns, Christopher Columbus instead stumbled across the Americas—and chile peppers. Noting that the pungent fruits were "as long as cinnamon" and "full of small grains as biting as pepper," he brought loads of them back to Spain and is credited with their rapid spread across Europe and into Africa and Asia. It is the chile pepper's fiery heat that has made it so timeless, so popular, and so useful.

The terms *chile*, *chile pepper*, and *hot pepper* are all synonymous, and refer to fruits of plants in the same genus, *Capsicum*. Culinarily speaking, sweet, mild peppers—bell peppers and pimientos, for instance—are usually called "peppers," while hot ones such as habanero or jalapeño are usually referred to as "chiles." The latter's heat comes from a substance called capsaicin, and the amount of capsaicin a chile contains is measured in Scoville heat units. A bell pepper, for example, has a Scoville rating of almost zero, while a Scotch Bonnet can clock in at a blistering 300,000. But even within one variety, a chile's heat can swing from mild to medium or from hot to very hot, as determined by the weather, soil, and other growing conditions.

Depending on the variety of chile used, and whether it is fresh or dried, its heat will be balanced by an alluring back note of flavor—sweetness, for instance, or smokiness. Fresh green jalapeños give the hominy stew called posole an uncomplicated spiciness, but when paired with dried ancho and guajillo chiles in a bowl of "Texas red," the end result is more mellow and fruity. You will discover that both types of heat are equally habit-forming.

PICKLED CUCUMBERS AND JALAPEÑOS In a bowl, toss 2 pounds Kirby cucumbers and 4 red jalapeño chiles, both sliced diagonally ¼ inch thick; 3 small onions, cut into ½-inch wedges; and 3 tablespoons coarse salt. Cover; refrigerate 2 hours. In a saucepan over medium heat, cook 2 cups cider vinegar, 1¾ cups packed light-brown sugar, 1 tablespoon mustard seeds, and ¾ teaspoon each celery seeds and turmeric, stirring to dissolve sugar. Rinse and drain cucumber mixture, then divide among jars (or place in a large container) and add vinegar mixture. Let cool completely. Refrigerate, covered, up to 3 weeks. **MAKES 2 QUARTS**

SALSA VERDE

14 tomatillos (about 14 ounces), husks removed, rinsed

½ large white onion, coarsely chopped

3 garlic cloves

3 chiles de árbol or other dried red chiles

Coarse salt

1 Place tomatillos in a large saucepan, and cover with water by 1 inch. Bring to a boil, and reduce heat to simmer; cook until tomatillos have softened but not burst, about 5 minutes. Reserve 1 cup cooking liquid. Pass tomatillos through a fine sieve into a bowl, pressing to release as much liquid as possible.

2 In a blender or food processor, purée tomatillos, onion, garlic, chiles, 2 teaspoons salt, and ½ cup reserved cooking liquid until smooth. For a thinner consistency, add more cooking liquid as desired. Season with salt. (Salsa can be refrigerated up to 2 weeks in an airtight container.)

MAKES 4 CUPS

ROASTED TOMATO SALSA

9 plum tomatoes, cut into ½-inch pieces

1 large white onion, quartered

3 jalapeño chiles

2 garlic cloves (unpeeled)

Coarse salt

1 Heat broiler. Combine tomatoes, onion, jalapeños, and garlic on a rimmed baking sheet, and spread in a single layer. Broil until tomatoes and jalapeños are charred, about 7 minutes. Let stand until cool enough to handle.

2 Peel the roasted garlic. Transfer to a blender along with the charred tomatoes, onion, jalapeños, and 1 tablespoon salt. Purée until smooth. For a thinner consistency, add water as needed. Season with more salt. (Salsa can be refrigerated up to 2 weeks in an airtight container.)

MAKES 4 CUPS

PICO DE GALLO

4 ripe tomatoes, finely chopped

½ large white onion, finely chopped

2 serrano or jalapeño chiles, minced

¾ cup finely chopped cilantro

1 cup water

Coarse salt

In a bowl, stir together tomatoes, onion, chiles, cilantro, and the water; season with salt. (Salsa can be refrigerated up to 3 days in an airtight container.)

MAKES 4 CUPS

THE SOUTHWEST

BACKSTORY

Within minutes of being seated at a Mexican restaurant in the Southwest, you are likely to be presented with a basket of still-warm tortilla chips and a bowl—or two or three—of salsa, either red or green. Pico de gallo, a chopped fresh tomato salsa, is the all-purpose classic; tomatoes are roasted for extra flavor and a hint of smokiness in another familiar red salsa; and salsa verde (or "green sauce") is made from tomatillos—those tart green relatives to the tomato—puréed to an almost-smooth consistency. You needn't choose just one; each member of the trio plays off another's qualities beautifully. For spicier salsas, increase the amount of chiles as desired.

SALSA VERDE

PICO DE GALLO

ROASTED TOMATO SALSA

TEQUILA-GRILLED SHRIMP

CHEESE-STUFFED JALAPEÑOS

CHEESE-STUFFED JALAPEÑOS

4 ounces cream cheese, softened

½ cup grated sharp cheddar

Coarse salt and freshly ground pepper

6 large jalapeño chiles, halved lengthwise, ribs and seeds removed

Preheat oven to 450°F. In a small bowl, mix cream cheese and cheddar; season with salt and pepper. With a small spoon, fill each jalapeño half with about 1 tablespoon cheese mixture. Place chiles on a parchment-lined baking sheet and cook until cheese is browned and bubbling, rotating sheet halfway through, about 10 minutes. Let cool slightly before serving.

SERVES 4 TO 6

THE SOUTHWEST

BACKSTORY

No happy hour in the Lone Star State would be complete without an assortment of spicy finger foods to wash down with a pitcher of margaritas and some ice-cold beer. Here, jalapeños, ubiquitous in kitchens throughout the Southwest, lend their fiery heat to two refreshingly simple starters. In this streamlined version of jalapeño "poppers," the chiles are simply halved, seeded, and stuffed with a two-cheese filling before baking until melted and golden—no roasting, breading, or deep-frying required. Gulf shrimp, Texas's claim to seafood fame, is the real star of the other dish, with diced jalapeños serving as a mere (but requisite) garnish; before a brief session on the grill, the shrimp are marinated in a mixture of citrus juice and tequila, also the makings of a welcome chaser.

TEQUILA-GRILLED SHRIMP

1 pound large shrimp, peeled and deveined

¼ cup (2 fluid ounces) tequila

¼ cup fresh lime juice (from 2 to 3 limes), plus wedges for serving

¼ cup fresh orange juice

Coarse salt and freshly ground pepper

Vegetable oil, for grill

1 jalapeño chile, halved lengthwise, ribs and seeds removed, minced

1 In a medium nonreactive bowl, stir together shrimp, tequila, and both juices; season with salt and pepper. Cover with plastic wrap and refrigerate 20 minutes.

2 Heat grill to medium-high. (If you are using a charcoal grill, coals are ready when you can hold your hand 5 inches above grates for just 3 to 4 seconds.) Lightly oil hot grates. Remove shrimp from marinade, letting excess drip off; discard marinade. Grill shrimp until opaque throughout, 4 to 6 minutes, flipping once. Transfer to a platter and sprinkle with jalapeño. Serve shrimp with lime wedges.

SERVES 4

BLACK-EYED PEAS

Food historians believe that the black-eyed pea, which is really a bean, may have come from China, India, or Africa. From one of those starting points, the black-eyed pea ended up in enough corners of the globe to be considered the Marco Polo of legumes; it is now found in the cuisines of a large percentage of the world's population.

In the last quarter of the seventeenth century, black-eyed peas made their way from Africa to the New World on slave-trading ships, arriving in the southern states by way of the Caribbean. Because they need hot weather and lots of sun to flourish, their growing area is limited to a swath running from the coast of the Carolinas all the way to Texas, where they are a feature of hot, dusty farm country. In many Texas communities, a high-school football game followed by dinner at a barbecue restaurant is what makes a Friday night. One such town is Athens, about sixty miles east of Dallas, which bills itself the black-eyed pea capital of the world. The town even throws a festival each October to celebrate the harvest.

Most of us find the black-eyeds at the supermarket, dried and sealed in a plastic bag. They look like all the other dried beans on the shelf—or perhaps just a little cuter, with their distinctive oval spots on curved beige bodies. But it's worth seeking out fresh black-eyeds if you can—they are as much a summer treat as that first bite of just-picked corn on the cob. Fresh black-eyeds have a more toothsome texture than dried ones, and their flavor is slightly nutty, with a silky, buttery quality. Although their season is brief, if you shell them (as you would peas) and seal them in an airtight container, the beans keep beautifully in the freezer for about six months. Then they can be used in all sorts of relishes, salads, and side dishes.

Whether you are using fresh or dried black-eyed peas, they taste wonderful simply cooked with a ham hock or other assertive flavors such as hot chiles, green bell peppers, spicy sausage, or fresh thyme, oregano, or rosemary. But some folks believe the best way to eat them is in the local specialty known as Texas caviar; it is vibrant, satisfying, and a little surprising—a lot like the Lone Star State itself.

TEXAS CAVIAR Texas caviar is often served as a dip for tortilla chips, but it also makes a quick side dish for pork or chicken (use a slotted spoon when serving). In a large bowl, toss together 2 rinsed and drained cans (15.5 ounces each) black-eyed peas, ½ cup finely diced red bell pepper, ½ cup finely diced celery, ¼ cup finely chopped red onion, 1 finely diced jalapeño (seeded, if desired, for less heat), 2 tablespoons chopped fresh flat-leaf parsley or cilantro, 2 tablespoons safflower oil, 1 tablespoon Worcestershire sauce, ½ teaspoon finely chopped fresh oregano, 2 teaspoons cider vinegar, ½ teaspoon sugar, and a dash of hot sauce. Season with coarse salt and ground pepper. Drizzle with a little more vinegar before serving. **SERVES 4**

SEVEN-LAYER DIP

    2   teaspoons fresh lime juice
    2   tablespoons water
    2   cups refried beans, preferably homemade (see below)
        Coarse salt and freshly ground pepper
    ½   cup sour cream
    ½   cup grated cheddar (2 ounces)
    1   can (4.5 ounces) chopped green chiles
    2   plum tomatoes, seeded and chopped
    1   ripe but firm avocado, halved, pitted, peeled, and
        cut into small dice
    1   cup shredded romaine lettuce
    2   scallions, trimmed and finely chopped
        Tortilla chips, for serving

In a medium bowl, stir lime juice and the water into refried beans; season with
salt and pepper. Transfer to a serving dish. Spread sour cream on top, then layer
evenly with cheese, chiles, tomatoes, avocado, lettuce, and scallions. Serve with
tortilla chips.

SERVES 4

THE SOUTHWEST

BACKSTORY

*In football country, on any
given weekend during the fall,
diehard fans get together to
root for their favorite teams.
Wherever they gather, there's
sure to be chips and dip. The
seven-layer dip is a venerable
crowd-pleaser of the Tex-Mex
variety that some believe
will bring good luck (because
of lucky number 7). Most
recipes call for canned refried
beans, which are a perfectly
acceptable shortcut; making
your own, however, takes
very little effort, and you'll
have extra for serving with
other Tex-Mex favorites.*

REFRIED BEANS

    2   tablespoons olive oil
    2   small onions, very finely chopped
    1   dried bay leaf
        Coarse salt and freshly ground pepper
    2   garlic cloves, minced
    1   teaspoon chili powder
    3   cans (15.5 ounces each) pinto beans, drained and rinsed
    ⅔   cup water, plus more if needed

1 In a medium saucepan, heat olive oil over medium-high. Add onions and bay
leaf; season with salt and pepper. Cook, stirring, until onion is translucent,
about 6 minutes. Add garlic and chili powder; cook, stirring, until garlic is
softened and mixture is fragrant, about 3 minutes.

2 Remove bay leaf and discard. Add two-thirds of the pinto beans and stir to
coat. Add the water, and mash mixture using a potato masher. Add remaining
pinto beans and stir to combine; add more water, if necessary, to thin. Season
with salt and pepper and keep warm until ready to use.

SERVES 6

lobster CORN DOGS

THE SOUTHWEST

BACKSTORY

The State Fair of Texas, with the largest attendance among all state fairs in the United States, has spawned some pretty large legends over the years. There's the annual showdown between Texas and Oklahoma college football teams at the Cotton Bowl in Fair Park. Big Tex, the 52-foot-tall mascot, greets visitors with a "Howdy, folks!" And, in 1942, brothers Neil and Carl Fletcher introduced a newfangled snack called the "corny dog." The Fletcher family has been selling hundreds of thousands at the fair every year since. Whether or not the brothers actually invented the deep-fried hot dog on a stick, they certainly created a much-touted local institution. The secret to achieving an even coating: Put the batter in a tall container, such as a Mason jar, for dipping each hot dog. True fans like to swirl the corn dogs in mustard before taking the first bite.

2⅔ cups yellow cornmeal

1⅓ cups all-purpose flour, plus more for rolling

3 tablespoons sugar

2 teaspoons baking powder

Coarse salt and freshly ground pepper

4 large eggs, lightly beaten

1½ cups milk

Vegetable or peanut oil, for frying (about 2 quarts)

12 hot dogs

Yellow mustard, for serving

1 Whisk together cornmeal, flour, sugar, baking powder, 1 teaspoon salt, and 1 teaspoon pepper. Stir in eggs and milk. (You will have about 5 cups batter.) Fill a large heavy pot, Dutch oven, or deep-fryer with enough oil to submerge hot dogs; heat until a deep-fry thermometer registers 360°F.

2 Meanwhile, pat hot dogs dry and insert a 10-inch bamboo skewer through each lengthwise; roll in flour to coat.

3 Dip a hot dog into batter, turning until completely coated; let any excess batter drip off and wipe away extra batter using your fingers so that hot dog is coated evenly. Holding it by the skewer, carefully add hot dog to hot oil. Immediately repeat with remaining hot dogs.

4 Cook corn dogs, turning with tongs to cook evenly, until deep golden brown, 5 to 7 minutes for each. Transfer to a paper towel–lined platter, turning to blot oil. Serve warm, with mustard.

MAKES 12

Tattered Cover
Book Store

Books Are
Humanity
in Print.
—Barbara Tuchman

Colfax Avenue 303-322-7727
Historic LoDo 303-436-1070
Highlands Ranch 303-470-7050
1-800-833-9327
www.tatteredcover.com

BO OK sense™
*Independent Bookstores for
Independent Minds*

SOUTHWESTERN CORN CHOWDER

5   slices bacon (5 ounces), cut into ½-inch pieces

1   onion, cut into ½-inch dice

1   large carrot, cut into ½-inch dice

2   celery stalks, cut into ½-inch dice

1   small fresh poblano chile, ribs and seeds removed, cut into ¼-inch dice

½   teaspoon ground cumin

    Pinch of cayenne

    Coarse salt and freshly ground pepper

1   cup dry white wine

1   pound Yukon Gold potatoes, peeled and cut into ½-inch pieces

5   cups chicken stock, preferably homemade (page 410)

3   cups fresh (about 6 ears) or frozen corn kernels (do not thaw)

1   cup heavy cream

¼   cup coarsely chopped fresh cilantro, plus more for garnish

    Hot sauce, such as Tabasco, for serving (optional)

1 Heat a large pot over medium. Add bacon, and cook, stirring occasionally, until crisp, about 5 minutes. Transfer with a slotted spatula or spoon to a paper towel–lined plate to drain.

2 Add onion to pot; cook, stirring occasionally, until just softened, about 4 minutes. Add carrot, celery, and poblano; cook until vegetables are just tender, about 5 minutes. Stir in cumin and cayenne, and season with salt and pepper. Raise heat to high; add wine. Cook, stirring frequently, until most liquid has evaporated, 2 to 3 minutes. Add potatoes and stock; bring to a boil. Reduce heat to medium-low; gently simmer until all vegetables are tender, about 20 minutes.

3 Stir in corn and cream; cook until corn is tender (do not let cream boil), about 5 minutes more. Stir in cilantro. Season with salt and pepper. Garnish with more cilantro and the bacon pieces; serve with hot sauce, if desired.

SERVES 4 TO 6

THE SOUTHWEST

BACKSTORY

Chowder may be thought of as a Yankee dish, but Southwesterners have made this spicy, chunky version all their own with local ingredients—namely, fresh corn, jalapeño chiles, and cilantro. Here, bacon adds smokiness, and poblanos and cayenne contribute fiery heat. It's hearty enough to win over meat-loving locals and far-flung visitors alike.

TEXAS CHILI

BACKSTORY

A "bowl of red" in the Southwest refers to this signature brick-colored, bean-free beef chili (this is cattle country, after all). Indeed, the simplest forms of the dish contain little more than beef and spices, although you'll find spruced-up versions at any of the countless cook-offs held throughout the region. And forget about ground beef; Texas chili is all about chunks of tender, melting chuck. You can serve the chili with a handful of tortilla chips or saltines, or a side of cornbread, but a bowl on its own, most agree, is all the sustenance you need.

8 dried chiles (about 3 ounces), such as a mix of ancho and guajillo

3 tablespoons neutral-tasting oil, such as safflower, plus more as needed

3 pounds trimmed beef chuck, cut into small pieces (½ inch or smaller)

   Coarse salt and freshly ground pepper

2 large onions, coarsely chopped (about 4 cups)

7 to 8 garlic cloves, minced (¼ cup plus 1 tablespoon)

2 fresh jalapeño or serrano chiles, minced (ribs and seeds removed for less heat, if desired)

2½ teaspoons ground cumin

1½ teaspoons dried oregano

1 can (28 ounces) whole peeled tomatoes, puréed with their juice (to yield 3½ cups)

2 to 3 teaspoons distilled white vinegar

   Avocado, for serving (optional)

   Cilantro leaves, for garnish

1 Toast dried chiles in a dry skillet over medium-high heat until fragrant and blistered, 2 to 3 minutes per side. Let cool, then remove stems and seeds; discard. Transfer chiles to a large liquid measuring cup or bowl, and add hot water to cover. Rest a small bowl on top to keep chiles submerged and let soak 30 minutes. Remove chiles and purée in a blender with ½ cup soaking liquid.

2 Heat a large, heavy-bottomed pot over high; add 2 tablespoons oil. Season beef with salt and pepper. Working in batches, cook beef until browned all over, about 10 minutes; use a slotted spoon to transfer to a plate. Add more oil as needed between batches.

3 Add remaining 1 tablespoon oil to the pot. Cook onions, garlic, and fresh chiles over medium-high heat, stirring occasionally, until onions are translucent, about 5 minutes. (If the pan gets too dark, add a little water, and scrape up browned bits with a wooden spoon to deglaze.) Add cumin and oregano, and cook, stirring constantly, until fragrant, 30 to 60 seconds.

4 Stir in puréed chiles and tomatoes, then add browned beef and accumulated juices. Season with salt and bring to a boil. Reduce heat and simmer gently, partially covered, until meat is very tender and juices are thick, 2½ to 3 hours. (Check pot every hour, adding a little water if mixture seems too dry.) Season chili with more salt and stir in vinegar to taste. Serve immediately, topped with avocado, if desired, and garnished with cilantro. (Chili can be refrigerated up to 3 days or frozen up to 3 months; let cool completely before transferring to airtight containers. Thaw frozen chili overnight in the refrigerator; reheat over medium, stirring occasionally.)

SERVES 6 TO 8

GREEN CHILE POSOLE

- 12 ounces dried hominy, rinsed
- 3 pounds country-style pork ribs, or 2 pounds cubed pork shoulder plus 1 pound baby back ribs or spareribs
- 8 sprigs flat-leaf parsley, tied in a bundle with kitchen twine
- 4 garlic cloves, thinly sliced
- 1½ teaspoons dried oregano, preferably Mexican
- 1 pound tomatillos, husks removed, rinsed
- 2¼ cups (10 ounces) pepitas (hulled green pumpkin seeds)
- 3 large jalapeño chiles, quartered
- 1 cup packed cilantro sprigs
- 1 white onion, coarsely chopped
- 2 tablespoons neutral-tasting oil, such as safflower
- Coarse salt
- Assorted garnishes, such as avocado, onion, cilantro, and lime wedges, for serving

1 In a large pot, bring hominy and 6 quarts water to a boil (do not add salt). Reduce heat to medium-low and simmer until hominy is tender (the pointed tip should easily be pinched off), about 2 hours. Transfer hominy to a bowl using a slotted spoon; let cool 5 minutes, then pinch off pointed tip from each kernel. Return hominy to pot and simmer 1½ to 2 hours more. Remove from heat. Use slotted spoon to transfer hominy to bowl; reserve cooking liquid.

2 Meanwhile, place pork in a large pot; cover with water by 2 inches (about 3 quarts). Add parsley and garlic and bring to a boil. Skim top layer of foam and fat using a ladle. Reduce heat to medium-low; stir in oregano. Simmer, partially covered, until meat is falling off the bone, about 3 hours. Remove pork; reserve broth (you should have 8 cups; add some reserved hominy cooking liquid, if needed). Trim excess fat and remove meat from bones. Shred meat and cover to keep warm.

3 While pork is cooking, bring a small pot of water to a boil. Add tomatillos; simmer until tender, about 10 minutes. Transfer tomatillos to a bowl using slotted spoon.

4 Heat a large skillet over medium. Toast pepitas, shaking and stirring often, until golden and popping, 10 to 12 minutes. Add to tomatillos along with jalapeños, cilantro, onion, and 1½ cups reserved hominy cooking liquid. Let cool 5 minutes. Working in batches, purée mixture in a blender until smooth, adding up to ½ cup more cooking liquid if needed.

5 Heat oil in a large skillet over medium-high until surface shimmers. Add tomatillo purée and ½ teaspoon salt, stirring constantly. Reduce heat to medium; simmer gently, stirring occasionally, until thick and color deepens, about 15 minutes.

6 Stir 1 tablespoon salt and the tomatillo mixture into reserved pork broth. Bring to a boil; add pork. Reduce heat, and simmer gently until heated through, about 10 minutes. Stir in hominy, and season with salt and pepper. Simmer until heated through, about 5 minutes. Serve immediately, with garnishes.

SERVES 12

THE SOUTHWEST

BACKSTORY

Ring in the New Year in New Mexico, and you are likely to be served a steaming bowl of posole for good luck. This hearty stew—also a year-round option throughout the state—gets its name from posole, or hominy, prepared by soaking hard corn kernels in lime water until swollen, and the hull and germ removed and then the kernels allowed to dry (an ancient process called nixtamilization). Dried hominy can be found at Mexican grocers and many supermarkets; canned hominy (you'll need four 15.5-ounce cans) may be substituted, in which case you can skip the first step and reserve tomatillo cooking liquid to use in place of hominy cooking liquid in step 4. Variations on the stew are many; pork, chicken, and even meatless versions are common, and posole can be red or green depending on the chiles used. The toppings—avocado, onion, cilantro, and lime wedges—are integral to the dish.

CHICKEN-FRIED STEAK

THE SOUTHWEST

BACKSTORY

The lore surrounding chicken-fried steak is that it came about as a way to tenderize tough cuts of meat by pounding it before frying and then smothering it with cream gravy made with the pan drippings. The dish is, not coincidentally, similar to Wiener schnitzel, a favorite among the large population of Germanic settlers in central Texas, where beef was much more readily available than pork. No matter how it was born, chicken-fried steak has become a Texas institution, and it's easy to see why: It's down-home cooking that folks everywhere can surely appreciate. Mashed potatoes are a must on the side; blanched green beans make a crisp, wholesome accompaniment.

2 large eggs

1 cup plus 1 teaspoon all-purpose flour

½ teaspoon paprika

Coarse salt and freshly ground pepper

4 "minute" steaks (each about 2 ounces and ¼ inch thick)

¼ cup neutral-tasting oil, such as safflower

1½ cups milk

1 Preheat oven to 250°F. Lightly beat eggs in a wide, shallow bowl. In another bowl, combine 1 cup flour with the paprika. Season eggs and flour mixture with salt and pepper.

2 Pat dry steaks with paper towels and season both sides with salt and pepper. Dredge each steak in flour mixture, then dip in egg; allow excess to drip off, then dredge in flour again.

3 In a large cast-iron skillet, heat oil over medium-high. Add steaks, working in batches if necessary, and cook until crust is golden, 3 to 4 minutes per side. Transfer to a baking sheet and place in oven to keep warm.

4 Pour off all but 1 tablespoon oil from skillet. Add remaining teaspoon flour; cook, whisking, until golden, about 30 seconds. Whisking constantly, gradually add milk; raise heat to high and boil until gravy is thickened, 4 to 5 minutes. Season gravy with salt and pepper and serve immediately with steaks.

SERVES 4

TAMALE PIE

5½ cups water

Coarse salt and freshly ground pepper

1¼ cups yellow cornmeal

1 tablespoon unsalted butter, plus more for dish

¼ cup extra-virgin olive oil

1 onion, coarsely chopped

3 garlic cloves, coarsely chopped

1 green bell pepper, ribs and seeds removed, cut into ¼-inch dice

1 serrano chile, finely chopped

1½ pounds ground turkey meat (7% fat)

1 can (14 ounces) plum tomatoes, coarsely chopped, juices reserved

½ cup chicken stock, preferably homemade (page 410)

1 teaspoon ground cumin

¾ teaspoon dried oregano

¼ teaspoon cayenne

8 pimiento-stuffed green olives, rinsed and coarsely chopped

4 ounces Monterey Jack, grated (1¼ cups)

Crisp lettuce leaves, for serving

Assorted garnishes, such as chopped avocado, tomatoes, red onion, and cilantro, for serving

BACKSTORY

Authentic tamales, a product of Mexico, can seem quite labor-intensive to those who have never made them before: Meats are cooked until meltingly tender, then shredded and mixed with a cornmeal batter; the mixture is wrapped in cornhusks, sealed, and steamed. Enter the tamale pie, a casserole layered with the flavors that make tamales so wonderful, but with a distinctly American ease. This is the official casserole of Texas and as fine an example of Tex-Mex cooking as you're likely to find. Serve with a salad of crisp Romaine leaves, and top with a colorful assortment of garnishes.

1 Bring the water to a boil in a medium saucepan. Add 2 teaspoons salt. Whisking constantly, add cornmeal in a slow, steady stream, switching to a wooden spoon when cornmeal becomes too thick to whisk. Reduce heat to medium and cook, stirring often, until thick and creamy, about 15 minutes. Stir in butter; cover and keep warm over low heat.

2 Preheat oven to 350°F. Lightly butter a 2-quart baking dish. Heat olive oil in a large skillet over medium-high, then add onion, garlic, bell pepper, chile, and a pinch of salt. Cook, stirring often, until onion is golden and vegetables are tender, 10 to 12 minutes. Add turkey and cook, breaking up large pieces with a wooden spoon, until cooked through, 5 to 7 minutes. Stir in tomatoes and juices, stock, cumin, oregano, and cayenne. Reduce heat to medium and cook, stirring, until most of the liquid has evaporated and the mixture resembles chili, about 10 minutes. Stir in olives and season with salt and pepper.

3 With a wet spatula, spread 1½ cups cornmeal into bottom of prepared dish. Spread turkey mixture on top, then spread remaining cornmeal on top. Sprinkle evenly with cheese. Bake until golden brown and cheese is melted, 35 to 40 minutes. Let stand 15 minutes. Serve with lettuce and garnishes.

SERVES 6 TO 8

STEAK FAJITAS

THE SOUTHWEST

BACKSTORY

No wonder this steak-in-a-skillet dish is so popular: It is quick and simple to prepare, literally sizzles when brought to the table, and allows guests to engage in the fun of assembling their own plates. It also makes excellent use of less costly cuts of meat, which is how the dish came to be created. Vaqueros *(cowboys) working on ranches would grill these inexpensive cuts, including skirt steak (this long strip was referred to as* faja, *or "belt"), to eat with tortillas and grilled onions, and which were then dubbed* tacos de fajitas. *While you may find versions made with chicken or even shrimp, beef is still the preferred choice in Longhorn country.*

1   teaspoon ground cumin

½   teaspoon ground coriander

    Coarse salt and freshly ground pepper

1   pound skirt steak, cut crosswise into 2 equal pieces

2   red bell peppers, halved crosswise, ribs and seeds removed, and thinly sliced

1   red onion, halved and thinly sliced

1   to 2 jalapeño chiles, very thinly sliced lengthwise (ribs and seeds removed for less heat, if desired)

2   tablespoons fresh lime juice

8   flour tortillas (6-inch)

    Sour cream and lime wedges, for serving

1 In a small bowl, combine the cumin, coriander, 2 teaspoons salt, and ½ teaspoon pepper. Pat dry steaks with paper towels, then rub steaks all over with spice mixture.

2 Heat a large skillet over medium-high; add meat (if necessary, cut into smaller pieces to fit in skillet, and work in batches to avoid crowding pan). Cook 2 to 4 minutes per side for medium-rare. Transfer to a cutting board. Tent steaks with foil and let rest 5 to 10 minutes.

3 Meanwhile, reduce heat to medium. Add bell peppers, onion, and chiles to skillet; season with salt and pepper. Cook, stirring occasionally, until crisp-tender, 8 to 10 minutes. Add lime juice and stir, scraping up browned bits in skillet with a wooden spoon.

4 Working with one at a time, heat tortillas in a dry skillet over medium-high 5 seconds, then flip and heat 5 seconds more. (Alternatively, stack tortillas and wrap in a damp kitchen towel or paper towels; heat in microwave 30 seconds.) Thinly slice steaks crosswise, and serve with tortillas, bell pepper mixture, sour cream, and lime wedges.

SERVES 4

BARBECUED BRISKET WITH BEER-BATTERED ONION RINGS

1 first-cut beef brisket (5 to 6 pounds), with a layer of fat at least ¼ inch thick, but preferably ½ inch thick

1 tablespoon dark-brown sugar

1 tablespoon coarse salt

1 tablespoon ground dried chile, preferably ancho

1 teaspoon freshly ground pepper

1 teaspoon ground cumin

1 teaspoon dry mustard powder

Texas Barbecue Sauce (recipe follows)

1 Rinse brisket and pat dry with paper towels. Whisk together brown sugar, salt, and the spices in a bowl. Rub all over meat. Wrap in plastic and refrigerate at least 4 hours, but preferably 24 (especially if cooking in the oven).

2 Prepare a charcoal grill (see page 409). When ready to cook, toss 1½ cups mesquite, hickory, or other smoked wood chips on the coals (¾ cup per side). Place the brisket, fat side up, in a disposable aluminum foil pan (or make a pan with a double sheet of heavy-duty aluminum foil). Place in the center of the top rack, directly over another aluminum pan. Cover the grill.

3 Smoke the brisket until tender enough to shred with your fingers—anywhere from 6 to 8 hours (the cooking time will depend on the size of the brisket and heat of the grill). Baste the brisket from time to time with the fat and juices that accumulate in the pan. You'll need to add 10 to 12 fresh coals to each side every hour and toss more wood chips on the fresh coals; add about ¾ cup chips per side every time you replenish the coals during the first 3 hours.

4 Remove the brisket pan from the grill and let rest 15 minutes. Transfer the brisket to a cutting board and thinly slice it across the grain, using a sharp knife, electric knife, or cleaver. Transfer the sliced meat to a platter, pour the pan juices on top, and serve immediately, with barbecue sauce.

Alternate oven method: After marinating brisket (preferably for 24 hours), place in a roasting pan or Dutch oven fitted with a rack (to keep the meat from stewing in its juices), with the fat side down. Cook (uncovered) in a 300°F oven 4 to 8 hours, depending on size of brisket (plan on about 1 hour per pound of meat), basting with pan juices every hour. Remove brisket and place pan on the stove to use for making the barbecue sauce, incorporating the juices and browned bits.

SERVES 8

(Continued on next page)

TEXAS BARBECUE SAUCE

- ¼ teaspoon cumin seeds
- ½ teaspoon coriander seeds
- ⅓ cup neutral-tasting oil, such as safflower
- 3 small sweet onions, diced (about 3 cups)
- 6 garlic cloves, minced (about 3 tablespoons)
  Coarse salt and freshly ground pepper
- 1 tablespoon ground dried chile, preferably ancho
- ½ cup unsulfured molasses
- ½ cup packed dark-brown sugar
- 4 cups crushed tomatoes (from two 28-ounce cans)
- ¾ cup cider vinegar
- ¼ cup distilled white vinegar
- 2 tablespoons Worcestershire sauce
- 2 cups water, plus more if needed

1 Heat a dry skillet over medium-high until hot. Add cumin and coriander seeds and cook, swirling pan occasionally, until fragrant, 30 to 60 seconds. Let cool, then grind in a spice grinder or clean coffee mill.

2 Heat oil in a medium pot over medium. Add onions and garlic, and sauté until translucent and tender, stirring occasionally, about 10 minutes. Add 1 teaspoon salt, ½ teaspoon pepper, the spices, molasses, and brown sugar; stir to combine. Cook, stirring frequently, 3 minutes. Add tomatoes and cider vinegar and bring to a simmer. Reduce heat to medium-low and simmer gently, stirring occasionally, until mixture is thick and dark, about 1 hour. Reduce heat to low if sauce is simmering too quickly.

3 Let cool slightly, then purée sauce in a blender. Add 1 tablespoon salt, 1 teaspoon pepper, the white vinegar, and Worcestershire; purée until smooth. With blender running, carefully add the water in a slow, steady stream. Blend until mixture is smooth and emulsified, adding more water if needed. Season with more salt and pepper. (Sauce can be refrigerated up to 3 days in an airtight container; let cool completely before storing, and reheat over medium before serving.)

MAKES 8 CUPS

BEER-BATTERED ONION RINGS

- 1 cup plus 2 tablespoons all-purpose flour
- 1 teaspoon ground cumin
  Pinch of cayenne
  Coarse salt
- ¾ cup buttermilk
- ¾ cup beer
- 1 large egg
- 4 cups peanut oil
- 2 large sweet white onions (about 2 pounds), sliced crosswise ½ inch thick and separated into rings

1 Preheat oven to 200°F. Combine flour, cumin, cayenne, and 1 teaspoon salt in a medium bowl. Slowly whisk in buttermilk, beer, and egg until smooth. Let batter stand 15 minutes.

2 In a large saucepan over medium-high, heat oil until a deep-fry thermometer registers 375°F. Working in batches, dip onion slices in batter, turning to coat. Carefully drop slices into hot oil. Cook, turning rings once, until golden brown, about 2 minutes. (Adjust heat between batches as necessary to keep oil at a steady temperature.)

3 Use a slotted spoon or mesh spider to transfer rings to a paper towel–lined baking sheet to drain. Season immediately with salt. Keep warm in the oven until ready to serve.

SERVES 4 TO 6

CHICKEN ENCHILADAS VERDES

1½ pounds bone-in chicken breast halves, skin removed

½ white onion, halved crosswise

1 garlic clove (peeled)

Coarse salt

2 cups loosely packed cilantro leaves

1½ pounds tomatillos, husks removed, rinsed

1 jalapeño chile

1 poblano chile

8 corn tortillas (6-inch)

1 cup grated Monterey Jack (2 ounces)

½ cup sour cream

2 tablespoons water

1 Place chicken, half the onion, and garlic in a medium saucepan. Add enough water to cover by 1 inch and season with salt. Bring to a boil, then reduce heat. Simmer until chicken is cooked through, 18 to 22 minutes. Transfer chicken to a plate. Reserve ¾ cup cooking liquid (discard garlic and onion). When cool enough to handle, shred chicken meat; discard bones. Coarsely chop ½ cup cilantro, and toss with chicken.

2 Heat broiler, with rack about 6 inches from heat source. Broil tomatillos and chiles on a rimmed baking sheet, rotating as they blacken, 10 to 12 minutes. Let cool. Remove blackened skins from chiles with paper towels; remove ribs and seeds if desired for less heat. Reduce oven to 375°F.

3 Combine tomatillos and chiles in a blender with remaining 1½ cups cilantro and the reserved cooking liquid; season with salt. Purée to a coarse consistency, then transfer salsa to a large bowl.

4 Working with one at a time, heat tortillas in a dry skillet over medium-high 5 seconds, then flip and heat 5 seconds more. (Alternatively, stack tortillas and wrap in a damp kitchen towel or paper towels; heat in microwave 30 seconds.)

5 Dip a tortilla into salsa to coat on both sides lightly. Place ⅓ cup chicken on half of tortilla. Sprinkle 2 tablespoons cheese on top and roll up. Place seam side down in a 9-by-13-inch baking dish. Repeat with remaining tortillas, chicken, and cheese, arranging enchiladas side by side in dish. Spoon remaining salsa on top and bake until heated through, about 20 minutes.

6 Thinly slice remaining onion and scatter over the top of the enchiladas. Stir the water into sour cream and spoon on top. Serve immediately.

SERVES 4

GRILLED CHILE-CITRUS TURKEY BREAST

BACKSTORY

A bone-in turkey breast might seem an unlikely choice for grilling, but it slow-cooks beautifully and feeds a crowd with ease. The Mexican chile called cascabel gives its nutty, smoky flavor to the bird, producing a deeply flavorful result; ancho chiles, or dried poblanos, are an easier-to-find substitute. For indirect cooking on a charcoal grill, rake hot coals onto opposite sides before grilling; place a foil pan in the center to catch the drippings. Set the turkey breast on the grates over the pan; keep the grill covered during cooking, but with the vents partially opened. Corn cobs and fresh green chiles (such as serrano or jalapeño) can be cooked alongside the turkey. Before grilling the corn, pull back the husks and remove the silks, then spread the cobs with softened butter, if desired; replace husks, securing tip with a small strand of husk (or simply twist to seal). Serve the turkey with warm corn tortillas so guests can make their own tacos, topping each with more chile-citrus sauce.

12	dried cascabel chiles or 5 ancho chiles
	Juice of 2 navel oranges
	Juice of 1 lime
5	garlic cloves
1	small white onion, coarsely chopped
	Coarse salt
1	bone-in turkey breast (4 to 6 pounds)
	Vegetable oil, for grill
24	corn tortillas (6-inch)

1 Toast chiles in a large, dry skillet over medium heat, turning occasionally, until slightly softened and pliable, about 5 minutes. Remove seeds and ribs. Place chiles in a small bowl and cover with boiling water. Let stand 15 minutes.

2 Using a slotted spoon, transfer chiles to a blender. Add both citrus juices, the garlic, and onion; season with salt and blend until smooth. Transfer ¾ cup sauce to a bowl and refrigerate, covered.

3 Rub turkey with remaining sauce. Transfer to a plate and cover with plastic wrap. Marinate in refrigerator at least 2 hours or up to 12 hours.

4 Heat grill to medium. (If you are using a charcoal grill, coals are ready when you can hold your hand 5 inches above grates for 5 to 6 seconds.) Meanwhile, remove turkey from refrigerator; let stand at room temperature 30 minutes.

5 Lightly oil hot grates. Grill, covered, over indirect heat (see backstory) until an instant-read thermometer inserted into thickest part of breast registers 165°F, 1 to 1½ hours. (Alternatively, roast in a 400°F oven for about 1 hour 20 minutes.) Transfer to a cutting board; let stand at least 15 minutes before slicing.

6 Using tongs, toast tortillas on the grill, 5 to 10 seconds per side. (Or heat the tortillas in a dry skillet over medium-high, flipping once.) Reheat reserved sauce, stirring, in a small saucepan over medium. Serve turkey with warm tortillas and sauce.

SERVES 8

JÍCAMA AND ORANGE SALAD

1 jícama (1½ pounds)
2 navel oranges
1 English cucumber
1 cup nasturtium flowers and leaves (optional)
  Coarse salt and freshly ground pepper
½ cup Creamy Orange Vinaigrette (recipe follows)

1 Prepare an ice-water bath. Peel jícama; cut into 4-inch batons (¼ inch thick). Let soak in the ice bath. With a paring knife, remove peel and bitter white pith from oranges, following the curve of the fruit. Cut flesh into ¼-inch-thick rounds; halve or quarter larger rounds.

2 Drain jícama; pat dry. Arrange all ingredients on a platter. Season with salt and pepper and drizzle with vinaigrette. Serve immediately.

SERVES 6 TO 8

CREAMY ORANGE VINAIGRETTE

1 teaspoon cumin seeds
1 navel orange
2 teaspoons Dijon mustard
2 teaspoons honey, preferably orange flower
3 tablespoons champagne vinegar
  Coarse salt and freshly ground pepper
½ cup extra-virgin olive oil
¼ cup heavy cream

1 Toast cumin seeds in a small, dry skillet over medium-high heat, shaking pan gently to keep them from burning, until fragrant, 2 to 3 minutes. Let cool, then finely grind with a mortar and pestle or in a spice grinder (or clean coffee mill).

2 Use a citrus zester to remove zest from orange; reserve zest. With a paring knife, remove bitter white pith from orange, following the curve of the fruit. Working over a bowl to catch the juices, cut orange segments from membrane, letting them fall into bowl. Squeeze any remaining juice from membrane into bowl. Remove segments and coarsely chop; return to bowl.

3 Whisk together mustard, honey, vinegar, and cumin; season with salt. Pour in oil in a slow stream, whisking until emulsified. Whisk in orange flesh, juice, and zest, then whisk in cream until thickened. Season with salt and pepper.

MAKES 1 CUP

THE SOUTHWEST

BACKSTORY

Visitors to New Mexico fall hard for the earthy, smoky, and often overtly spicy food, but locals are just as likely to celebrate some of the state's other, less well known ingredients—peppery nasturtium blossoms, for instance, or subtly sweet, crisp jícama. Cultivated in South America for centuries, jícama made its way north into Mexico, where it is a popular street food—cut into sticks, marinated in lime juice, and sprinkled with ground dried chile—and eventually to the southwestern United States. Jícama has a crisp texture and mild flavor reminiscent of pears or apples; here, the root vegetable is combined with cucumber and orange in a crunchy, refreshing salad. Nasturtium flowers can be found at nurseries and some farmers' market or from online sources; be sure to buy only those free of pesticides.

SKILLET CORNBREAD

THE SOUTHWEST

BACKSTORY

Just like in the South, where it originated, cornbread is the go-to accompaniment for barbecued meats in this part of the country. When it comes to texture and authenticity, a well-seasoned cast-iron skillet is key: first, you heat it in the oven; then, you pour in the batter so it forms the proper golden-brown crust. Putting buttermilk in the batter is also a must. In the Southwestern states, cornbread is often embellished with chiles, as in this version, and sometimes shredded cheese.

Vegetable oil, for pan
1 cup fine yellow cornmeal, preferably stone-ground
¼ cup all-purpose flour
⅓ cup sugar
1 teaspoon baking powder
½ teaspoon baking soda
½ teaspoon coarse salt
1 cup buttermilk
½ cup milk
1 large egg, lightly beaten
2 tablespoons unsalted butter, melted and cooled
¼ cup chopped canned jalapeños

1 Preheat oven to 425°F. Lightly oil an 8-inch cast-iron pan and heat in oven. Meanwhile, whisk together cornmeal, flour, sugar, baking powder, baking soda, and salt in a large bowl. Combine buttermilk, milk, and egg; add to cornmeal mixture and whisk to combine. Add melted butter and jalapeños, whisking to incorporate.

2 Remove pan from oven and pour in batter (it will sizzle). Bake until dark golden around the edges and set in center, 25 to 30 minutes. Let cool slightly in pan before cutting into squares or wedges. Serve warm or at room temperature.

MAKES ONE 8-INCH ROUND

SPICED PUMPKIN FLAN

- 1 cup sugar
- ¼ cup water
- 1 can (15 ounces) solid-pack pumpkin
- 1 can (14 ounces) sweetened condensed milk
- 1½ cups milk
- 4 large whole eggs plus 1 large egg yolk
- ¾ teaspoon ground cinnamon
- ½ teaspoon salt
- ¼ to ½ teaspoon ground dried chipotle chile
- ⅛ teaspoon ground cloves
- Pinch of cayenne

1 Preheat oven to 325°F. In a small saucepan with an ovenproof handle, bring sugar and the water to a boil over medium heat, stirring to dissolve sugar. Brush down sides of pan with a wet pastry brush to prevent crystals from forming. Cook, without stirring, until caramel turns dark amber, about 8 minutes. Pour into a 9-inch round cake pan. Let cool.

2 Blend pumpkin, condensed milk, and milk in a blender until smooth. Add whole eggs and yolk, cinnamon, salt, ground chile, cloves, and cayenne; blend until smooth. Pour mixture over caramel in pan. Carefully transfer cake pan to a roasting pan. Pour enough hot water into roasting pan to come 1 inch up sides of cake pan.

3 Bake until set and beginning to turn golden brown, about 1½ hours. Carefully remove cake pan from the water bath and let cool completely on a wire rack. Refrigerate until chilled, at least 6 hours or up to overnight. To unmold, run a knife around edges to loosen, then invert onto a platter. Scrape remaining sauce from pan over flan. Serve immediately.

SERVES 8 TO 10

THE SOUTHWEST

BACKSTORY

This cool, creamy dessert makes a perfect ending to a spicy meal. As such, flan has a devoted following in the Southwest, where it shares a Spanish heritage with other local dishes. This version of the baked custard is flavored with pumpkin, a favorite local fruit. Its subtly sweet taste is a natural partner for smoky spices, including ground chipotle and cayenne pepper, both used sparingly in this recipe.

BISCOCHITOS WITH MEXICAN HOT CHOCOLATE

3 cups all-purpose flour, plus more for dusting

½ teaspoon baking powder

¼ teaspoon salt

1¾ cups sugar

1¼ cups lard, preferably leaf lard, or solid vegetable shortening

1 large egg

1 teaspoon pure vanilla extract

2 tablespoons (1 fluid ounce) Triple Sec

Finely grated zest of 1 orange

2 teaspoons anise seeds

2 to 4 tablespoons water

½ teaspoon ground cinnamon

1 Into a bowl, sift together flour, baking powder, and salt. With an electric mixer on medium-high speed, mix 1 cup sugar and the lard until light and fluffy, 3 minutes. Add egg; beat to combine. Beat in vanilla, Triple Sec, and zest.

2 With mixer on low, gradually beat flour mixture into sugar mixture. Beat in anise seeds. Raise speed to medium; add 2 tablespoons water, beating until dough comes together. If necessary, add up to 2 more tablespoons water, a little at a time. Turn out dough onto a piece of plastic; shape into a disk. Wrap in plastic; refrigerate 30 minutes.

3 Preheat oven to 350°F. In a small bowl, combine the cinnamon and remaining ¾ cup sugar. On a lightly floured surface, roll out dough to ¼ inch thick. Cut dough into crescent moons, stars, and other shapes with 2-inch cookie cutters; lightly sift cinnamon-sugar over dough. Place on parchment-lined baking sheets, 1 inch apart.

4 Bake, one sheet at a time, until firm but not brown, rotating sheet halfway through, 12 to 14 minutes. Transfer cookies on parchment to a wire rack to cool completely. (Cookies can be stored between layers of parchment in an airtight container at room temperature up to 1 week.)

MAKES 4 DOZEN

MEXICAN HOT CHOCOLATE

4 cups milk

1 dried ancho chile, quartered, seeds removed

6 cinnamon sticks, preferably Mexican

4 ounces Mexican chocolate, such as Ibarra, finely chopped

Whipped cream, for serving

Ground cinnamon, for sprinkling

1 In a saucepan, heat milk, chile, and 2 cinnamon sticks over medium just until milk begins to steam. Remove from heat; cover and let steep 10 minutes.

2 Place chocolate in a heatproof bowl. Strain milk mixture into bowl, whisking to combine. Discard cinnamon. Return mixture to saucepan; whisk until chocolate has completely melted. Divide among four mugs. Top with whipped cream and sprinkle with ground cinnamon. Garnish with cinnamon sticks, and serve.

SERVES 4

THE SOUTHWEST

BACKSTORY

In New Mexico, it wouldn't be Christmas without a platter of biscochitos. The cookies, with their signature anise-scented flavor and crumbly texture (which results from the use of lard), are also eaten year-round, and in 1989 they became the official state cookie (the nation's first). Mexican hot chocolate makes the perfect partner. Look for Mexican chocolate, which is laced with canela (Mexican cinnamon), and the cinnamon sticks at Mexican food markets and from online retailers. Serve the cocoa with cinnamon-stick stirrers.

TEXAS SHEET CAKE

- 1 cup (2 sticks) unsalted butter, plus more, softened, for pan
- 2 cups all-purpose flour
- 2 cups sugar
- 1 teaspoon baking soda
- ¾ teaspoon coarse salt
- ½ teaspoon ground cinnamon
- ¼ cup unsweetened cocoa powder
- 1 cup water
- 2 large eggs, lightly beaten
- ½ cup buttermilk
- 1 teaspoon pure vanilla extract
  Boiled Chocolate Icing (recipe follows)
- 1¼ cups coarsely chopped toasted (page 408) pecans (6 to 7 ounces)

1 Preheat oven to 375°F. Lightly butter a 9-by-13-inch baking pan. Whisk together flour, sugar, baking soda, salt, and cinnamon in a large bowl.

2 Melt butter in a saucepan over medium-low; whisk in cocoa, then the water. Raise heat and bring to a boil, whisking occasionally. Pour over flour mixture and stir until thoroughly combined. Stir in eggs, buttermilk, and vanilla.

3 Pour batter into prepared pan and tap firmly on counter to release air bubbles. Bake until sides pull away from edges of pan and a cake tester inserted in center comes out clean, 12 to 14 minutes. Transfer pan to a wire rack and pour icing over cake while still warm. Sprinkle evenly with pecans and let cool before slicing into squares and serving.

MAKES ONE 9-BY-13-INCH CAKE

BOILED CHOCOLATE ICING

- ½ cup (1 stick) unsalted butter
- ¼ cup unsweetened cocoa powder
- ½ cup heavy cream
- 2 teaspoons pure vanilla extract
- 2½ cups confectioners' sugar

Bring butter, cocoa, and cream to a boil in a small saucepan, stirring occasionally. Remove from heat, and stir in vanilla and confectioners' sugar. Use while still warm.

MAKES ENOUGH FOR ONE 9-BY-13-INCH CAKE

BACKSTORY

This is one of the nation's, if not the world's, great chocolate cakes. The basic supermarket ingredients yield a moist, tender crumb. You can put it together at the drop of a hat and it's out of the oven in no time. Made in an old-fashioned rectangular pan, it is easy to tote to a potluck, birthday party, or backyard barbecue. If you have any Texans in your life, surprise them with this, and you're sure to secure their undying love and affection.

PLUM AND PIÑON STREUSEL CAKE

FOR THE STREUSEL

- 3 tablespoons cold unsalted butter
- ½ cup packed dark-brown sugar
- 1 teaspoon ground canela (Mexican cinnamon) or regular cinnamon
- ½ cup pine nuts, toasted (page 408)
- Pinch of salt

FOR THE CRUMB TOPPING

- 1½ cups all-purpose flour
- ¾ cup (1½ sticks) unsalted butter, softened
- ¾ cup confectioners' sugar, plus more for dusting
- ¼ teaspoon salt

FOR THE CAKE

- ¾ cup (1½ sticks) unsalted butter, softened, plus more for pan
- 2½ cups all-purpose flour, plus more for dusting
- 2 teaspoons baking powder
- 1 teaspoon baking soda
- ½ teaspoon salt
- 1¼ cups granulated sugar
- 3 large eggs, lightly beaten
- 1½ cups sour cream
- 12 ounces small plums, such as Italian prune plums, cut into ½-inch pieces
- 1 tablespoon plus 1 teaspoon pure vanilla extract

1 Prepare the streusel: Combine all streusel ingredients in a bowl. Using a pastry blender or two knives, blend until mixture resembles coarse meal. Cover and refrigerate.

2 Prepare the crumb topping: Combine all of the topping ingredients in a bowl. Using a pastry blender or two knives, blend until mixture resembles coarse meal. Cover and refrigerate.

3 Make the cake: Preheat oven to 375°F. Brush a 10-inch tube pan with butter and dust with flour; tap out excess. Sift together flour, baking powder, baking soda, and salt into a bowl. With an electric mixer on medium-high speed, cream butter and granulated sugar until light and fluffy. Add beaten eggs in two batches, mixing well. Add the flour mixture in three batches, alternating with two additions of sour cream and mixing until combined after each. Fold in plums.

4 Pour half the batter into prepared pan; sprinkle evenly with streusel. Top with remaining batter, then drizzle vanilla evenly over batter. Bake 20 minutes. Remove from oven; sprinkle with crumb topping. Bake until topping is golden brown, 25 to 30 minutes more. Let cool completely on a wire rack before removing from the pan. Dust with confectioners' sugar just before serving.

SERVES 8 TO 10

THE SOUTHWEST

BACKSTORY

Dotting the dusty desert plains of New Mexico and Arizona are short-statured piñon trees, a native pine whose nuts remain a source of regional pride. The nuts, long a part of the Native American diet in the Southwest, are more often today used in a variety of sweets, including cookies and this rich, dense cake. The streusel is flavored with canela, a more delicate-tasting cinnamon. If you can find piñon nuts, by all means use them here; otherwise, regular pine nuts will work just fine.

NECTARINE FRIED PIES

2 cups all-purpose flour, plus more for dusting

1 teaspoon baking powder

½ teaspoon salt

½ cup (1 stick) chilled unsalted butter, cut into small pieces

½ cup ice water

1¾ pounds large, ripe nectarines (about 4)

¼ cup granulated sugar

¼ cup honey

2 to 3 cups neutral-tasting oil, such as safflower, for frying
   Confectioners' sugar, for dusting

1 Into a large bowl, sift together flour, baking powder, and salt. Using your fingertips, work the butter into the flour mixture until it resembles coarse meal. Pour in the ice water; toss lightly, gathering the dough into a ball. Turn out dough onto a piece of plastic wrap; shape into a disk. Wrap dough in plastic; refrigerate at least 1 hour or up to overnight.

2 Halve nectarines lengthwise and discard pits. Leaving the skins on (to give the filling a pretty rose color), chop the fruit into ½-inch chunks.

3 In a large, heavy skillet, combine the nectarines, granulated sugar, and honey and fold to evenly coat. Bring to a boil over high heat; reduce heat to medium-low. Simmer, stirring frequently, until mixture is thick enough to hold its shape on the spoon, about 25 minutes. Transfer filling to a bowl and let cool.

4 On a lightly floured work surface, roll out the dough as thin as possible (about ¹⁄₁₆ inch). With a 4-inch fluted cutter, cut out as many rounds as possible from the dough. If the dough becomes too soft to work with, return to the refrigerator for 15 minutes. Gather scraps into a ball, and roll out dough as before. Again, cut out as many rounds as possible.

5 Place about 1 tablespoon filling on the lower third of each round. Moisten the edges of rounds lightly with cold water. Fold rounds in half over filling and press edges together tightly. Dip a fork in flour and use the tines to seal edges.

6 Preheat oven to 250°F. In a large, heavy skillet, heat 1 inch of oil over medium-high heat until a deep-fry thermometer registers 350°F. Cook the pies in batches, turning them occasionally with tongs or a slotted spoon, until crisp and golden, about 4 minutes. Transfer pies to a paper towel–lined baking sheet to drain; keep warm in the oven. Return oil to 350°F between batches. Serve warm, dusted with confectioners' sugar.

MAKES ABOUT 18

THE SOUTHWEST

BACKSTORY

Old-fashioned fried pies are as much a part of Texas and Oklahoma culture as state fairs, cookouts, and tailgating parties. In fact, that's where you'll likely find these portable fruit-filled pastries, as well as at many bakeries and restaurants specializing in honest, down-home food. Frying takes much less time than baking and produces the most delicious crisp, golden crust. This recipe calls for nectarines, but peaches and other stone fruits, berries, apples, or pears are other welcome options.

PECANS

Pecan trees cast shadows like slatted shutters along the loamy banks of the San Marcos and the Guadalupe rivers. Here, almost 100 miles east of San Antonio, it takes three Texas-size men, their fingertips barely touching, to form a circle around the trunks of some of these trees.

The pecan harvest in Georgia might be the biggest in the country, but Texans know that their state is the true home of the pecan. Given all the streams, creeks, bayous, islands, churches, schools, cemeteries, and parks that bear the word *pecan* in their name, their claim is plausible.

Although pecans were once harvested entirely by hand, nowadays ranchers use a shaker—a truck fitted with a giant lobster claw that clamps hold of a tree trunk. It rattles the trunk so fiercely that the nuts, along with leaves and branches, hurtle to the ground. A blower/sweeper machine whisks the nuts into a row before they're delivered to a cleaner, which spits out twigs, leaves, and cracked nuts. Any remaining debris or off-quality pecans are removed by hand. Some varieties of nuts require a final sizing—done by machine—while others are simply bagged in burlap sacks and sold.

Harvesting goes on all day, and 15,000 pounds of pecans might be gathered by nightfall. But sometimes a mishap—a snapped chain or a flat tractor tire—causes a major disruption. Any worker hopes that if anything breaks down, it doesn't happen until close to quitting time. That way he has the night to make the repairs.

The buttery goodness of new-crop pecans ensures a stellar pie—either a traditional version or something more fanciful, such as a chocolate-bourbon variation (see page 216) or one with a butter-pecan ice cream filling (see page 336)—as well as cookies and candies like turtle fudge and pecan pralines. Texans also like to use pecans to make mole (where ground nuts help to thicken the sauce), as a crisp coating for seared meat and fish, and in slaws and salads. And of course there are many sweet and/or savory versions of spiced nuts, including the one at right; combined with pepitas and chili powder (other local favorites), the pecans make a salty snack worthy of the best fresh-squeezed lemonade—or icy margaritas.

SPICED PECANS AND PEPITAS
Preheat oven to 375°F. On a rimmed baking sheet, toss together 2 cups pecans (8 ounces), ¾ cup pepitas (hulled green pumpkin seeds), 1 teaspoon neutral-tasting oil (such as safflower), 2 teaspoons chili powder, and 1¼ teaspoons coarse salt. Spread in a single layer and bake, stirring once, until well toasted, about 10 minutes. Let cool completely before serving or storing in an airtight container at room temperature, up to 1 week.

BUTTER-PECAN ICE CREAM PIE

FOR THE CRUST

- 1 cup pecans
- ¼ cup sugar
- ¾ cup all-purpose flour
- 2 tablespoons unsalted butter

FOR THE FILLING

- 1¼ cups pecans, coarsely chopped
- 3 tablespoons unsalted butter, cut into tablespoons
- ¼ teaspoon plus a pinch of salt
- 2½ cups heavy cream
- 2 cups milk
- 8 large egg yolks
- ½ cup granulated sugar
- ½ cup packed dark-brown sugar
- ½ teaspoon pure vanilla extract

1 Make the crust: Preheat oven to 375°F. Reserve ½ cup pecans for topping pie. Finely grind remaining ½ cup pecans with the sugar in a food processor. Add flour and butter; process until moist clumps form. With wet fingers, press crust evenly into bottom and up sides of a 9-inch pie plate. Pierce all over bottom of crust with a fork. Freeze until firm, about 20 minutes. Bake until golden, 20 to 25 minutes (if crust puffs up, gently press down with the back of a spoon). Transfer to a wire rack and let cool completely. Reduce oven to 350°F.

2 Meanwhile, prepare the filling: Spread pecans on a rimmed baking sheet and toast in oven 7 minutes, tossing occasionally. Add butter and a pinch of salt to sheet and toss with pecans until butter melts; continue toasting until fragrant and lightly browned, about 8 minutes more. Let cool completely. Heat cream and milk in a medium saucepan over medium-high until hot (do not let simmer), about 2 minutes. Remove from heat.

3 Prepare an ice-water bath. With an electric mixer, whisk egg yolks, granulated sugar, and remaining ¼ teaspoon salt on high speed until mixture has tripled in volume and can hold a ribbon on surface for 2 seconds when whisk

is lifted, about 3 minutes. Mix in brown sugar until well combined. Reduce speed to medium. Ladle 1 cup hot cream mixture in a slow stream into yolk mixture to temper it. Add another 1 cup cream mixture; beat to combine. Return mixture to saucepan; cook over medium-high heat, stirring constantly, until it is thick enough to coat the back of the spoon and an instant-read thermometer registers 180°F, 5 to 7 minutes. Stir in vanilla. Pour cream mixture through a fine sieve into a bowl set in the ice bath. Let cool completely, stirring often.

4 Freeze the mixture in an ice-cream maker according to the manufacturer's instructions. In the last minute of churning, add the sugared pecans and churn just until blended in. Transfer to an airtight container and freeze 1 hour before assembling pie. (Ice cream can be frozen up to 1 month; let stand at room temperature 15 to 20 minutes before using.)

5 Using an offset spatula, spread ice cream evenly in the cooled crust, smoothing top. Chop reserved ½ cup pecans; sprinkle on top. Freeze, covered loosely with plastic wrap, until firm, at least 6 hours or up to overnight.

MAKES ONE 9-INCH PIE

THE SOUTHWEST

BACKSTORY

With its press-in-the-pan crust and ice cream filling (you can swap in a good-quality store-bought variety instead of making your own, if you like), this dessert has just the right laid-back appeal during scorching summer months. Butter-pecan ice cream makes a delectably crunchy-creamy filling, ground pecans mixed with butter and sugar form the crust, and more pecans are sprinkled on top. The formula is endlessly adaptable; think peanut butter ice cream with a chocolate cookie crumb crust and a sprinkling of salted peanuts on top, or rum raisin ice cream with a gingersnap crust. Any way you slice it, ice cream pie provides cooling relief on a plate.

WEST

The Western states are paradise for home cooks and chefs alike. Whether you live in Los Angeles, San Francisco, Seattle, or on the the Big Island of Hawaii, you decide what you want for dinner while shopping for ingredients. The world—or, rather, the farmers' market—is your oyster. There might be plump, deep-purple Black Mission figs, just-picked wild blackberries, or buttery avocados that will finish ripening on your kitchen counter.

California cuisine has long been about celebrating the good life. Crab Louis, for instance, is a sumptuous dish that epitomizes the Gilded Age in San Francisco. Since the late nineteenth century, California has been known as the "land of salads," and Cobb salad—bright, beautiful, and rich with chicken, avocado, bacon, and blue cheese—is just as famous as the glossy Hollywood players who lunched at the Brown Derby. The date shake became a cool-as-an-oasis symbol of ever-hip Palm Springs. The sheer abundance of top-quality ingredients available throughout the United States today—including artichokes, garlic, almonds, pistachios, raisins, and olives—is due to the renewed emphasis on organically grown produce and sustainably harvested foodstuffs.

There is an inviting informality and interplay of cultures about this food that speaks to all Americans. The cuisines of China and Japan are two big influences on the food of California, but the most important is that which comes from Mexico; in fact, recipes for tacos first appeared in California cookbooks around 1914. In the twentieth century, a distinctive category called "Cal-Mex" emerged, making guacamole, burritos, and rice-and-bean combination plates standard fare across the land. Vegetable oil replaced the lard that is used in Mexican and Tex-Mex dishes, and Monterey Jack supplanted Mexican cheeses. One influential proponent of Cal-Mex food was Victor J. Bergeron, or "Trader Vic," who founded his eponymous chain of restaurants in 1933. Although the mai-tai is perhaps his most famous cocktail, Bergeron did a great deal to promote and popularize the margarita as well.

Nowadays, fish tacos might be considered "fast food," but they are as superb an example as you'll ever find, and a great excuse for a party. Also made for sharing is the rustic seafood stew called cioppino, invented out of necessity by San Francisco's Italian and Portuguese fishermen. It is, by design, enormously adaptable, so use whatever seafood is freshest.

It's easy to think of pineapple as the quintessential Hawaiian fruit, but, in fact, it wasn't introduced to the islands until the 1800s. The creation of a canning industry, along with the founding of the Hawaiian Pineapple Company in 1901, made the exotic tropical fruit affordable to every American and fueled a nationwide obsession with homey pineapple upside-down cake.

Like the indigenous inhabitants of the Hawaiian islands, those of the Pacific Northwest feasted on the bounty of the ocean; the cold waters stretching from Oregon up to Alaska have always teemed with salmon and halibut, oysters, clams, and Dungeness crab. Although there is also an abundance of blueberries and blackberries that grow wild on the western slopes of the Cascades, it is the cultivated fruit—including cherries, apples, grapes, apricots, raspberries, blackberries (and blackberry hybrids such as the marionberry, grown primarily in Oregon's Willamette Valley)—that the region is renowned for today. In addition to having world-class vineyards that rival those in California, the Pacific Northwest is also home to what are arguably the country's finest micro-breweries. The ideal growing conditions found there have made the region a center of hops cultivation since the late nineteenth century.

Impeccably fresh ingredients and freshly imagined dishes that bring out their best—the West has a brio that is all its own. It makes you want to go to the market, seek out the most delicious things available, then go home, get into the kitchen, and cook.

RECIPES

MARTINI

MAI TAI

PISCO PUNCH

SPRITZERS

DRINKS

MAI TAI

Mai tai *is Tahitian for "the very best," and that's just what Californian "Trader Vic" had in mind when mixing the first version in the 1940s. It's a combination of light and dark rums, curaçao (a citrus-flavored liqueur), orgeat syrup (made with almonds and citrus), and lime juice. Although much of America came to associate it with Hawaii, the mai tai didn't land there until a decade later.*

Fill a cocktail shaker with cracked **ice** and add 3 tablespoons (1 fluid ounce) each **light rum** and **dark rum**, 1 tablespoon (½ fluid ounce) each orange **curaçao** and **orgeat syrup**, 1½ teaspoons **simple syrup** (page 412), and juice of 1 **lime**. Shake vigorously, then strain into a rocks glass filled with crushed **ice**. Garnish with **mint**. MAKES 1

MARTINI

New Yorkers, hold on to your olives: the most urbane of cocktails was most likely invented on the West Coast, not in the Big Apple. San Francisco and the city of Martinez both claim ownership, the latter lending its name to the drink that would eventually evolve into the martini, that utterly appealing mix of salty and refreshing, with the unmistakable fragrance of juniper that comes from gin.

Fill a cocktail shaker with cracked **ice**. Add ¼ cup (2 fluid ounces) **gin** and 2 teaspoons **vermouth**. Shake vigorously, then strain into a stemmed glass. Garnish with skewered oil-cured pitted **olives**. Serve immediately. MAKES 1

PISCO PUNCH

Back when merchant ships plied the waters between California and South America, Peruvian pisco brandy found favor in bars all over San Francisco, where pisco punch and pisco sours were served day and night. Nowhere was pisco punch more revered than at a saloon called the Bank Exchange, whose tight-lipped owner took the recipe to his grave in 1926. There it stayed until an enterprising historian reconstructed the drink in the 1970s. Ever since, pisco punch has reclaimed its status as the cocktail of the City by the Bay.

Combine 1 peeled and cored **pineapple**, cut into 1-inch cubes, with 1 bottle (750 ml) **pisco** in a nonreactive (glass or ceramic) bowl. Cover and refrigerate 3 days. Stir ½ cup **simple syrup** (page 412) and ½ cup fresh **lime juice** (from 4 limes) into pisco mixture. Fill six glasses with **ice** and punch. Garnish with soaked pineapple. SERVES 6

SPRITZERS

Whether nonalcoholic or embellished with an unassuming white table wine, a spritzer makes a refreshing apéritif. It is also infinitely adaptable. The two versions below, for instance, make good use of California ingredients: Meyer lemons and lavender, which thrives on the Central Coast of California. Used judiciously, lavender adds a lovely, unexpected flavor to the second spritzer.

Meyer Lemon Spritzers: Bring 4 cups **water** and ½ cup **sugar** to a boil in a large saucepan, stirring until sugar dissolves. Add 6 **Meyer lemons**, thinly sliced, and 2 **rosemary sprigs**. Reduce heat and simmer 10 minutes. Remove from heat; cover and let steep 20 minutes. Strain through a fine sieve, discarding solids, and return liquid to pan. Boil until reduced by half, 10 to 15 minutes. Let cool completely. (Syrup can be refrigerated in an airtight container up to 1 week.) Pour ¼ cup syrup into each of six glasses and top with ¾ cup **sparkling water** (or ½ cup dry white wine and ¼ cup sparkling water). Serve immediately, garnished with a **lemon slice** if desired. MAKES 6

Lavender Spritzers: Bring 4 cups **water** and ½ cup **sugar** to a boil in a large saucepan, stirring until sugar dissolves. Add 3 tablespoons dried **lavender blossoms**. Remove from heat; cover and let steep 30 minutes. Strain through a fine sieve, discarding solids, and return liquid to pan. Boil until reduced by half, 10 to 15 minutes. Let cool completely. (Syrup can be refrigerated in an airtight container up to 1 week.) Pour ¼ cup syrup into each of six glasses and top with ¾ cup **sparkling water** (or ½ cup dry white wine and ¼ cup sparkling water). Serve immediately, garnished with a lavender stem if desired. MAKES 6

ORANGE JULIUS

TRIPLE-BERRY SMOOTHIE

DATE SHAKE

MANGO-PAPAYA SMOOTHIE

DATE SHAKE

1 cup dates, such as Deglet Noor or Medjool, pitted and coarsely chopped

1 cup milk

2 cups quality vanilla ice cream

In a blender, purée dates and milk until smooth. Add ice cream, and puree again. Divide between 2 tall glasses.

SERVES 2

ORANGE JULIUS

1¼ cups fresh orange juice

1 cup milk

1 large egg white or 3 tablespoons pasteurized egg whites

1 teaspoon pure vanilla extract

¼ cup sugar

1½ cups ice

Purée all ingredients except ice in a blender until frothy, about 10 seconds. Add ice and blend until slushy, about 10 seconds more.

SERVES 2

TRIPLE-BERRY SMOOTHIE

½ cup each blueberries, raspberries, and hulled strawberries

1 banana, peeled and cut into pieces

½ cup plain yogurt

1 cup milk

½ cup ice cubes

Purée all ingredients in a blender until smooth.

MAKES 2

MANGO-PAPAYA SMOOTHIE

½ cup pitted and peeled mango chunks

½ cup peeled papaya chunks

½ cup plain yogurt

¼ cup pineapple juice

Purée all ingredients in a blender until smooth.

SERVES 2

THE WEST

BACKSTORY

America's enthusiasm for blended fruit drinks started (where else?) in health-conscious California in the 1930s. These early versions were largely based on the vitamina of Brazil and liquada of Mexico, both of which were made with tropical fruits, including avocado, and sold in health-food stores in the Southern part of the state. When Waring introduced the blender to the U.S. market in the 1940s, the company included a couple of smoothie recipes in a cookbook designed to promote sales. Yet it wasn't until the 1970s, and the nationwide fervor for health food, that the trend really took off. At the same time, the Smoothie King and California Smoothie began selling shakes to the masses, and a humble little shop that Julius Freed opened in the 1920s in Los Angeles had grown into the national chain called Orange Julius, after the drink that it made famous. While not quite the nutritional drink that smoothies purported to be, it was nevertheless a less sugary option than Californians' other favorite blended drink, the milkshake. Chalk it up to car culture; over the years, drive-throughs and roadside stands opened up all along major routes to supply thirsty travelers with shakes. One of the more well-known (and sought-after) specialty shakes can still be found on the drive from Los Angeles to Palm Springs—the date shake is a regional favorite of the Coachella Valley, smack in the middle of the date-producing capital of the United States.

GUACAMOLE

TOMATILLO
GUACAMOLE

PEAR AND
POMEGRANATE
GUACAMOLE

GUACAMOLE

 2 tablespoons finely chopped white onion

 1 tablespoon plus 2 teaspoons finely chopped fresh cilantro

 1¼ teaspoons finely chopped jalapeño chile (ribs and seeds removed for less heat, if desired)

 Coarse salt

 1 ripe avocado, halved lengthwise, pitted, peeled, and coarsely chopped

 Juice of 1 lime

With a large mortar and pestle, mash onion, 1 tablespoon cilantro, the jalapeño, and ½ teaspoon salt until smooth and juicy. Add avocado and mash slightly (avocado should remain somewhat chunky). Stir in remaining 2 teaspoons cilantro and the lime juice. Season with more salt as desired. Serve immediately.

MAKES 1½ CUPS

PEAR AND POMEGRANATE GUACAMOLE

 1 tablespoon finely chopped white onion

 ½ jalapeño chile, finely chopped (ribs and seeds removed for less heat, if desired)

 Coarse salt

 1 ripe avocado, halved lengthwise, pitted, peeled, and cut into ½-inch dice

 ½ small ripe Anjou pear, peeled and cut into ½-inch dice

 2 tablespoons pomegranate seeds

With a large mortar and pestle, mash onion, jalapeño, and ¼ teaspoon salt until smooth and juicy. Gently stir in avocado and pear, and sprinkle with pomegranate seeds. Season with more salt as desired. Serve mmediately.

MAKES 1½ CUPS

TOMATILLO GUACAMOLE

 6 tomatillos (about 12 ounces), husks removed, rinsed, and halved

 ½ jalapeño chile (ribs and seeds removed for less heat, if desired)

 ¼ cup finely chopped white onion

 2 tablespoons finely chopped fresh cilantro

 Coarse salt

 1 ripe avocado, halved lengthwise, pitted, peeled, and coarsely chopped

Purée tomatillos, jalapeño, onion, cilantro, and ¾ teaspoon salt in a food processor or blender until smooth. Reserve ½ cup salsa mixture in food processor; transfer remaining salsa to a serving dish. Add avocado to blender and purée until smooth. Season with more salt as desired. Serve immediately, with salsa alongside.

MAKES 1 CUP

THE WEST

BACKSTORY

Guacamole has to be one of the very best ways to enjoy avocados. The Hass variety of the tropical fruit, common in Mexico and California, is distinguished by its wonderful flavor, long shelf life, and year-round availability. It's on the small side, with a dark, leathery rind ranging from purplish green to brownish black. The fruit's flesh is buttery with a delicate herbal flavor. The molcajete is a traditional Mexican mortar made from rough volcanic rock, used for preparing guacamole and salsas and for grinding spices. If you don't have a mortar and pestle, mash the ingredients in a heavy bowl with a fork. Place a damp kitchen towel underneath the bowl to hold it steady.

ARTICHOKES

Rarely is a vegetable so closely identified with a particular town: If you find yourself in Castroville, California, about a hundred miles south of San Francisco, you can't help but notice the artichoke-themed murals splashed across buildings or the artichoke hats and tattoos adorning proud locals. Or if you happen to visit in May, you can attend a harvest festival featuring an artichoke queen. (The first beauty to wear the crown, incidentally, was one Norma Jean Baker, later known as Marilyn Monroe.)

The Italian immigrants who arrived here in the 1920s quickly discovered that the mild climate of coastal Monterey County provided the perfect environment for growing what they called *carciofi*, beloved throughout the Mediterranean region since Roman times. Today, if you've ever eaten an artichoke grown in the United States, it most likely came from the fields around Castroville.

To many Americans, though, artichokes are still a bit of a mystery. For one thing, with all those layers of impenetrable-looking spiny green leaves, they seem more like pine cones than something edible. The spines, along with a spiky purple bloom, affirm the artichoke's membership in the thistle family. What we call an artichoke is actually the flower bud of the plant. The thick outer leaves are the bracts that protect the incipient flower within. Nestled among the leaves is the fuzzy, inedible choke. (So-called baby artichokes are just smaller buds that grow lower on the stalk and have undeveloped, edible chokes.) Under the choke lies the tender, pale heart, which bears the seeds and which, in American kitchens at least, is more likely to be procured from a jar or can than from the vegetable itself.

But steaming fresh artichokes, divested of their toughest leaves, is really very simple, and the flavor of the remaining leaves—typically plucked one by one and dipped in a sauce or melted butter, then scraped between the teeth to remove the flesh—is haunting and complex. Dig out the choke with a spoon and savor (at last!) the prized heart.

STEAMED ARTICHOKES WITH TARRAGON MAYONNAISE Squeeze juice of 1 lemon into a large bowl of cold water. Trim stem of 1 artichoke flush with bottom. Snap off outer leaves. Using kitchen shears, cut off tips of remaining leaves. Place in lemon water. Repeat with 7 more artichokes. Drain artichokes, and place in a pot in a single snug layer (in batches if necessary). Add ¼ cup water. Bring to a simmer, cover, and steam until tender, about 35 minutes. Remove from pot. Let cool. Cover and refrigerate up to 2 hours. Meanwhile, zest and juice another lemon. Whisk to combine zest, 2 tablespoons juice, 2 cups mayonnaise, 1½ teaspoons chopped fresh tarragon, and 3 dashes of hot sauce; season with salt and freshly ground pepper. Serve alongside artichokes. **SERVES 6 TO 8**

GRILLED ARTICHOKES WITH LEMON-OREGANO MAYONNAISE

1½ lemons

4 large artichokes (2½ pounds total)

Coarse salt and freshly ground pepper

Extra-virgin olive oil, for drizzling

8 thin slices cured ham, such as serrano or prosciutto

Lemon-Oregano Mayonnaise, for serving (recipe follows)

1 Heat grill to medium-high. (If you are using a charcoal grill, coals are ready when you can hold your hand 5 inches above grates for just 3 to 4 seconds.) Bring a large pot of water to a boil.

2 Meanwhile, squeeze juice of one lemon half into a large bowl of water. Trim artichoke stems to ½ inch. Remove tough outer leaves. Working with one artichoke at a time, trim pointy tips of artichoke leaves using kitchen shears; cut artichoke in half lengthwise and remove fuzzy chokes by scraping with a small spoon. Transfer artichoke to bowl of lemon-water as you work to prevent discoloration.

3 Once water in pot is at a boil, add salt. Squeeze juice of remaining lemon half into pot, then drop in lemon half. Using a slotted spoon, transfer artichokes to pot and cook until easily pierced with a sharp knife, about 12 minutes. Drain and let cool.

4 Drizzle artichokes with olive oil and season with salt and pepper; toss to coat. Grill, turning as needed with tongs, until lightly browned, about 5 minutes. Arrange ham on a platter; top with artichokes. Serve with lemon mayonnaise.

SERVES 4

LEMON-OREGANO MAYONNAISE

1 large egg yolk

2 tablespoons fresh lemon juice

1 tablespoon Dijon mustard

1 tablespoon fresh oregano leaves, chopped

½ cup plus 2 tablespoons extra-virgin olive oil

Coarse salt and freshly ground pepper

Whisk together egg yolk, lemon juice, mustard, and oregano (or pulse in a food processor). Slowly pour in olive oil in a slow, steady stream, whisking (or processing) constantly until emulsified; season with salt and pepper. Serve immediately.

MAKES ½ CUP

Note The egg yolk in this recipe is not cooked. It should not be prepared for pregnant women, babies, young children, the elderly, or anyone whose health is compromised.

THE WEST

BACKSTORY

It's easy to understand Americans' hesitation when it comes to fresh artichokes. But armed with a pair of kitchen shears, a knife, and some lemon halves, you can quickly conquer this seemingly formidable foe. The globes take well to practically every cooking method—steaming, roasting, sautéing, even deep-frying. Grilling seems especially appropriate for this West Coast specialty, resulting in an easygoing dish with sophisticated flavors thanks to a layer of cured-ham underneath the artichokes and the lemony mayonnaise sidekick.

ASPARAGUS WITH PROSCIUTTO AND LEMON SABAYON

1   bunch asparagus (about 1 pound), tough ends trimmed
    Coarse salt and freshly ground pepper

¼   cup heavy cream

4   large egg yolks
    Finely grated lemon zest, for garnish,
    plus 3 tablespoons fresh lemon juice

4   ounces thinly sliced prosciutto

1 Prepare an ice-water bath. Cook the asparagus in a large pot of boiling salted water until bright green and just tender, 3 to 4 minutes. Transfer asparagus to the ice bath to stop the cooking. When cool, transfer to paper towels to drain.

2 Whip cream until soft peaks form. In a heatproof bowl set over (not in) a pan of simmering water, combine egg yolks, lemon juice, and a pinch of salt. Whisk constantly, occasionally removing bowl from heat to prevent mixture from curdling, until thick enough to hold a trail from the whisk, about 4 minutes. Remove from heat and gently but thoroughly fold in whipped cream.

3 Divide asparagus among four serving plates and drape prosciutto over bottom portion of spears. Spoon lemon sauce over the tips. Garnish with lemon zest and season with pepper. Serve immediately.

SERVES 4

THE WEST

BACKSTORY

Cultivated since ancient times, asparagus was first grown in California in the 1850s, and the state now leads the United States in production. Paper-thin slices of just-salty-enough prosciutto pair well with the tender green spears, but what really makes this dish sensational is the addition of the smooth, airy custard called sabayon.

CITRUS VINAIGRETTE

2 tablespoons finely grated lemon zest (from 2 lemons), plus 3 tablespoons fresh lemon juice

2 tablespoons finely grated orange zest, plus 3 tablespoons fresh orange juice

2 tablespoons finely grated grapefruit zest, plus 3 tablespoons fresh grapefruit juice

1 shallot, minced (about 2 tablespoons)

1 tablespoon plus 1 teaspoon white-wine vinegar

Coarse salt

½ cup extra-virgin olive oil

In a small bowl, combine citrus zests and juices, shallot, vinegar, and ¼ teaspoon salt; let sit 15 minutes. Gradually add olive oil, whisking until combined and dressing is emulsified. Season with more salt if desired. (Vinaigrette can be refrigerated in an airtight container up to 1 day; whisk again before serving.)

MAKES 1½ CUPS

THE WEST

BACKSTORY

In large part, we have California to thank for the fact that the salad has evolved from "diet food" to a celebration of ultra-fresh produce. Our citrus vinaigrette (above)— made with a bright blend of orange, lemon, and grapefruit zests—is versatile (and a celebration of a major California crop). It's wonderful with soft green butterhead lettuces like Bibb and Boston (and topped with sliced avocado and orange, as shown above), and it also works well with bitter greens like chicory or endive. Green goddess dressing (opposite, right), created by the chef at San Francisco's Palace Hotel in the 1920s for a banquet honoring the lead actor of the film The Green Goddess, *is vibrant with herbs and creamy with mayonnaise and sour cream. It gives a salad enough substance to serve as a main course, and it is also lovely as a sauce for poached chicken and fish, or boiled shrimp. Buttermilk is the secret to ranch dressing (opposite, left), invented in the 1950s by the owner of the notable development in Hidden Valley Ranch, California, who eventually capitalized on its popularity by creating the well-known powdered mixes sold in every supermarket across the country. But it would be a shame to rely on those packets when from-scratch versions are so easy to make and taste so much fresher. You'll want to add all three of the dressings on this page to your repertoire, for salads that really shine.*

RANCH DRESSING

- ½ shallot, minced (about 1 tablespoon)
- 1 garlic clove, minced
- ½ cup buttermilk
- ½ cup mayonnaise
- Juice of 1 lemon
- 3 tablespoons finely chopped fresh flat-leaf parsley
- 3 tablespoons minced fresh chives
- Pinch of cayenne, plus more to taste
- Coarse salt

Stir together all ingredients until combined, seasoning with salt and more cayenne as desired. (Dressing can be refrigerated in an airtight container up to 1 day; stir again before serving.)

MAKES 2¼ CUPS

GREEN GODDESS DRESSING

- 1 small garlic clove, pressed in a garlic press or mashed to a paste
- 2 anchovy fillets, preferably salt-packed, rinsed and chopped
- 1 cup sour cream
- ½ cup mayonnaise
- 1 tablespoon white-wine vinegar
- Coarse salt
- Pinch of cayenne, plus more to taste
- ¼ cup finely chopped fresh flat-leaf parsley
- 3 tablespoons minced fresh chives
- 1½ teaspoons finely chopped fresh tarragon
- 2 tablespoons thinly sliced trimmed scallion

Pulse garlic and anchovies in a food processor to combine. Add sour cream, mayonnaise, vinegar, ½ teaspoon salt, and the cayenne; pulse a few times to combine. Add herbs and scallion and process until fully incorporated and mixture is pale green. Season with more salt and cayenne, as desired. (Dressing can be refrigerated in an airtight container up to 1 day; stir before serving.)

MAKES 1¼ CUPS

CRAB LOUIS

That crab Louis is a West Coast classic is about all that can be agreed on about the popular salad. At last count, the recipe was credited to at least three different chefs named Louis in three different cities—San Francisco, Portland, and Seattle—at the turn of the twentieth century. The dish is essentially cooked fresh crabmeat mixed with a creamy dressing flavored with onion, chili sauce, and cayenne. Use Dungeness crab if you can get it; otherwise, jumbo lump or peekytoe crabmeat works just fine. Although not as traditional, the salad can also be made with an equal amount of baby shrimp for similar delicious results. Whichever version you make, be sure to serve it the way they do out West: scooped onto a bed of crisp iceberg lettuce, with hard-cooked eggs, celery, and tomato served alongside.

2 large eggs
1 head iceberg lettuce, shredded
1½ pounds cooked crabmeat (about 6 cups)
1 tablespoon finely chopped fresh flat-leaf parsley
1 to 2 ripe tomatoes, cut into wedges
4 celery stalks
   Lemon wedges, for serving
   Louis Dressing (recipe follows)

1 Place eggs in a small saucepan; fill with enough cold water to cover by 1 inch. Bring to a boil over medium-high heat; turn off heat. Cover; let stand 11 minutes. Transfer to a small bowl and cover with cold water; let cool and peel. Slice eggs in half lengthwise.

2 Divide lettuce among four plates. Scoop crabmeat on top of lettuce and sprinkle with parsley. Arrange tomato wedges, celery stalks, egg halves, and lemon wedges around crab. Spoon dressing on top or serve on the side.

SERVES 4

LOUIS DRESSING

1 cup mayonnaise
3 tablespoons grated mild sweet onion, such as Walla Walla
¼ cup tomato-based chili sauce, such as Heinz
¼ cup sweet pickle relish, drained
1 tablespoon fresh lemon juice
   Pinch of cayenne
   Coarse salt

Stir together mayonnaise, onion, chili sauce, relish, lemon juice, and cayenne; season with salt. (Dressing can be refrigerated, covered, up to 2 days; stir before using.)

MAKES ABOUT 2 CUPS

COBB SALAD

2 boneless, skinless chicken breast halves

2 large eggs

3 slices turkey bacon

1 head romaine lettuce, stalk and tough outer leaves removed, sliced crosswise into ¼-inch-wide strips

1 cup finely chopped fresh watercress, tough stems discarded

3 ripe tomatoes, cut into ½-inch pieces

1 ripe but firm avocado, halved lengthwise, pitted, peeled, and cut into ½-inch pieces

¼ cup finely chopped fresh flat-leaf parsley

¼ cup snipped fresh chives

¼ cup crumbled blue cheese (1 ounce)

3 tablespoons red-wine vinegar

1 teaspoon Dijon mustard

Coarse salt and freshly ground pepper

1 tablespoon extra-virgin olive oil

1 Bring a medium saucepan of water to a boil. Add chicken and reduce heat to a bare simmer; poach until chicken is cooked through, about 15 minutes. Transfer to a plate and let cool. Cut into ½-inch cubes.

2 Place eggs in a small saucepan; fill with enough cold water to cover by 1 inch. Bring to a boil over medium-high heat; turn off heat. Cover; let stand 11 minutes. Transfer to a small bowl and cover with cold water; let cool and peel. Slice eggs in half lengthwise. Pass yolks through a fine sieve into a small bowl. Slice each egg white half into three wedges.

3 Cook bacon in a medium sauté pan over medium-low heat until browned and fat is rendered, turning once, about 3 minutes per side. Transfer to paper towels to drain. Let cool; coarsely chop.

4 Spread lettuce on a serving platter. Arrange chicken, eggs, bacon, watercress, tomatoes, avocado, and parsley and chives in separate rows atop lettuce.

5 In a small bowl, whisk together cheese, vinegar, and mustard; season with salt and pepper. Slowly whisk in the olive oil until mixture is emulsified. Drizzle vinaigrette over salad and serve immediately.

SERVES 4 TO 6

THE WEST

BACKSTORY

This salad is named for Robert Cobb of Hollywood's Brown Derby restaurant, who purportedly threw it together as a late-night meal in the 1930s, using leftovers from dinner service. Typically you'll find grilled chicken, bacon, lettuce, avocado, hard-cooked egg, tomato, and blue cheese; you can—and should—adapt the recipe to use what's in your own kitchen, in the spirit of the original. Beans are a nice addition or substitution, as are other types of cheeses. This leaner version of the original uses poached chicken and turkey bacon, and just a smidgen of blue cheese in the vinaigrette; watercress adds bright, peppery flavor. What makes Cobb salad recognizable is not so much the individual components as the way they are presented: Unlike other so-called chopped salads, which might be tossed with dressing before serving, each ingredient is arranged neatly in rows over the lettuce, and the dressing drizzled on top. The result? A salad that's easy to pull together yet special enough for company.

ENDIVE AND PEAR SALAD WITH OREGON BLUE CHEESE AND HAZELNUTS

THE WEST

BACKSTORY

If you could sum up the bounty of the Pacific Northwest in one dish, this winter salad might well be it. Crisp, pale leaves of endive—the mildest bitter green—provide a welcome counterpoint to sweet pears, rich blue cheese, and crunchy toasted hazelnuts. We used Caveman Blue cheese from the Rogue Creamery in Oregon, but any blue-veined cheese, such as Roquefort, Stilton, or Danablu, would be a worthy alternative. Toasting hazelnuts in the oven is the easiest way to loosen their tight, papery skins, and it also intensifies their flavor. A light olive oil works best with the assertive flavors in the salad.

1 cup hazelnuts

1 tablespoon sherry vinegar

1 tablespoon balsamic vinegar

Coarse salt and freshly ground pepper

2 tablespoons light olive oil

2 tablespoons hazelnut oil

6 large or 8 small heads Belgian endive

4 ripe pears, such as Anjou, Bartlett, or Comice

8 ounces blue cheese, such as Caveman Blue

1 Preheat oven to 350°F. Spread hazelnuts in a single layer on a rimmed baking sheet, and toast in the oven until skins begin to split, 10 to 12 minutes. Remove from oven. While still warm, rub nuts vigorously with a clean kitchen towel to remove skins. Discard skins, and return nuts to baking sheet. Return to oven, and continue toasting until they are fragrant and golden, about 1 minute more. Remove from oven, let cool, then coarsely chop.

2 Combine both vinegars in a bowl and season with salt and pepper. Whisking constantly, slowly pour in olive oil and then hazelnut oil in a steady stream until vinaigrette is thick and emulsified.

3 Discard large outer leaves of endive; separate interior leaves and cut each in half. Place in a large salad bowl. Quarter the pears, discarding core and seeds. Using a sharp knife, cut each quarter into ⅛-inch-thick slices, and add them to the bowl.

4 Drizzle endive and pears with half the vinaigrette and gently toss to coat. Add toasted hazelnuts, cheese, and the remaining vinaigrette; toss to combine. Season with salt and pepper; gently toss again. Serve immediately.

SERVES 8

FIG PIZZA

½ pound sliced pancetta, cut into ¾-inch pieces

2 onions, thinly sliced

2 teaspoons sugar

Freshly ground pepper

Pizza Dough (recipe follows)

All-purpose flour, for dusting

Yellow cornmeal, for sprinkling

12 ripe Mission figs, sliced lengthwise ¼ inch thick

½ cup Niçoise or Kalamata olives, pitted and coarsely chopped

½ cup fresh ricotta

1 Preheat oven to 400°F. Sauté pancetta in a medium skillet over medium heat, stirring occasionally, until golden brown and crisp and most of the fat is rendered, 15 to 20 minutes. Use a slotted spoon to remove the pancetta from the skillet and let drain on paper towels.

2 Pour off all but 3 tablespoons of fat from pan. Add onions, sprinkle with sugar, and season with pepper; raise heat to medium-high. Sauté onions, stirring occasionally, until golden brown and lightly caramelized, 15 to 20 minutes. Remove from heat.

3 Divide pizza dough into four equal pieces. On a lightly floured surface, roll out each portion into a 6- to 7-inch oval about ¼ inch thick. Sprinkle two heavy baking sheets with a generous amount of cornmeal. Arrange pizza dough on sheets. Pierce each round of dough several times with a fork, leaving a ¾-inch border.

4 Divide onions among rounds, and spread out over dough, leaving border uncovered. Arrange figs over onions, sprinkle with pancetta and olives, and dot with ricotta. Bake until crust is crisp and golden and topping is hot, 20 to 25 minutes. Remove from oven, season with pepper, and serve immediately.

MAKES 4 INDIVIDUAL PIZZAS

PIZZA DOUGH

1 package active dry yeast (1 scant tablespoon)

¾ cup warm water (100°F)

2 cups all-purpose flour, plus more for dusting

1 teaspoon salt

1 tablespoon plus 1½ teaspoons extra-virgin olive oil, plus more for bowl

1 Sprinkle yeast over the warm water; let stand until creamy, about 5 minutes. Stir well to combine.

2 Combine flour and salt in a food processor. Add yeast mixture and olive oil and process just until dough comes together. Turn out onto a lightly floured surface, knead for 1 minute, and shape into a ball.

3 Place dough in a well-oiled bowl, turn to coat with olive oil, and cover loosely with plastic wrap. Let rise in a warm place until dough has doubled in bulk, 45 to 60 minutes. Punch down dough and use immediately.

MAKES ENOUGH FOR 4 INDIVIDUAL PIZZAS

THE WEST

BACKSTORY

Figs—rich, jammy, and not too sweet—make a great topping for pizza. Grown in the Mediterranean for thousands of years, the fruit was planted early on at Spanish missions in California. Those "Mission figs" were the only ones cultivated there until the 1850s, when other varieties were brought from the East Coast and Europe. Any variety of fresh fig will work here, and is sure to produce a pizza that's a big hit; in fact, it just might become one of your signature dishes.

WHOLE-WHEAT SPAGHETTI WITH MEYER LEMON, ARUGULA, AND PISTACHIOS

½ cup shelled unsalted pistachios
   Sea salt or coarse salt and freshly ground pepper
½ pound whole-wheat spaghetti
 1 small shallot, cut into eighths
 1 Meyer lemon, cut into eighths and seeded
 3 tablespoons extra-virgin olive oil
 2 cups packed baby arugula

1 Preheat oven to 375°F. Spread pistachios on a rimmed baking sheet. Toast in oven until fragrant, tossing occasionally, about 8 minutes. Transfer pistachios to a plate to cool.

2 Bring a pot of water to a boil; add salt. Cook pasta until al dente according to package instructions. Reserve ½ cup cooking water, and drain pasta.

3 While pasta is cooking, pulse pistachios and shallot in a food processor until finely chopped. Transfer to a large bowl. Without cleaning processor bowl, add lemon, and pulse to finely chop. Add to pistachios and shallot; stir to combine. Stir in 2 tablespoons olive oil.

4 Toss pasta with pistachio mixture, adding just enough reserved cooking water to form a sauce that coats pasta. Stir in arugula and remaining tablespoon olive oil; season with salt and pepper. Serve immediately.

SERVES 4

THE WEST

BACKSTORY

A round, smooth-skinned Meyer lemon—tangy yet sweeter than a regular lemon—gives this light, quintessentially Californian dish a certain sassy quality. The combination of earthy whole-wheat pasta and crunchy toasted pistachios makes a wonderfully satisfying first course during the winter, when Meyer lemons are available. If possible, use a fragrant extra-virgin olive oil (from California, if you like) for the nut "pesto" and for tossing. Or to reinforce the flavor, use an olive oil that has been cold-pressed with citrus.

CIOPPINO

THE WEST

BACKSTORY

A pot of cioppino is the sort of thing Bay Area fishermen used to simmer on their boats as they headed back to the harbor after a long day's work. After all, the brothy stew was created by Italian and Portuguese immigrants as a way to make the most of the catch of the day, and it remains a restaurant favorite in the city's North Beach neighborhood. There are many versions of cioppino, but they all heed to a basic formula: Make a tomato-based broth flavored with onion and garlic and usually a bit of wine, and then stir in the freshest seafood you can find. This recipe calls for clams, crab legs, shrimp, and halibut, but nearly any type of seafood can be used, including mussels, lobster, and any firm white fish, such as grouper, sea bass, or red snapper. Just be sure to add each type of seafood at different times so it will be cooked to the proper degree— and no further—before the stew is ready for serving. Here, toasted baguette slices spread with roasted garlic and topped with shaved parmesan are served alongside.

¼ cup extra-virgin olive oil

1 large onion, coarsely chopped

4 garlic cloves, minced

2½ teaspoons fresh thyme leaves

2 teaspoons dried oregano

½ teaspoon crushed red-pepper flakes

1 dried bay leaf

1 can (28 ounces) whole peeled tomatoes, crushed, juice reserved

1¼ cups dry white wine

1¼ cups water

1 cup bottled clam juice

2 pounds shell-on King crab legs (or Dungeness crab legs), cut into 2-inch pieces (optional)

24 littleneck clams, scrubbed

1 pound halibut or other firm white-flesh fish, cut into bite-size pieces

Coarse salt and freshly ground pepper

1¼ pounds large shrimp, peeled and deveined, tails left on if desired

½ cup coarsely chopped fresh flat-leaf parsley, plus more for garnish

1 Heat olive oil in a large stockpot over medium. Cook onion and garlic until onion is translucent, stirring frequently, 3 to 4 minutes. Stir in thyme, oregano, red-pepper flakes, and bay leaf.

2 Add crushed tomatoes and their juice, wine, the water, and clam juice; bring to a simmer. Add crab legs, if using, and clams. Simmer, covered, until crab shells turn bright pink and clams are open, about 10 minutes.

3 Season halibut with salt and pepper. Add to stockpot along with shrimp. Cover and simmer gently until fish and shrimp are opaque throughout, 2 to 3 minutes. Remove from heat. Discard bay leaf and any unopened clams. Stir in parsley and season with salt and pepper. Divide among bowls and serve immediately, garnished with more parsley.

SERVES 6 TO 8

MARINATED TOFU WITH COLD PEANUT NOODLES

Coarse salt

1 package (8 ounces) soba or other thin Asian noodles

Coconut Peanut Sauce (recipe follows)

¼ cup tamari soy sauce

¼ cup mirin (Japanese cooking wine)

2 tablespoons grated peeled fresh ginger

2 packages (12.3 ounces each) firm silken tofu

12 radishes, trimmed and sliced paper-thin

8 ounces jícama, peeled and cut into 1-inch-long matchsticks

Chopped peanuts, for garnish

Pea shoots or sprouts, for garnish

1 Bring a large pot of water to a boil and add salt. Cook soba noodles until just tender according to package instructions. Drain in a large colander; rinse with cold water until completely cool, then drain again. Transfer noodles to a large bowl; add peanut sauce, tossing to coat.

2 Combine soy sauce, mirin, and ginger in a bowl. Cut tofu into 8 equal pieces; place one piece on each plate. Drizzle with soy mixture. Divide noodles among plates; top with radishes, jícama, and pea shoots. Serve immediately.

SERVES 8

COCONUT PEANUT SAUCE

¼ cup canned coconut milk (well shaken)

2 tablespoons smooth peanut butter

1 tablespoon tamari soy sauce

1 tablespoon mirin (Japanese cooking wine)

½ inch piece fresh ginger, peeled and coarsely chopped

1½ teaspoons dark-brown sugar

Blend all ingredients in a food processor or blender until smooth. (Sauce can be stored in an airtight container in the refrigerator up to 5 days; stir before using.)

MAKES ABOUT ½ CUP

THE WEST

BACKSTORY

Although tofu—soybean curd—was first made in China more than 2,000 years ago, it's now eaten throughout Asia, Southeast Asia, and many other parts of the world. In the United States, we call it by its Japanese name because immigrants from Japan first popularized it here. Today, artisanal tofu makers in California are among those who have turned the food from a predictable joke into what Asians have known virtually forever: It sops up flavors like the proverbial sponge. In this treatment, the silky marinated tofu and Japanese soba noodles get an appealing contrast in texture from radish slices and crunchy matchsticks of jícama. This is a fabulous supper for a sultry evening.

GRILLED FISH TACOS

THE WEST

BACKSTORY

There are places where tourists insist on visiting a street vendor or some hole-in-the-wall for a taste of the local specialty. Philadelphia has its cheesesteaks, for example, and New Orleans its po'boys. In sun-drenched Baja California, you can buy a taco de pescado—*the day's catch, batter-fried, wrapped in a fresh corn tortilla and topped with your choice of salsas and chopped vegetables. At home, skip the deep-frying and try your fish grilled instead, then topped with a zesty slaw made with green cabbage, radishes, and scallions. Ground dried chipotle chile can be purchased at many supermarkets and from online retailers. Well-chilled Mexican beer, with lime wedges on the side, is just the right refresher.*

1   garlic clove, minced

    Coarse salt

¼   cup finely chopped cilantro, plus whole leaves for serving

1   teaspoon ground dried chipotle chile

1   teaspoon dried oregano, preferably Mexican

2   limes, zested and juiced, plus lime wedges for serving

1   teaspoon extra-virgin olive oil

4   skin-on red snapper fillets (about 5 ounces each)

8   radishes, trimmed and julienned

¼   head green cabbage, finely shredded (about 2 cups)

3   scallions, trimmed and julienned

1   ripe avocado, halved lengthwise, pitted, and peeled

4   flour tortillas (6-inch)

1 Mash garlic and 1 teaspoon salt into a fine paste using a mortar and pestle (or use the side of a chef's knife on a cutting board) and transfer to a bowl. Stir in cilantro, ground chipotle, oregano, lime zest, and olive oil. Cut two slashes in the skin of each fish fillet. Turn skin side down and rub half the spice mixture onto fish.

2 Heat grill to medium-high. (If you are using a charcoal grill, coals are ready when you can hold your hand 5 inches above grates for just 3 to 4 seconds.) Place fish, skin side up, on grill; cook until opaque throughout, about 4 minutes per side, flipping once.

3 Remove skin from fish and discard. Flake fish into large pieces, discarding any bones. Combine fish with remaining spice mixture and toss with 2 teaspoons lime juice.

4 Toss together radishes, cabbage, and scallions in a bowl. Mash avocado in another bowl; stir in 1 tablespoon lime juice.

5 Toast tortillas on the grill to soften, 5 to 10 seconds per side, turning with tongs. (Or heat them one at a time in a dry skillet over medium-high heat.)

6 Dividing evenly, spread mashed avocado onto each tortilla, then top with fish and slaw. Fold tortillas over filling, garnish with cilantro leaves, and serve with lime wedges.

SERVES 4

FRIED RICE WITH SHRIMP AND SNOW PEAS

¼ cup plus 1 teaspoon peanut oil

2 large eggs, lightly beaten

12 large shrimp (about 12 ounces), peeled and deveined, tails on
Coarse salt and freshly ground pepper

3 tablespoons finely chopped trimmed lemongrass (yellow and pale green parts only)

4 large garlic cloves, minced

2 tablespoons minced peeled fresh ginger (from one 2-inch piece)

½ teaspoon finely chopped Thai chile

12 shiitake mushrooms, stemmed, cleaned, and sliced ½ inch thick (1½ cups)

1 cup snow peas, trimmed

4 cups day-old cooked long-grain rice, preferably jasmine (from 1⅓ cups dry)

3 tablespoons soy sauce

5 scallions, white and pale green parts only, sliced crosswise (⅓ cup), plus more, thinly sliced, for garnish
Lime wedges, for serving

1 Heat 1 teaspoon oil in a wok or large skillet over medium-high; swirl to coat. Add eggs and cook until softly scrambled, stirring constantly, about 30 seconds; transfer to a plate.

2 Season shrimp with salt and pepper. Add 1 tablespoon oil to wok and heat until shimmering. Cook shrimp, tossing occasionally, just until seared on both sides, 1 to 2 minutes; transfer to a plate.

3 Add remaining 3 tablespoons oil, the lemongrass, garlic, ginger, and chile to wok. Cook, tossing, 1 minute. Add mushrooms and cook 2 minutes. Add shrimp; cook until opaque throughout, 1 to 2 minutes. Add peas; cook until bright green but still crisp, about 1 minute. Stir in rice, and cook until heated through, then stir in soy sauce to coat. Toss in scrambled eggs, breaking up any large clumps, and scallions. Season with salt and pepper. Garnish with scallions and serve with lime wedges.

SERVES 6 TO 8

TRI-TIP STEAKS

3 tri-tip sirloin steaks (each 1½ to 2 pounds and 1½ inches thick)

2 cups strongly brewed coffee

1 cup (8 fluid ounces) bourbon

½ cup extra-virgin olive oil

½ cup packed light-brown sugar

2 onions, coarsely chopped

8 garlic cloves, coarsely chopped

6 fresh bay leaves, plus more for garnish, or 3 dried bay leaves

2 fresh Anaheim chiles or banana peppers, cut into ¼-inch rings, plus more for garnish

2 dried chile peppers, crumbled, or ½ teaspoon crushed red-pepper flakes

2 tablespoons coarsely chopped fresh oregano, plus sprigs for garnish

Coarse salt and freshly ground pepper

Chimichurri, for serving (recipe follows)

Roasted Garlic Aïoli, for serving (recipe follows)

1 Arrange steaks in a single layer in a shallow nonreactive dish. Whisk together coffee, bourbon, olive oil, brown sugar, onions, garlic, bay leaves, fresh and dried chiles, and chopped oregano; season with salt and pepper. Pour over steaks. Cover and marinate in the refrigerator, flipping occasionally, at least 6 hours or up to 2 days.

2 Set up grill for direct and indirect heat. Heat grill to medium-high. (If using a charcoal grill, coals are ready when you can hold your hand 5 inches above grates for just 3 to 4 seconds.) Transfer steaks to plates and pat dry; reserve marinade. Season steaks on both sides with salt and pepper. Cook over direct heat (hotter part of grill) until browned, about 4 minutes per side; move to indirect heat (cooler part of grill) and cook until a meat thermometer registers 135°F for medium-rare, about 5 minutes more. Transfer to a platter, cover, and let rest 10 to 15 minutes.

3 Bring the marinade to a boil in a saucepan; let it boil for 5 minutes. Season steaks with more salt and pepper. Pour marinade over steaks, or serve on the side along with chimichurri and aïoli. Garnish with fresh bay leaves, fresh chiles, and oregano sprigs.

SERVES 10 TO 12

BACKSTORY

Santa Maria, California, is renowned for tri-tip—a deeply flavorful boneless cut of beef from the bottom sirloin—that is grilled over fragrant red oak from the Central Coast. (Other cuts of beef, such as sirloin steaks or New York strip steaks, will work, too.) Here, we've changed things a bit by first marinating the meat in a blend of coffee, bourbon, brown sugar, and fresh and dried chiles, then serving the grilled steak with two sauces that may be untraditional but sure are sensational. Chimichurri is a thick sauce, redolent of fresh green herbs, typically served with steaks of the renowned grass-fed cattle of Argentina. A creamy aïoli from the South of France is also robust and rich in flavor, yet in a different way. Making both sauces ensures that everyone can try a little of this, a little of that. Round out the meal with a platter of summer vegetables and mushrooms roasted over the same coals as the steak.

CHIMICHURRI

- 2 jalapeño chiles
- 2 tablespoons chopped fresh oregano
- 2 tablespoons chopped fresh flat-leaf parsley
- 2 tablespoons chopped fresh mint
- 3 garlic cloves
- 2 teaspoons sweet paprika
- Coarse salt and freshly ground pepper
- ¾ cup extra-virgin olive oil
- 2 teaspoons red-wine vinegar

1 Roast jalapeños directly over the flame of a gas-stove burner on high heat or on a hot grill, turning with tongs, until blistered. Let cool, then rub off skins with paper towels. Coarsely chop chiles (first remove ribs and seeds if less heat is desired).

2 Mash together herbs, garlic, paprika, and 1 teaspoon salt with a mortar and pestle or in a food processor. Heat olive oil over medium-low heat. Stir in herb mixture, jalapeños, and vinegar; season with pepper. Cook until just heated through. Season with more salt, if desired. (Sauce can be refrigerated in an airtight container up to 1 week; let cool completely before storing, and reheat over low before serving.)

MAKES ABOUT 1 CUP

ROASTED GARLIC AÏOLI

- 1 small head garlic
- 2 cups extra-virgin olive oil, plus more for drizzling
- 4 large egg yolks, room temperature
- ¾ teaspoon coarse salt
- 2 tablespoons plus 2 teaspoons fresh lemon juice
- 2 tablespoons heavy cream

1 Preheat oven to 375°F. Place garlic on a piece of parchment and drizzle generously with olive oil. Wrap in parchment, then in foil. Roast until tender, about 1 hour. When cool enough to handle, squeeze cloves from skins.

2 Process garlic, egg yolks, and salt in a food processor until combined. With machine running, gradually add olive oil, drop by drop at first and then in a slow, steady stream, until emulsified. Stir in lemon juice and cream. (Aïoli can be refrigerated in an airtight container up to 2 days; stir before serving.)

MAKES ABOUT 2 CUPS

Note The egg yolks in this recipe are not cooked. It should not be prepared for pregnant women, babies, young children, the elderly, or anyone whose health is compromised.

SALMON

The winding, glacier-fed Copper River travels nearly 300 miles across the landscape of southeastern Alaska before reaching the Gulf of Alaska and, beyond it, the Pacific Ocean. Though its waters are frigid, this great river is part of one of the richest watersheds in the nation, where a tremendous variety of wildlife resides. And at its mouth, generations of fishermen have made their living harvesting one of the state's most precious natural resources: wild salmon.

Native Alaskans have revered the buttery, red flesh of wild salmon for millennia, and do not let even the smallest morsel go to waste. They prize the king salmon above all, but sockeye and coho also abound here; the three species use the freshwaters of the Copper River and its tributaries as breeding ground. The fish live most of their lives in the ocean, returning to freshwater only to spawn (and then, in a sad if inevitable natural cycle, to die). In order to have the energy required to fight their way upriver, against the current, they must first build up their fat reserves in the ocean. By the time the fish are preparing to leave the ocean and travel the long Copper River, they have some of the highest fat content anywhere—and that's what contributes to their incredible flavor.

Those reserves are also home to rich stores of omega-3 fatty acids (and other essential nutrients), so prized for promoting heart health and healthy aging. Its nourishing properties and excellent flavor have made salmon one of the most popular fish in the world. But today, the supply of wild salmon is being depleted.

Fortunately, the state of Alaska has the sustainability of salmon written into its constitution, so every aspect of fishing for it is closely regulated—from who can fish, when and where, to the size of nets used for the catch. These efforts are preserving this vibrant wild food source, though perhaps only for the time being. However you're enjoying wild salmon—smoked and served on a cracker, stirred into a chowder, roasted on a cedar plank—it's wise to think of it as the delicacy it is, and savor every bite.

SOY-SESAME SALMON Heat broiler. Whisk together ¼ cup each soy sauce, honey, and fresh orange juice with ½ teaspoon toasted sesame oil and 1 piece (1 inch) peeled fresh ginger, thinly sliced, in a glass baking dish. Add 4 skin-on wild salmon fillets (4 ounces each), skin side up. Let marinate 15 minutes at room temperature. Transfer salmon to a rimmed baking sheet, skin side down; reserve marinade. Broil salmon until flesh is slightly firm to the touch, 5 to 6 minutes. Meanwhile, bring marinade to a boil in a small saucepan. Cook until reduced by half, about 3 minutes. Drizzle glaze over salmon and serve, with steamed baby bok choy, and udon noodles tossed with thinly sliced cucumber and red onion. **SERVERS 4**

CEDAR PLANK-ROASTED SALMON

BACKSTORY

Some twenty years ago, Alaskan king salmon from the Copper River and the Pacific was still relatively unknown outside of the region; today, the world vies for the fish, caught wild and only available in season. The health benefits of eating wild-caught salmon are well documented; the flavor of the fish is almost indescribably rich, smooth, and sweet. One of the best ways to enjoy the natural nuance of this treasure is to cook it in the style of the Native Americans of the Northwest: on a cedar plank, which imparts some of its aroma and the subtlest of smoky flavors to the fish.

⅓ cup coarse sea salt

1 bunch fresh thyme

1 bunch fresh rosemary

1 whole side of salmon (3 pounds), skin left on, boned and trimmed of excess fat

1 tablespoon freshly ground pepper

Lemon wedges, for serving

1 Heat grill to high (see note below; if using a charcoal grill, the coals are ready when you can hold your hand about 4 inches above the grill for only 2 to 3 seconds). Prepare cedar plank by toasting it over hot coals until it begins to blacken slightly on one side; remove from heat and let cool completely.

2 Place board, toasted side up, with both ends resting on supports. Sprinkle with one-third salt and a few sprigs each thyme and rosemary. Place salmon on plank, skin side down. About 2 inches from each end, tap one nail horizontally into side of plank, leaving nail head protruding for the wire. Season salmon with remaining salt and the pepper; arrange remaining herbs across the top.

3 Starting at the larger end of fish, twist wire around the nail several times to secure. Wrap wire entirely around salmon and plank at 2-inch intervals, making sure that it is tight enough to hold fish in place without slicing through the tender flesh. When you reach the other end of the plank, twist the wire several times around other nail, and trim any excess wire with wire cutters.

4 Arrange plank supports near the fire and rest the plank, fish side down, on top, 15 to 20 inches above the coals. Cook until thicker part of fish is firm to the touch, 25 to 35 minutes, depending on the heat of the fire, the distance from the heat during cooking, and the thickness of the fish. Turn over the plank several times during cooking to check for doneness.

5 Remove plank from heat and let cool slightly. Remove wire and herbs and discard. Cut fish on the diagonal, or flake the flesh with a fork into large pieces, and serve it directly from the plank, with lemon wedges.

Using the Grill Stack fire-resistant supports, such as bricks, stones, or cinder blocks, on each side of a charcoal or gas grill so that the cedar plank will rest at least 15 inches above the hot coals. The longer the salmon cooks, the more pronounced the wood-roasted flavor, so avoid cooking it too close to the heat. If at any time the fish or plank begins to smolder, spritz it with water. You will need an untreated cedar plank that is at least 8 by 5 inches and 1 inch thick; two fire-resistant supports; two small nails or screws; and at least 15 feet of picture wire.

SERVES 8 TO 10

ROASTED CHICKEN WITH GARLIC AND LEMON

1 whole chicken (3 to 4 pounds)
    Roasted Garlic Heads (recipe follows)
½ cup (1 stick) unsalted butter, softened and cut into pieces
    Coarse salt and freshly ground pepper
8 sprigs flat-leaf parsley
4 sprigs rosemary, plus more for garnish
2 lemons, halved

1 Let chicken stand at room temperature 30 minutes. Squeeze 10 roasted garlic cloves from their skins into a small bowl. Add the butter and stir together until well blended and smooth.

2 Preheat oven to 350°F. Remove and discard giblets and any excess fat from chicken cavity. Rinse chicken inside and out with cold water; pat dry with paper towels. Tuck wing tips under body. Season cavity with salt and pepper; stuff with parsley, rosemary, and 2 lemon halves. Using your hands, gently separate skin from chicken breast; spread garlic butter over entire surface of chicken and under skin. Generously season with salt and pepper. Tie legs together with kitchen twine. Transfer chicken to a roasting pan. Arrange remaining 2 lemon halves around bird.

3 Roast chicken, basting occasionally with accumulated pan juices, until skin is crisp and deep golden brown and an instant-read thermometer inserted into thickest part of thigh registers 165°F, about 1 hour.

4 Transfer chicken and lemon halves to a platter. Let chicken stand 10 to 15 minutes. Garnish with rosemary sprigs and roasted garlic heads.

SERVES 4

ROASTED GARLIC HEADS

4 heads garlic, papery outer skins discarded
4 sprigs thyme
2 tablespoons extra-virgin olive oil

Preheat oven to 425°F. Place garlic heads on a piece of parchment; arrange thyme on top. Drizzle with olive oil. Wrap parchment to seal, then wrap in foil. Roast garlic until tender and golden, about 1 hour.

MAKES 4 HEADS

THE WEST

BACKSTORY

Most of our country's garlic is grown in the California's Central Valley, and we know a good thing when we see it— consumption has increased fourfold in the past generation. Whole roasted garlic bulbs are simultaneously robust and mellow. You will want to slip the sweet, soft cloves out of their skins, blend them with butter, and then slather the result over and under the skin of a chicken before roasting. Or simply smear the garlic cloves on forkfuls of the juicy bird, crisp and browned from the oven, and on pieces of crusty bread served alongside.

PIKE PLACE FISH AND CHIPS

2 large eggs

1 cup lager beer

1½ cups cake flour (not self-rising)

1 tablespoon coarse salt

Neutral-tasting oil, such as safflower, for frying

8 pieces (each 3 to 5 ounces and 3 by 4 inches) skinless firm white fish, such as halibut or cod

1 Whisk eggs in a small bowl, then gradually whisk in the beer. In another bowl, whisk together cake flour and salt; slowly whisk in egg mixture, just until the batter is thick and creamy (do not overmix; batter should be slightly lumpy like pancake batter). Cover and refrigerate at least 20 minutes or up to 2 hours.

2 Preheat oven to 200°F, and line a baking sheet with a double layer of paper towels. Pour 3 inches of oil into a heavy, large (6-quart) pot and heat over medium until a deep-fry thermometer registers 375°F.

3 Working in batches, dip fish in the batter to completely coat and allow excess to drip back into the bowl. Use tongs to carefully lower each fish piece into the hot oil; fry until the crust is deep golden brown, turning once or twice, about 7 minutes. Adjust the heat as needed so oil remains between 350°F and 375°F (add more room-temperature oil, if necessary, to cool the oil quickly). Use a mesh spider or slotted spoon to transfer fish to prepared baking sheet to drain; season with salt and keep warm in the oven while frying remaining fish. After each batch is removed, remove any loose bits from oil so they don't burn and stick to fish, and return oil to the proper temperature before adding next batch. Serve fish warm.

SERVES 4

CHIPS

3 Yukon Gold potatoes, cut into ¼-inch-thick rounds

4 cups neutral-tasting oil, such as safflower

Coarse salt

1 Place potatoes in a large bowl and cover with cold water. Refrigerate 8 hours. Drain, rinse, and pat dry.

2 Preheat oven to 200°F. Heat oil in a large pot over medium until a deep-fry thermometer registers 310°F. Line two baking sheets with paper towels. Carefully add potatoes to oil in small batches. Cook 3 to 4 minutes, turning occasionally. (They will not color much.) Using a mesh spider or a slotted spoon, transfer fries to prepared baking sheets to drain. Let cool.

3 Increase heat so oil reaches 350°F. Fry potatoes again in small batches until golden brown, 3 to 4 minutes. Transfer chips to baking sheets (replace paper towels) and season with salt. Keep warm in the oven while frying remaining potatoes.

SERVES 4

THE WEST

BACKSTORY

Throughout the Pacific Northwest, in all types of eateries, fresh fish takes center stage, and nowhere is this more obvious than in the many seafood shacks that offer a local specialty: deep-fried, beer-battered fish with a side of "chips," in the British tradition. Just about every type of local catch—particularly halibut, but also Pacific cod, salmon, prawns, and crab—is fair game for the fryer. Using cake flour instead of all-purpose flour produces a lighter, more delicate crust. Enjoy this version (named for the famous fish market) Seattle-style, with a cup of coleslaw (page 50) and a frosty glass of microbrewed beer.

VENISON CHILI

  4 ounces slab bacon, cut into ¼-inch dice

  3 pounds venison stew meat (from shoulder),
     cut into ¾-inch pieces

  2 teaspoons cumin seeds

  1 tablespoon neutral-tasting oil, such as safflower

  1 large onion, coarsely chopped

  6 garlic cloves, coarsely chopped

  1 celery stalk, cut into ¼-inch dice

  2 tablespoons tomato paste

1½ teaspoons dried oregano

1¼ teaspoons chili powder

  1 teaspoon crushed red-pepper flakes

     Coarse salt and freshly ground pepper

  5 cups hot water, or more as needed

  5 cups cooked (or canned) pinto or kidney beans,
     or a combination

1 Cook bacon in a large Dutch oven or heavy pot over medium heat, stirring occasionally, until fat has rendered and bacon is cooked but not crisp, 8 to 10 minutes. Use a slotted spoon to remove bacon from pot and place on a plate.

2 Raise heat to medium-high. Working in three batches, cook venison in a single layer until browned, stirring occasionally, about 3 minutes per batch. Remove venison with a slotted spoon and place on a plate, and wait until fat is hot again between batches.

3 Add cumin seeds to pot and cook, stirring, until fragrant, about 30 seconds. Reduce heat to medium and add oil. Cook onion, garlic, and celery, stirring occasionally, until softened and golden brown, about 5 minutes.

4 Stir in tomato paste and return bacon and venison to pot. Add oregano, chili powder, and red-pepper flakes; season with salt and pepper and stir in the hot water (add more water if needed to cover by 1 inch). Raise heat to medium-high and bring to a boil; stir and reduce heat to a gentle simmer. Cover and cook 1½ hours, stirring occasionally. Add beans and continue cooking until venison is tender and chili is thick and rich, 30 to 45 minutes more. Season with more salt and pepper and serve hot.

SERVES 8

BACKSTORY

Venison may be lean and low in fat, but it's also rich in flavor and tender in texture, making it a natural for chili. One spoonful will conjure a log cabin somewhere in the Rockies, a cozy flannel shirt, and a dog snoozing in front of a crackling fire. Top each generous serving with chopped onion and grated cheese, as desired.

OYSTERS

America bumps headlong into the ocean in western Marin County, where hills tumble recklessly into the waves. The Pacific spills inland, too, filling lagoons and bays with marine creatures, blanketing valleys with milk-white fog and flavoring the air with seaweed and salt. Nothing captures this essence as perfectly as an oyster on the half shell from Tomales Bay, a marine sanctuary and home to some of the West's most renowned oyster harvesters. It lies in the swath of a freshwater stream, which lowers the salinity of the water by a mere few parts per million, just enough to make the oysters sweeter. In fact, among the area's most popular oyster is the Hog Island Sweetwater, named after the stream and an island in the bay.

Each oyster "variety" is named after the place where it is harvested because it takes on the flavor characteristics—sweet, briny, metallic, buttery—of the water and of the plankton the oysters feed on. But every one of those oyster varieties come from just five species cultivated in North America: Kumamoto, Pacific, Olympia, European Flat, and Eastern. A connoisseur can detect variations even between oysters from the same region, such as Skookums, from an inlet in southern Puget Sound, and Quilcenes, from a bay farther north.

Thanks to advances in refrigerated shipping, oysters are no longer an indulgence exclusive to coastal dwellers. They can be harvested and sold fresh year-round (and there's no need to limit eating them to months with an *r* in their name, as once believed). Buy them the day you plan to eat them, then serve them raw on the half shell with nothing more than a squeeze of lemon (except maybe a glass of Champagne), or with the sauces at right.

To shuck an oyster, hold it over a bowl with the flat side up and the tapered hinge end pointing toward you. Wearing a work glove on the hand gripping the oyster, ease the tip of an oyster knife into the hinge and apply levering pressure to loosen it. Slide the knife around the edge of the oyster to separate the shell and pry the halves apart. Slip the knife under the flesh to detach it from the bottom shell. As you follow these steps, don't let the oyster's precious liquid, called its liquor, spill; it's as much a part of the wonderful eating experience as the oyster itself.

OYSTERS ON THE HALF SHELL WITH TWO SAUCES Shuck oysters as described (left), then serve in shells with one or both of the following sauces. **Cocktail Sauce:** Mash 1 garlic clove with ¼ teaspoon coarse salt. Coarsely purée 2 chopped tomatoes in a food processor. Drain purée in a fine sieve for 10 minutes, reserving liquid. Return tomatoes to food processor. Add 4½ teaspoons prepared horseradish, ½ teaspoon grated lemon zest, 4 teaspoons lemon juice, 1 teaspoon coarse salt, 1¼ teaspoons Worcestershire sauce, 1½ teaspoons hot sauce, and the garlic paste. Pulse to combine. Add 2 tablespoons extra-virgin olive oil and process until combined. Add up to ¼ cup reserved liquid to adjust to desired consistency. Chill, covered, up to 1 day. **Mignonette Sauce:** Stir together 1 finely chopped shallot, 1½ teaspoons coarsely ground pepper, ½ cup sherry vinegar, and ½ cup champagne or white-wine vinegar. Let stand 20 minutes before serving. **EACH MAKES ABOUT 1 CUP**

HANGTOWN FRY

THE WEST

BACKSTORY

The opulence of oysters and the familiar smoky goodness of bacon come together in this extravagant omelet. The odd name comes from the city where it was created (now known as Placerville) during the going-for-broke days of the California Gold Rush. It didn't take long before the omelet appeared on menus all over San Francisco, where oysters were in plentiful supply. For authenticity, you can seek out West Coast varieties, such as Kumamoto, Olympia, and Pacific; otherwise, any fresh oysters will do.

 6 slices thick-cut bacon
 4 large eggs
 2 tablespoons heavy cream
 1 teaspoon coarsely chopped fresh flat-leaf parsley
    Coarse salt and freshly ground pepper
 ¼ cup all-purpose flour
12 fresh oysters, shucked
 2 tablespoons unsalted butter

1 Heat broiler with rack 8 inches from heat source. Cook bacon in a large skillet over medium heat until crisp, flipping once, about 8 minutes. Drain on paper towels. Cover to keep warm.

2 Meanwhile, in a bowl, whisk together eggs, cream, and parsley; season with salt and pepper. In another bowl, combine flour and a pinch each of salt and pepper. Dredge oysters in flour mixture, shake off excess, and transfer to a plate.

3 Heat 1 tablespoon butter in an 8-inch ovenproof skillet over medium-high until foamy. Add half the oysters and cook, flipping once, until golden, about 3 minutes. Reduce heat to medium, and pour half the egg mixture over oysters in skillet. Cook until set on bottom, about 1 minute. Transfer to broiler and broil until top and center are just set, 30 seconds to 1 minute. Slide omelet onto a plate and cover to keep warm. Wipe skillet clean and repeat with remaining oysters and egg mixture. To serve, top each omelet with 3 bacon slices.

SERVES 2

HUCKLEBERRY MUFFINS

6 tablespoons unsalted butter, melted, plus more for tin

2 cups all-purpose flour

⅔ cup sugar

1 teaspoon baking powder

½ teaspoon baking soda

1¼ teaspoons coarse salt

2 large eggs, lightly beaten

1 cup sour cream

¼ cup milk

1 cup fresh or frozen wild huckleberries

1 Preheat oven to 375°F. Lightly butter a 12-cup standard muffin tin. Whisk together 1¾ cups flour, the sugar, baking powder, baking soda, and salt. In a separate bowl, whisk together eggs, butter, sour cream, and milk; stir into flour mixture just until combined.

2 Toss huckleberries with remaining ¼ cup flour, then fold into batter. Divide among prepared cups, filling each about three-fourths full. Bake until tops are golden and a tester inserted in center of a muffin comes out clean, 20 to 22 minutes. Let cool in tin 10 minutes before turning out onto a wire rack to cool completely. (Muffins can be stored in an airtight container at room temperature up to 4 days.)

MAKES 1 DOZEN

THE WEST

BACKSTORY

The small, sweet huckleberries foraged from the wild, mountainous parts of Montana and Wyoming (as well as in neighboring Idaho, where it is the state fruit) are a true seasonal delicacy in the late summer and early fall. They give warm muffins an appealing, tart flavor that is completely irresistible. The muffin recipe itself is highly versatile; feel free to swap in other berries, such as blueberries, raspberries, or cranberries, or other fruit, including cut-up peaches or plums.

MINIATURE BLACKBERRY PIES

1½ pounds (5 cups) fresh blackberries
¾ cup sugar, plus more for sprinkling
2 tablespoons cornstarch
⅛ teaspoon salt
All-purpose flour, for dusting
Tender Pie Dough (page 412)
2 tablespoons unsalted butter, cut into pieces
1 large egg yolk
1 tablespoon heavy cream

1 Preheat oven to 425°F. In a large bowl, gently toss blackberries with sugar, cornstarch, and salt.

2 On a lightly floured surface, roll out 1 disk of dough to about ⅛ inch thick. Using a 5½-inch biscuit cutter, cut out six rounds. Drape each round over a 4-inch fluted tart pan with a removable bottom and press dough into bottom and up sides of pan. Roll out remaining disk of dough to a ⅛-inch thickness. Cut out six more 5½-inch rounds.

3 Fill each tart pan with ¾ cup blackberry mixture, mounding berries in the center. Dot berries with butter. Center one of the remaining dough rounds on top of a tart pan. Gently press top and bottom edges of dough together to seal and then pinch sealed edges. Repeat with remaining rounds. Transfer pies to a rimmed baking sheet and freeze or refrigerate until firm, 15 to 20 minutes.

4 Lightly whisk together yolk and heavy cream. Using a pastry brush, coat the top of each pie with egg wash and sprinkle with sugar. Cut four vent holes in the top of each.

5 Bake 30 minutes. Rotate baking sheet, and reduce oven to 375°F. Continue baking until filling is bubbling and crust is deep golden brown, about 30 minutes. Tent with foil if crust is browning too quickly. Transfer tart pans to wire racks and let cool 30 minutes. Remove pies from pans and let cool completely on racks.

MAKES 6

WASHINGTON WALNUT PIE

All-purpose flour, for dusting
Tender Pie Dough (page 412; 1 disk reserved for another use)
4 large eggs
1 cup sugar
1 cup light corn syrup
1 teaspoon pure vanilla extract
½ teaspoon salt
1¼ cups chopped toasted walnuts (page 408) (about 4 ounces)

1 Preheat oven to 325°F. On a lightly floured surface, roll out disk of dough to an 11-inch round, about ⅛ inch thick. Fit into a 9-inch pie plate. Trim edges, leaving a 1-inch edge; fold edge under flush with rim, and crimp as desired. Lightly pierce bottom of dough with a fork. Freeze or refrigerate until firm, about 15 minutes.

2 In a medium bowl, stir together eggs, sugar, corn syrup, vanilla, and salt until well combined. Stir in walnuts, and spread mixture evenly over dough in dish.

3 Bake, rotating halfway through, until filling is just set in the center and crust is golden brown, about 1 hour and 10 minutes. Transfer pie plate to a wire rack to cool completely.

MAKES ONE 9-INCH PIE

THE WEST

BACKSTORY

These pies pay homage to a couple of Washington specialties: walnuts and wild blackberries, the latter picked from brambles bursting with fruit from the Olympic Mountains to Seattle. Recipes for these regional favorites have been passed down through the Evergreen State families for generations, and the recipes are appealing in their simplicity. Serve both pies topped with whipped cream, which will offset the jammy sweetness of the berries and the richness of the walnut filling.

ORANGE CHIFFON CAKE

  2 cups all-purpose flour

  1 tablespoon plus 1 teaspoon baking powder

  ½ teaspoon salt

1½ cups sugar

  ½ cup neutral-tasting oil, such as safflower

  6 large eggs, separated

  2 tablespoons finely grated orange zest and ½ cup fresh orange juice (from 2 to 3 navel or Valencia oranges)

  ¼ cup cold water

  ¼ teaspoon cream of tartar

     Whipped cream, for serving

     Candied Orange Zest, for serving (optional; recipe follows)

1 Preheat oven to 325°F. In a large bowl, whisk together flour, baking powder, salt, and 1 cup sugar. Make a well in center of flour mixture. Add oil, egg yolks, orange zest and juice, and the cold water; whisk batter until smooth.

2 With an electric mixer on medium-high speed, whisk egg whites and cream of tartar until soft peaks form. Gradually add the remaining ½ cup sugar, 1 tablespoon at a time; continue to beat until stiff peaks form. Using a flexible spatula, gently fold half of egg-white mixture into batter. Fold in remaining egg-white mixture just until combined (do not overmix).

3 Pour batter into a 10-inch footed angel food cake pan with a removable bottom; bake until a cake tester inserted near center of cake comes out clean, 55 to 60 minutes. Remove from oven; invert, still in pan, onto a baking sheet. Let cool completely. Run a sharp knife around edges to release cake. Serve with whipped cream and candied zest, if desired.

SERVES 10

CANDIED ORANGE ZEST

  1 orange

  ½ cup plus 2 tablespoons sugar

Using a vegetable peeler, remove orange zest in strips (leaving white pith behind); slice lengthwise into matchsticks. In a saucepan, bring ½ cup sugar and 1 cup water to a boil. Add zest; reduce heat to medium. Cook until zest is soft, about 15 minutes. With a slotted spoon, transfer zest to a waxed paper–lined baking sheet; let cool. Toss with remaining 2 tablespoons sugar. Zest can be stored up to 1 day in an airtight container at room temperature.

MAKES ENOUGH FOR A GARNISH

One secret to this moist, tall cake is its use of vegetable oil instead of butter, an unprecedented choice when the recipe was invented in the 1920s in Hollywood. Along with egg yolks, oil gives the cake an exceptionally fine, soft crumb, while beaten egg whites folded into the batter lend lightness and result in a cake with impressive scale. Do not overbeat the egg whites, or they will become grainy, and use a gentle hand when adding them to the batter, or else they deflate. This version of the cake bears the flavor and scent of oranges, from the zest and juice added to the batter, as well as the candied peel used as a garnish.

PINEAPPLE

There's a reason a pineapple wears a crown. It is an appropriate headdress for this most regal of fruits, with its upright stature and golden flesh elaborately clothed in diamond-patterned skin. And as anyone who has sampled a pineapple can attest, the inimitable, sweet flavor with just a hint of tartness is truly a treat befitting royalty.

Indeed, there was a time when only royalty had access to pineapples, which Christopher Columbus brought to Queen Isabella of Spain from the Caribbean island of Guadeloupe in 1493. In the late 1600s, King Charles II of England was so enamored of pineapples that he commissioned a portrait of himself accepting one as a gift. And among American colonists, a pineapple was a status symbol: Those who couldn't afford to buy the fruit rented it from grocers to display at parties and other celebratory occasions.

Despite its storied pedigree, the pineapple has long been an emblem of warmth and welcome. In Columbus's day, the people who inhabited the Caribbean islands placed the fruit outside their homes as a gesture of hospitality. The American sea captains who later traveled this trade route began a similar tradition in New England, putting pineapples near their houses to let their neighbors know that they had returned safely.

Today, pineapples are widely associated with Hawaii, where they have been cultivated for nearly two centuries. James Dole launched the first commercial pineapple farm on the island of Oahu in 1901. Thanks to the year-round mildness of the climate there, residents of the continental United States can buy pineapples in any season. Pineapples stop ripening once they are picked, so choose those that yield to gentle pressure and have firm green leaves and a sweet aroma.

Lively and refreshing, pineapple complements a range of flavors, including coconut, papaya, ginger, rosemary, allspice, and rum. Its astringency makes it a boon to savory foods, such as chicken or ham, and guarantees that it is never cloying in desserts, even in brown sugar–laden upside-down cakes. And when it is grilled or roasted, pineapple turns caramel and smoky in flavor, the ultimate bed for a scoop of vanilla ice cream. No matter how you slice it, you're sure to relish every bite of this marvelous, majestic fruit.

ROASTED PINEAPPLE WITH RUM-VANILLA GLAZE Preheat oven to 375°F. Peel and core a pineapple and cut lengthwise into wedges. Place wedges on a rimmed baking sheet. In a small bowl, stir together 2 tablespoons (1 fluid ounce) dark rum and 2 tablespoons light-brown sugar; scrape seeds from ½ vanilla bean (split lengthwise) into bowl. Brush rum mixture onto pineapple wedges and dot tops with small pieces of unsalted butter (about 2 tablespoons). Roast until liquid has evaporated and pineapple has caramelized, about 30 minutes. Transfer sheet to a wire rack and let pineapple cool slightly. Serve warm or at room temperature, with vanilla ice cream. **SERVES 4**

PINEAPPLE UPSIDE-DOWN CAKE

THE WEST

BACKSTORY

Just ten years after Jim Dole founded the Hawaiian Pineapple Company in 1901, canned pineapple slices were available in every state of the union at an affordable price, allowing homemakers everywhere to bake a popular dessert of the day, pineapple upside-down cake. A recipe contest sponsored by the company in 1926 reportedly resulted in more than 2,000 entries, and this cemented the cake's place in the canon of American desserts. The contrast of the syrupy fruit on the "bottom" and the buttery cake layer on top is what keeps it so popular today. In fact, you'll find variations using other types of fruit in place of the pineapple, including mangoes, pears, apples, and berries. But pineapple remains the nostalgic choice, the one and only among the dessert's most devoted followers.

1½ cups all-purpose flour

2 teaspoons baking powder

¼ teaspoon salt

6 tablespoons unsalted butter, softened, plus 3 tablespoons cut into small pieces

1⅔ cups sugar

2 large eggs

1 teaspoon pure vanilla extract

½ cup milk

7 thin rounds cored pineapple (from ½ small pineapple)

1 Preheat oven to 350°F. In a large bowl, combine flour, baking powder, and salt. With an electric mixer on medium speed, cream 6 tablespoons butter and 1 cup sugar until light and fluffy. Add eggs and vanilla; beat until combined. Add flour mixture in three additions, alternating with the milk and beginning and ending with the flour. Mix just until combined.

2 Place remaining ⅔ cup sugar in a 10-inch cast-iron or heavy ovenproof skillet and heat over medium until beginning to liquefy, then stir with a wooden spoon until completely melted and golden, 2 to 3 minutes. Remove pan from heat; add remaining 3 tablespoons butter, stirring to incorporate. Place a pineapple round in center of pan; arrange remaining rounds in a circle around center slice, overlapping slightly as needed.

3 Carefully spoon batter over pineapples in skillet. Bake until a cake tester inserted in the center comes out clean, about 45 minutes. Transfer pan to wire rack and let cool 5 minutes. Run a sharp knife around edge of cake, then carefully invert onto a platter. Serve warm or at room temperature.

SERVES 8

HAZELNUTS

Oregon's Willamette Valley is an agricultural dreamscape: long growing seasons, moderate temperatures, fertile land. One of the many crops that flourish in this Mediterranean-like climate is hazelnuts. In fact, if you're eating an American-grown hazelnut, you're almost certainly eating one from Oregon.

Also known as filberts, hazelnuts are versatile and appealing in countless sweet and savory preparations or simply eaten out of hand. They have a delicate crunch and a sweet, toasty flavor that can't be matched. And while many growers in the state produce them as a commodity crop, pooling their nuts and processing them in one huge facility for commercial sale, some small family farms still do things the old-fashioned way—overseeing their production from tree to table to ensure the best possible quality of nuts.

Hazelnut trees are biennials, meaning they have a high yield one year, and a lower one the next. But large crop or small, the harvesting process is essentially the same: As the weather cools in autumn, the nuts start to fall—slowly at first, then rapid-fire, like a hail storm. Fastidious farmers keep the ground beneath the trees swept clean, so nothing gets in the way of the bounty. The farmers then rush to get their crop off the ground before the seasonal rains start, since moisture can encourage mold.

Once gathered, the nuts are cracked and shelled and hand-sorted for quality before they're sold. Visit a Portland farmers' market on an October Saturday and you're in for a real treat: hazelnuts roasted, salted, and spiced; candied, or baked into cookies or pizza dough; or puréed into a paste and blended with chocolate for that famous (and addictive) spread called gianduja (and more commonly known by the brand name Nutella). However you find them, the farmers' market nuts will be nearly as fresh as if you stood beneath a tree and caught them as they dropped.

HAZELNUT-CHOCOLATE SPREAD
Purée 7 ounces toasted (see page 408) blanched hazelnuts (1½ cups) and ¼ teaspoon coarse salt until mixture is the texture of peanut butter. Add ½ cup confectioners' sugar and 2½ ounces semisweet chocolate, melted; pulse until combined. Refrigerate in an airtight container up to 1 week; serve chilled or at room temperature, spread on French bread, between buttery cookies, or as a cake filling. **MAKES 1 CUP**

HAZELNUT COOKIES

½   cup (1 stick) unsalted butter, softened

½   cup sugar

1¼ cups all-purpose flour

½   cup roasted hazelnut meal

½   teaspoon coarse salt

1 Preheat oven to 350°F. With an electric mixer on medium-high speed, cream butter and sugar until light and fluffy, 2 to 3 minutes. Add flour, hazelnut meal, and salt; beat until mixture comes together to form a dough. (Dough can be wrapped well in plastic and refrigerated up to 1 day or frozen up to 3 months; thaw in refrigerator before using.)

2 Roll dough into balls (each 1 inch in diameter) and transfer to baking sheets, spacing 2 inches apart. Press balls with tines of fork to flatten. Bake until edges are golden, rotating sheets halfway through, 12 to 15 minutes. Transfer sheets to a wire rack and let cookies cool completely. (Cookies can be stored in an airtight container at room temperature up to 3 days.)

MAKES ABOUT 2 DOZEN

THE WEST

BACKSTORY

Although only about three percent of the world's hazelnuts come from Oregon, they are widely considered to be the best. The deep flavor of these five-ingredient cookies belie their simplicity. You can find roasted hazelnut meal at specialty food stores and from online retailers, or make your own: pulse toasted and cooled blanched hazelnuts (page 408) in a food processor just until it reaches the consistency of cornmeal (do not grind it into a paste; two ounces whole nuts will yield half cup of ground).

APRICOT AND WALNUT ROLL CAKE

Unsalted butter, softened, for baking sheet

¾ cup sifted cake flour (not self-rising)

¾ teaspoon baking powder

½ teaspoon salt

4 large eggs, separated

¾ cup granulated sugar

1 teaspoon pure vanilla extract

½ cup walnuts, finely ground
Confectioners' sugar, for dusting

½ cup marsala or sweet sherry

1¾ cups Apricot-Honey-Ginger Jam
(recipe follows)

1 Preheat oven to 375°F. Butter a 12-by-17-inch rimmed baking sheet. Line with parchment, with overhang on both short sides. Butter parchment. Sift together cake flour, baking powder, and salt into a bowl.

2 With an electric mixer on medium speed, beat egg yolks until light, about 4 minutes. Gradually add granulated sugar and beat until thick and creamy, about 3 minutes more. Mix in vanilla. With mixer on low speed, gradually add flour mixture and beat until just combined.

3 Whisk egg whites on medium speed to form stiff but not dry peaks. Fold one-third of egg whites into batter to lighten, then gently fold in remaining whites, being careful not to overmix. Gently fold in walnuts.

4 With an offset spatula, spread batter evenly in prepared baking sheet, covering all corners. Bake 10 minutes. Remove from oven and loosen edges of cake with a knife. Invert sheet onto a kitchen towel that has been liberally dusted with confectioners' sugar. Peel off parchment. With a serrated knife, trim about ½ inch of the browned and hardened edges off cake.

5 Brush marsala generously over warm cake and spread the jam evenly on top. Starting from a short side, carefully roll up cake gently but firmly into a log. Place rolled cake on a serving platter, seam side down, and dust with confectioners' sugar. To serve, slice with a serrated knife.

SERVES 6 TO 8

APRICOT-HONEY-GINGER JAM

3 pounds small ripe apricots (about 24), halved, pitted, and cut into eighths

1½ cups sugar

¾ cup honey

2 tablespoons crystallized ginger, minced

2 tablespoons fresh lemon juice

1 Toss together all the ingredients in a bowl. Cover with plastic wrap and let stand at room temperature 3 hours, or refrigerate up to 1 day.

2 In a heavy-bottomed 2- to 3-quart pot, bring apricot mixture to a boil over medium-high heat. Reduce heat to medium-low; simmer, skimming foam from surface as needed, until fruit is transparent and falls apart slightly, about 20 minutes (cooking time will vary depending on ripeness of fruit). If mixture seems too watery, strain out fruit and continue cooking syrup about 5 minutes more, then return fruit to pan and let cool completely. (Jam can be refrigerated in an airtight container up to 3 weeks.)

MAKES ABOUT 4 CUPS

THE WEST

BACKSTORY

Apricots are a legacy of China, where they have been cultivated for more than four millennia. Growing the soft-fleshed, delicate fruit can be a challenge. To yield the most sumptuous fruit, the trees need a cold winter in which to lie dormant, followed by a warm spring and summer to concentrate the flavor of the developing crop. Accordingly, apricots do best in a temperate zone, such as in California's San Joaquin Valley. Alas, they have an all-too-brief season, lasting from about mid-May to early July. Celebrate their arrival, then, by making this lovely marsala-spiked walnut roll cake, which is filled with an apricot jam flavored with honey and candied ginger, and dusted with confectioners' sugar. Summer never tasted so sweet.

TIPS AND TECHNIQUES

MAKING BREADCRUMBS

Trim off crusts from a loaf of bread (such as Pullman, pan de mie, or other type), and tear the bread into large pieces. Pulse in a food processor to form coarse or fine crumbs, as desired. (For dried breadcrumbs, toast the crumbs in an even layer on a baking sheet at 250°F for 12 to 15 minutes.) Leftover breadcrumbs can be frozen, in an airtight container, for up to 6 months.

MELTING CHOCOLATE

Melt chopped chocolate in a heatproof bowl set over (not in) a pan of simmering water, or in a double-boiler. Alternatively, you can melt chocolate in the microwave: In a microwave-safe bowl, heat chopped chocolate in 30-second intervals, stirring after each, until almost melted; remove and stir until completely melted.

TOASTING NUTS

To toast nuts such as pecans, walnuts, and almonds, spread them on a rimmed baking sheet and toast in a 350°F oven until fragrant and darkened slightly, 7 to 10 minutes, tossing occasionally. Transfer to a plate to cool. Toast pine nuts 5 to 7 minutes. Toast hazelnuts until skins split, 10 to 12 minutes. When cool enough to handle, rub warm nuts in a clean kitchen towel to remove skins.

TOASTING SESAME SEEDS

Heat seeds in a small skillet over medium, shaking the pan occasionally, until golden and fragrant, 2 to 3 minutes (be careful not to let them burn). Transfer to a plate to cool.

TOASTING AND GRINDING SPICES

Toast whole spices just before grinding to release their flavorful oils: Heat a dry skillet over medium. Add spices in a single layer and toast, gently shaking or swirling pan constantly to keep spices from burning, until fragrant, 30 to 60 seconds, depending on the spice. Immediately transfer to a plate to cool before grinding in a spice grinder or clean electric coffee grinder (buy a separate grinder for spices only). Each time after using, run a few bits of soft bread or a handful of uncooked rice through the grinder to remove any residue.

WASHING LEEKS

Trim and discard root ends and dark green parts from leeks. Slice leeks to desired thickness, then place pieces in a bowl; wash leeks in several changes of cold water, swishing to loosen grit, until you no longer see any grit in bottom of bowl. Lift leeks out of water, and dry on a clean kitchen towel (or paper towels) before using.

PEELING TOMATOES AND PEACHES

Bring a pot of water to a boil and prepare a large ice-water bath. Using a sharp knife, lightly score the bottom (not the stem end) of each tomato or peach with an X. Working in batches of three or four, add fruit to boiling water and blanch just until skin splits and starts to pull away from fruit, 1 to 2 minutes. Use a slotted spoon to transfer fruit to the ice bath to stop the cooking. Let cool completely, then remove from ice bath and gently peel away skins, using a paring knife on any stubborn spots.

PEELING AND DEVEINING SHRIMP

Holding shrimp by the tail, peel shell from inside curve with your fingers, leaving tail intact (or remove, if desired). Gently run a paring knife from head to tail along the center of the back to expose the "vein." Then use the knife to remove the blackish vein in one piece.

CLEANING MUSSELS

Use a knife or your fingers to pull away the beards (tough fibers) from the mussels, and discard. Holding them under cold running water, scrub mussels with a stiff-bristle brush, then soak in cold water until ready to use, up to 30 minutes. When ready to use, lift shells out of water, leaving sediment behind (do not drain in a colander).

CLEANING CLAMS

Holding them under cold running water, scrub clams with a stiff-bristle brush, then place in a bowl of cold water. Add a handful of cornmeal (which helps draw out the grit) and let soak 15 to 30 minutes. Lift clams from water; rinse.

STERILIZING JARS

For complete instructions, see the U.S. Department of Agriculture's canning guidelines at foodsafety.cas.psu .edu/canningguide.html. If you are using jars with glass lids, follow the manufacturer's processing instructions.

- ☐ Discard any jars that have chips or cracks. Wash jars, metal lids, and screw bands in hot, soapy water; rinse.

- ☐ Place empty jars upright on a wire rack placed in the bottom of a large pot, leaving at least an inch of space between jars. Fill the pot with hot water until jars are submerged by 1 to 2 inches.

- ☐ Bring water to a boil. Continue to boil for 15 minutes. Turn off heat; leave the jars in the water until they are ready to be filled.

- ☐ Sterilize the lids according to manufacturer's instructions. Never reuse metal lids—the seals will not work a second time.

- ☐ Using a jar lifter or stainless-steel tongs, lift the jars from the pot, emptying the water back into the pot, and place the jars on a layer of clean towels.

HOT-SMOKING ON THE GRILL

Ordinary backyard grills can be used to hot-smoke foods, such as the ribs on page 246 and brisket on page 313. There are two ways to do this, depending on the type of grill you have. Gas grills require attachments, which are available for most models (follow the manufacturer's instructions). The instructions below are for kettle-style charcoal grills, such as those by manufactured Weber.

- ☐ Soak fragrant wood chips, such as mesquite, hickory, or pecan, in water for 1 hour before using.

- ☐ Heat coals and let them burn until whitish-gray, then rake the hot coals to opposite sides, leaving center free. Drain wood chips and place on top of coals. Let burn 5 minutes.

- ☐ Place a disposable 9-by-13-inch aluminum pan in center of the bottom grill rack.

- ☐ Fill the disposable pan halfway with hot water; this will create the steam to keep the meat moist.

- ☐ Place the top rack on grill, then place meat in center of rack (over the pan).

- ☐ Cover grill, closing all but one vent to create a hot environment; you will need to open and close other vents during cooking to maintain a grill temperature of 275°F to 325°F. If your grill doesn't have a built-in thermometer, insert a probe thermometer into one of the kettle's top vents.

- ☐ During cooking, stoke the fire every 30 minutes, adding more charcoal and wood chips as needed.

BASIC RECIPES

CHICKEN STOCK

- 5 pounds assorted chicken parts (backs, necks, and wings)
- 2 carrots, cut into 1-inch pieces
- 2 large celery stalks, cut into 1-inch pieces
- 2 yellow onions, cut into eighths
- 1 dried bay leaf
- 1 teaspoon black peppercorns

1 Place chicken parts in an 8-quart stockpot and add enough water to cover by 1 inch (about 3 quarts). Bring to a boil over medium-high heat, using a ladle or large spoon to skim foam from surface. Add carrots, celery, onions, bay leaf, and peppercorns, and reduce heat to a bare simmer. Cook, skimming frequently, about 2 hours.

2 Strain stock through a fine sieve (preferably lined with cheesecloth) into a large heatproof bowl or another pot, pressing on solids with a wooden spoon to release as much liquid as possible (discard solids). Skim off fat if using immediately, or let cool completely (an ice-water bath speeds this process) before transferring to airtight containers. Refrigerate at least 6 hours to allow fat to accumulate at the top. With a large spoon, remove and discard fat before using or storing stock. (Stock can be refrigerated in airtight containers for up to 3 days or frozen for up to 6 months; thaw in the refrigerator before using.)

MAKES ABOUT 2½ QUARTS

VEGETABLE STOCK

- 3 tablespoons olive oil
- 1 large onion, coarsely chopped
- 2 large celery stalks, coarsely chopped
- 2 medium carrots, coarsely chopped
- 2 garlic cloves, thinly sliced
- 10 cups water
- 8 sprigs flat-leaf parsley
- 4 sprigs thyme
- 1 dried bay leaf
- 1 teaspoon whole black peppercorns
  Coarse salt and freshly ground pepper

1 Heat oil in a 6-quart stockpot over medium. Add onion; cook, stirring often, until golden brown, 10 to 15 minutes. Add celery, carrots, and garlic. Cook, stirring occasionally, until vegetables are tender, about 10 minutes.

2 Stir in the water, herbs, and peppercorns; season with salt and pepper. Bring to a boil. Reduce heat, and simmer 1 hour.

3 Strain stock through a fine sieve (preferably lined with cheesecloth) into a large heatproof bowl or another pot, pressing on solids with a wooden spoon to extract as much liquid as possible (discard solids). Use immediately, or let cool completely before storing in airtight containers. Stock can be refrigerated in airtight containers up to 3 days or frozen for up to 6 months; thaw in the refrigerator before using.

MAKES ABOUT 2 QUARTS

BEEF STOCK

- 6 pounds beef bone-in short ribs, trimmed of excess fat

  Coarse salt and freshly ground pepper
- 1 can (28 ounces) whole peeled tomatoes, coarsely chopped, juice reserved
- 2 dried bay leaves
- 1 small bunch fresh thyme
- 10 whole black peppercorns

1 Preheat oven to 450°F. Arrange ribs in a roasting pan; season with salt and pepper. Roast until well browned, turning ribs halfway through, about 1½ hours.

2 Transfer ribs to an 8-quart stockpot and add enough water to cover by 1 inch (about 3 quarts). Pour off and discard fat from roasting pan. Pour 1 cup water into pan. Bring to a boil over medium-high heat, scraping any browned bits from the bottom with a wooden spoon, until water is reduced by half. Transfer liquid and bits to stockpot. Add tomatoes and their juice, bay leaves, thyme, and peppercorns.

3 Bring mixture to a simmer over high heat (do not boil). Reduce heat until liquid is at a gentle simmer, and place a smaller pot lid directly on surface of stock to keep ingredients submerged; cook until meat is very tender and pulls away from the bone, about 1½ hours. Skim foam from surface with a ladle or large spoon as needed. Remove ribs from pot. (Let cool slightly, then pull meat from the bones; refrigerate, covered, up to 3 days. Use the meat to make fillings for tacos, enchiladas, or quesadillas.)

4 Strain stock through a fine sieve (preferably lined with cheesecloth) into a large heatproof bowl or another pot, pressing on solids with a wooden spoon to release as much liquid as possible (discard solids). Skim off fat if using immediately, or let cool completely (an ice-water bath speeds the process) before transferring to airtight containers. Refrigerate at least 6 hours to allow fat to accumulate at the top. With a large spoon, remove and discard fat before using or storing stock.

5 Stock can be refrigerated in airtight containers for up to 3 days or frozen for up to 6 months; thaw in the refrigerator before using.

MAKES ABOUT 3 QUARTS

MARINARA SAUCE

- 3 tablespoons olive oil
- 1 small yellow onion, diced (about 1 cup)
- 4 garlic cloves, thinly sliced
- 2 cans (28 ounces each) whole peeled tomatoes in juice, preferably San Marzano, puréed
- ½ teaspoon red-pepper flakes

  Coarse salt and freshly ground pepper
- 1 tablespoon chopped fresh oregano
- ¼ cup fresh basil leaves, torn

In a large pot or Dutch oven, heat olive oil over medium. Add onion and garlic; cook until softened, stirring occasionally, about 8 minutes. Add puréed tomatoes and red-pepper flakes; season with salt and pepper. Bring to a simmer; cook, partially covered, until thickened, about 25 minutes. Stir in herbs. (If not using immediately, cool completely and refrigerate up to 3 days in an airtight container or freeze up to 2 months; thaw in refrigerator.)

MAKES 6 CUPS

KANSAS CITY BARBECUE SAUCE

- 1 tablespoon unsalted butter
- ½ small onion, finely grated
- 2 garlic cloves, minced

  Coarse salt and freshly ground pepper
- ½ cup packed light-brown sugar
- 2 tablespoons unsulfured molasses
- 1½ cups ketchup
- 1 tablespoon yellow mustard
- ⅓ cup cider vinegar
- 2 tablespoons Worcestershire sauce
- ½ teaspoon cayenne

In a medium saucepan, melt butter over medium heat. Add onion and garlic; season with salt and pepper. Cook, stirring occasionally, until onion is soft, 2 to 3 minutes. Add brown sugar, molasses, ketchup, mustard, vinegar, Worcestershire, and cayenne. Bring to a simmer. Cook, stirring occasionally, until thick, about 5 minutes. (Sauce can be cooled completely and refrigerated in an airtight container up to 2 weeks; reheat over low before serving.)

MAKES 1½ CUPS (ENOUGH FOR TWO 2½-POUND RIB RACKS)

SIMPLE SYRUP

2 cups sugar

2 cups water

Bring sugar and the water to a boil in a small saucepan, stirring to dissolve sugar. Boil 1 minute, then remove from heat; let cool completely. Syrup can be refrigerated up to 1 week in an airtight container.

MAKES 2½ CUPS

BASIC PIE DOUGH

3 cups all-purpose flour

1 teaspoon salt

1 tablespoon sugar

1 cup (2 sticks) plus 2 tablespoons cold unsalted butter, cut into small pieces

¼ to ½ cup ice water

1 Pulse together flour, salt, and sugar in a food processor to combine. Add butter; pulse until mixture resembles coarse crumbs with some larger pieces remaining, about 10 seconds. Evenly drizzle ¼ cup ice water over mixture. Pulse until mixture just begins to hold together (it should not be wet or sticky). If dough is too dry, add up to ¼ cup more water, 1 tablespoon at a time, and pulse to combine.

2 Divide dough in half. Wrap each in plastic; shape into disks. Refrigerate until chilled, at least 1 hour or up to overnight. (Dough can be frozen up to 1 month; thaw overnight in refrigerator before using.)

MAKES ENOUGH FOR ONE DOUBLE-CRUST OR TWO SINGLE-CRUST 9-INCH PIES

VARIATION

Herbed Pie Dough Omit sugar and add 2 tablespoons chopped mixed fresh herbs, such as thyme, oregano, and marjoram, along with the flour and salt in step 1.

Mile-High Pie Dough Use 3¾ cups all-purpose flour, 1½ teaspoons salt, 1½ teaspoons sugar, 1½ cups (3 sticks) cold unsalted butter, and ½ to ¾ cup ice water in step 1. Divide dough into two unequal pieces, one roughly twice as big as the other, in step 2.

TENDER PIE DOUGH

2 large egg yolks

¼ cup ice water

2½ cups all-purpose flour

3 tablespoons sugar

Pinch of salt

8 ounces (2 sticks) cold unsalted butter, cut into small pieces

1 Lightly beat yolks and the water in a bowl to combine. In a food processor, pulse together flour, sugar, and salt to combine. Add butter and process until mixture resembles coarse meal. With the machine running, add yolk mixture in a slow, steady stream. Process until mixture just begins to hold together (no longer than 30 seconds).

2 Divide dough in half. Wrap each in plastic; shape into disks. Refrigerate until chilled, at least 1 hour or up to overnight. (Dough can be frozen up to 1 month; thaw overnight in refrigerator before using.)

MAKES ENOUGH FOR ONE DOUBLE-CRUST OR TWO SINGLE-CRUST 9-INCH PIES

COOKIE-DOUGH CRUST

½ cup (1 stick) unsalted butter, softened

½ cup sugar

2 large egg yolks

2¼ teaspoons pure vanilla extract

1¼ cups all-purpose flour

Pinch of salt

With an electric mixer on medium speed, cream butter and sugar until pale and fluffy. Add yolks, one at a time, beating well after each and scraping down sides of bowl as needed. Beat in vanilla. Add flour and salt; beat until mixture comes together but still crumbles. If not using immediately, form into a disk; wrap in plastic. Refrigerate up to 5 days or freeze up to 1 month (thaw before using).

MAKES ONE 10-INCH SHELL

GRAHAM CRACKERS

Made with wheat germ and whole-wheat graham flour, these cookies are wholesome versions of the store-bought favorite. They are just the right shape for making the Tennessee-Style Marshmallow Cookies on page 220. You can also score each sheet of dough into 24 rectangles (each 3 by 1½ inches), then pierce dough all over with a fork to create dotted lines. Chill and bake as directed below.

- 1½ cups all-purpose flour, plus more for work surface
- 1 cup whole-wheat graham flour
- ½ cup toasted wheat germ
- 1 teaspoon ground cinnamon
- ¾ teaspoon baking soda
- ½ teaspoon salt
- 1 cup (2 sticks) unsalted butter, softened
- ⅔ cup packed light-brown sugar
- 2 tablespoons honey

1 Whisk together both flours, wheat germ, cinnamon, baking soda, and salt in a bowl. In a separate bowl, beat butter and sugar with an electric mixer on medium-high speed until fluffy, 3 to 4 minutes. Beat in honey. Scrape down side of bowl. Reduce speed to low, and gradually add flour mixture; beat until combined. Divide dough in half; shape into disks. Wrap each in plastic; chill 20 minutes.

2 On lightly floured parchment, roll out each disk of dough to a 9-inch square, about ⅛ inch thick. Chill 30 minutes.

3 Preheat oven to 350°F. Using a pastry wheel or pizza cutter, trim the edges if necessary, then mark 9 squares (each 3 inches) on each dough sheet, scoring but not cutting all the way through. Chill 30 minutes.

4 Transfer dough, still on parchment, to baking sheets. Bake, rotating sheets halfway through, until golden brown, 17 to 19 minutes. Let cool completely on sheet on a wire rack. Break graham crackers along scored lines. Crackers can be stored in an airtight container at room temperature up to 1 week.

MAKES ABOUT 1 DOZEN

GRAHAM-CRACKER CRUST

You will need about 9 store-bought graham-cracker sheets (each 3 by 6 inches) or 18 homemade squares (see left).

- 1¼ cups graham-cracker crumbs
- 4 tablespoons unsalted butter, melted and cooled
- 3 tablespoons sugar
-     Pinch of salt

Stir together all ingredients in a medium bowl to combine. Press into bottom and sides of a 9-inch pie plate.

MAKES ONE 9-INCH SHELL

CARAMEL FROSTING

- 5 cups sugar
- 1 cup water
- 2 cups heavy cream
- 1 teaspoon pure vanilla extract
- ¾ cup (1½ sticks) unsalted butter, cut into small pieces, softened

1 Bring 4 cups sugar and the water to a boil in a medium saucepan over medium heat, stirring until sugar has dissolved, about 8 minutes; wash down sides of pan with a wet pastry brush to prevent crystals from forming. Raise heat to high; gently swirl pan (do not stir) until caramel is a deep amber, about 10 minutes. Remove from heat.

2 Meanwhile, heat cream and remaining 1 cup sugar in a small saucepan over medium until sugar dissolves, stirring frequently, about 5 minutes. Turn off heat, and cover to keep warm. Prepare an ice-water bath.

3 As soon as caramel is desired color, add hot cream mixture in a slow, steady stream, stirring to combine. Be careful, as caramel may splatter when hot cream is added. Stir in vanilla and continue stirring until mixture no longer bubbles.

4 Transfer mixture to a mixing bowl and place in the ice bath, stirring until completely cool. Remove from ice bath; with an electric mixer on medium speed, beat 5 minutes. With machine running, gradually add butter, a few pieces at a time, beating to incorporate fully. Let frosting stand 20 minutes to thicken before using.

MAKES 5 CUPS (ENOUGH FOR A 9-INCH LAYER CAKE)

CHOCOLATE FROSTING

- 1½ pounds semisweet chocolate, finely chopped
- ½ cup plus 1 tablespoon unsweetened Dutch-process cocoa powder
- ½ cup plus 1 tablespoon boiling water
- 1 pound plus 4 tablespoons (4½ sticks) unsalted butter, softened
- ¾ cup confectioners' sugar
- Pinch of salt

1 Heat chocolate in a heatproof bowl set over (not in) a pan of simmering water, stirring occasionally, until completely melted, about 15 minutes. Remove from heat and let cool to room temperature, 25 to 30 minutes. Meanwhile, combine cocoa and the boiling water; stir until cocoa is dissolved.

2 With an electric mixer on medium-high speed, beat butter, confectioners' sugar, and salt until light and fluffy. Add melted chocolate; beat on low speed until combined, 1 to 2 minutes, scraping down sides of bowl as needed. Beat in cocoa mixture. Use immediately.

MAKES 7½ CUPS (ENOUGH FOR A 8-INCH LAYER CAKE)

VANILLA PASTRY CREAM

- 6 large egg yolks
- ¾ cup sugar
- ¼ cup plus 2 tablespoons cornstarch
- ⅛ teaspoon salt
- 3 cups milk
- 2 teaspoons pure vanilla extract

1 In a large bowl, whisk egg yolks until smooth. Combine sugar, cornstarch, and salt in a medium saucepan over medium heat. Gradually add milk in a slow, steady stream. Cook, stirring constantly, until mixture thickens and begins to bubble, about 5 minutes. Remove from heat.

2 Whisking, slowly pour one-third of the milk mixture into egg yolks. Return mixture to saucepan. Cook over medium heat, stirring, until mixture begins to bubble and thicken, 2 to 4 minutes. Remove from heat; stir in vanilla.

3 Transfer mixture to a bowl. Cover with plastic wrap, pressing it directly on surface to prevent a skin from forming; refrigerate until chilled, 1 hour or up to 3 days.

MAKES ABOUT 4 CUPS

CHOCOLATE GANACHE ICING

- 9 ounces bittersweet or semisweet chocolate, finely chopped
- 1½ cups heavy cream

Place chocolate in a medium heatproof bowl. In a small saucepan, heat cream until bubbles begin to appear around edges; pour over chocolate. Let stand 5 minutes, then stir until smooth. Set aside at room temperature until cool but pourable, stirring occasionally.

MAKES ABOUT 2 CUPS

ROYAL ICING

You can use this versatile icing to decorate all your rolled and cut sugar cookies, including the red, white, and blue ones on page 58. To apply the icing and make the spectacular bursts, you'll need three plastic squeeze bottles (available at craft supply stores) or three pastry bags—one for each color. Snip the tip of each squeeze bottle to form a small hole, making one slightly larger (for the white). If using pastry bags, fit one with a small round tip (we used Ateco #2 for the white icing), and the remaining two with very small tips (such as Ateco #0 for the colored icings).

- 1 cup water, plus more if needed
- ½ cup meringue powder
- 2 pounds confectioners' sugar, sifted
- Gel-paste food coloring (optional)

Whisk the water and meringue powder with a mixer on medium speed until soft peaks form, about 3 minutes. Add sugar, and mix until icing holds a ribbonlike trail on the surface for 5 seconds when beater is raised. Tint icing, if desired, and transfer to plastic squeeze bottles or pastry bags fitted with couplers and tips. Icing can be refrigerated in an airtight container (with a damp paper towel covering the surface) for up to 1 week.

MAKES ABOUT 4⅔ CUPS

SOURCES

The following is a list of producers and artisans our editors relied on again and again for food and equipment. Phone numbers and websites were verified at the time of publication, but are subject to change.

ALLEN'S BLUEBERRY FREEZER, INC.
207-667-5561
allensblueberries.com
Frozen wild blueberries

ANSON MILLS
803-467-4122
ansonmills.com
Organic grains, including stone-ground white and yellow cornmeal, grits, dried hominy, farro

BEVMO
877-772-3866
bevmo.com
Large selection of wine and spirits, including Laird's Applejack brancy, orgeat syrup, Pernod, pisco

BOB'S RED MILL
800-349-2173
bobsredmill.com
Whole grains and rice, including hard wheat berries, popcorn, stone-ground white and yellow cornmeal, wild rice

CAJUNGROCER
888-272-9347
cajungrocer.com
Cajun foods, including Andouille sausage, gulf shrimp, dried beans, filé powder

C.J. OLSON CHERRIES
800-738-2464
cjolsoncherries.com
Fresh and dried cherries

CRANBERRY HILL ORGANIC FARM
508-888-9179
organiccranberries.com
Fresh and frozen cranberries

D'ARTAGNAN
800-327-8246
dartagnan.com
Specialty meats, including venison

DESPAÑA BRAND FOODS
718-779-4971
despanabrandfoods.com
Spanish foods, including chorizo

ESPOSITO'S FINEST QUALITY SAUSAGE PRODUCTS
212-868-4142
espositosausage.com
Sweet Italian sausage

FLYING PIGS FARM
518-854-3844
flyingpigsfarm.com
Pork products, including slab bacon, ham hocks, leaf lard

FREDDY GUYS HAZELNUTS
503-606-0458
freddyguys.com
Hazelnuts, roasted hazelnut meal

FRISKE ORCHARDS
888-968-3554
friske.com
Fresh and frozen sour cherries, dried tart cherries

FROG HOLLOW FARM
888-779-4511
froghollow.com
Peaches

GIOVANNIS FRESH FISH MARKET
805-772-1276
giovannisfishmarket.com
Fresh seafood, including dungeness crab, kumamoto oysters, halibut

GREAT AMERICAN SPICE COMPANY
877-677-4239
americanspice.com
Spices and salts, including pink curing salt

HATCH CHILE EXPRESS
800-292-4454
hatch-chile.com
Hatch chiles

HERITAGE FOODS USA
718-389-0985
heritagefoodsusa.com
Heritage turkeys, seafood, beef, pork, honey

HOG ISLAND OYSTER CO.
415-663-9218
hogislandoysters.com
Pacific, Kumamoto, and Atlantic oysters

KENYON'S GRIST MILL
800-753-6966
kenyonsgristmill.com
Johnnycake cornmeal

KING ARTHUR FLOUR
802-649-3361
kingarthurflour.com
Baking ingredients, including rye flour, poppy seeds, pretzel salt, vanilla beans

LAVENDER WIND FARM
877-242-7716
lavenderwind.com
Dried culinary lavender

LAVIGNE ORGANICS
760-723-9997
lavignefruits.com
*Fresh fruit and juices,
including blood oranges,
Meyer lemons, persimmons*

LINTON'S SEAFOOD
877-546-8667
lintonseafood.com
*Fresh seafood, including
Maryland soft-shell crabs,
crab meat, gulf shrimp,
scallops, Chesapeake oysters*

LOBEL'S OF NEW YORK
877-783-4512
lobels.com
*Quality meats, including
prime beef, Berkshire pork,
and sausages*

MAYTAG DAIRY FARMS
800-247-2458
maytagdairyfarms.com
Blue cheese, white cheddar

MELISSA'S PRODUCE
800-588-0151
melissas.com
*Specialty produce, including
key limes, prickly pears,
persimmons (in season only)*

MEXGROCER.COM
877-463-9476
*Mexican foods, including
Maggi seasoning sauce,
Mexican chocolate, Mexican
oregano, canela (Mexican
cinnamon), fresh poblanos*

MILLICAN PECAN CO.
866-484-6358
pecancompany.com
Texas pecans

MURRAY'S CHEESE
888-692-4339
murrayscheese.com
*Wide variety of cheeses,
smoked bacon*

NATIVE HARVEST
888-274-8318
nativeharvest.com
Wild rice

**NATURAL IMPORT
COMPANY**
800-324-1878
naturalimport.com
*Mirin (Japanese
cooking wine)*

**THE NET RESULT FISH
MARKET**
800-394-6071
mvseafood.com
*Smoked bluefish, scallops,
quahogs, littleneck clams*

**NEW HAMPSHIRE
GOLD**
603-715-2259
nhgold.com
Maple syrup

**NEW MEXICO PIÑON
NUT COMPANY**
877-611-2274
newmexicopinonnut.com
Piñon nuts

**NORTHWEST WILD
FOODS**
866-945-3232
nwwildfoods.com
*Frozen huckleberries,
frozen lingonberries*

**THE OLD MILL OF
GUILFORD**
336-643-4783
oldmillofguilford.com
*Grits, stone-ground
cornmeal, rye flour*

PEARSON RANCH
888-667-2643
pearsonranch.com
*Meyer lemons
(in season only)*

PENZEYS SPICES
800-741-7787
penzeys.com
*Spices and dried herbs,
including pickling
spice, filé powder, vanilla
beans, dried chiles*

RANCHO GORDO
707-259-1935
ranchogordo.com
Heirloom dried beans

RED COOPER
800-825-8531
redcooper.com
Texas 1015 onions

ROGUE CREAMERY
866-396-4704
roguecreamery.com
Caveman blue cheese

RUSS & DAUGHTERS
800-787-7229
russanddaughters.com
*Smoked and cured fish,
including salmon and trout*

**SHIELDS DATE
GARDEN**
800-414-2555
shieldsdategarden.com
California dates

SHOPPERS VINEYARD
973-916-0707
shoppersvineyard.com
*Large selection of wine and
spirits, including Laird's
Applejack brancy, orgeat
syrup, Pernod, pisco*

SHOWCASE OF CITRUS
352-394-4377
showcaseofcitrus.com
Key limes (in season only)

**SOUTHERN GRACE
FARMS**
southerngracefarms.com
Peanuts

STONEWALL FARM
812-985-5510
stonewall-farms.com
*All-natural meats, including
pork chops and ribs, brisket*

**SUN VALLEY SMOKED
TROUT**
800-215-0646
smokedtrout.com
Smoked trout fillets

TEMPLE OF THAI
877-811-8773
templeofthai.com
Fresh and dried lemongrass

**WELLFLEET OYSTER
AND CLAM CO.**
800-572-9227
Wellfleetoysterandclam.com
*Fresh oysters and clams,
including quahogs*

**WILD ALASKAN
SALMON COMPANY**
724-344-7297
seabeef.com
Wild Alaskan salmon

**WILD EDIBLES
SEAFOOD MARKET**
212-687-4255
wildedibles.com
*Fresh seafood, including
lobsters, clams, mussels,
scallops, smoked fish*

WISCONSINMADE.COM
877-947-6233
wisconsinmade.com
*Sausages, including
kielbasa, bratwurst*

ACKNOWLEDGMENTS

This wonderful book—a love letter to American cuisine and all its regional and cultural diversity—required the efforts of numerous people at Martha Stewart Living Omnimedia, each of whom shared personal favorites from his or her home state (as noted).

In particular, the special projects group—Editorial Director Ellen Morrissey (Massachusetts), Executive Editor Evelyn Battaglia (Texas), Food Editor Anna Kovel (Massachusetts), Managing Editor Lisa Waddle (Connecticut), and editors Stephanie Fletcher (California) and Lindsey Stanberry (Ohio)—enthusiastically researched the different regions and pulled together the recipes accordingly. Under the astute guidance of creative director Eric A. Pike (New Jersey), art directors Jessica Blackham (Alaska) and William van Roden (Pennsylvania) developed the winning, spirited design, along with Yasemin Emory (Canada), who learned the most of anyone involved on the project, as did Flavia Schepmans (Venezuela).

We are grateful, as always, for the enduring support and enthusiasm of our publishing partners at Clarkson Potter—Amy Boorstein (New York), Angelin Borsics (Louisiana), Doris Cooper (New York), Derek Gullino (California), Maya Mavjee (Canada), Mark McCauslin (New Jersey), Donna Passannante (Florida), Marysarah Quinn (Minnesota), Lauren Shakely (Ohio), Jane Treuhaft (New York), and Kate Tyler (Connecticut).

And thank you to many others who generously lent their time, energy, and talent to the creation of this book, among them Jennifer Aaronson, Leigh Ann Boutwell, Monita Buchwald, Sarah Carey, Denise Clappi, Alison Vanek Devine, Catherine Gilbert, Heloise Goodman, Sarah Rutledge Gorman, Erin Fagerland, Pamela Morris, Ayesha Patel, Lucinda Scala Quinn, Megan Rice, Gael Towey, and Deb Wood. A special thanks to Jane Daniels Lear, Leslie Porcelli, and Laura Wallis for their contributions to the headnotes and other text, and to Maggie Ruggiero and Greg Lofts for food styling on several of the shoots.

INDEX

PHOTO CREDITS

ANTHONY AMOS page 81

SANG AN pages 82 (bottom left), 268, 288 (right), 370, 374

QUENTIN BACON pages 190, 319, 360

CHRISTOPHER BAKER pages 76, 77, 136, 137, 227, 228 (top left, bottom right), 239, 243, 253, 270 (right), 271, 273, 284 (left), 378, 379

ROLAND BELLO pages 292, 296

ALAN BENSON page 113

EARL CARTER page 258

PAUL COSTELLO pages 9, 432

CHRIS COURT page 337

BEATRIZ DA COSTA pages 151, 281

REED DAVIS page 199

PENNY DE LOS SANTOS page 284 (top right)

TARA DONNE page 250

STEVEN FREEMAN page 158 (left)

JASON FULFORD page 256 (left)

DANA GALLAGHER pages 23, 106, 204, 213, 369, 407

BRYAN GARDNER pages 62, 67

GENTL & HYERS pages 2, 17, 60, 61, 131, 339

ALASTAIR HENDY page 114 (right)

RAYMOND HOM pages 109, 196, 220

MATTHEW HRANEK pages 98, 344 (bottom left)

LISA HUBBARD pages 94, 115, 207, 261

DITTE ISAGER page 14 (right)

FRANCES JANISCH page 164

KARL JUENGEL pages 80 (center), 88

RICHARD JUNG page 248

JOHN KERNICK pages 21, 30, 95, 174, 175, 226 (top left), 231, 235, 260 (left), 300, 343, 350 (right), 398, 399

KEN KOCHEY pages 20 (right), 130, 185, 203

FRÉDÉRIC LAGRANGE page 80 (right)

DAVID LOFTUS page 332

JONATHAN LOVEKIN pages 143, 208, 214, 267, 324

MAURA MCEVOY page 14 (center)

ARTHUR MEEHAN page 158 (right)

WILLIAM MEPPEM page 382

JAMES MERRELL pages 10, 85, 138, 153, 226 (bottom left), 376

ELLIE MILLER page 350 (left)

JOHNNY MILLER pages 58, 79, 132, 167, 173, 257, 286 (bottom right), 316, 373

AMY NEUNSINGER pages 152 (right), 166, 169, 180, 183, 226 (right), 244, 259, 334

MARCUS NILSSON pages 20 (left), 33, 40, 41, 43, 90, 101, 110, 118, 152 (left), 176, 254, 263, 299, 304, 308, 389

HELEN NORMAN pages 154 (bottom left), 216, 217

VICTORIA PEARSON pages 6, 14 (left), 80 (left), 86, 87, 126, 148, 152 (center), 179, 210, 211, 222, 223, 236, 256 (right), 260 (right), 284 (bottom right), 311, 341, 342, 353, 388, 395, 402, 403, 404

JOSÉ MANUEL PICAYO RIVERA page 71

CON POULOS pages 4-5, 11, 13, 82 (bottom right), 247

DAVID PRINCE page 303

MARIA ROBLEDO pages 270 (left), 283, 288 (left)

DAVID SAWYER pages 285, 294

CHARLES SCHILLER pages 68, 112, 140

CLIVE STREETER pages 159, 289

EVAN SKLAR page 114 (left)

DAVID TSAY page 338

MIKKEL VANG pages 70, 125, 225, 286 (bottom left), 291, 331, 351

NICK WAPLINGTON page 149

ANNA WILLIAMS pages 15, 280, 286 (top left), 327, 335, 354, 366, 396

ROMULO YANES pages 18, 24, 27, 28, 35, 36, 39, 44, 47, 48, 51, 52, 55, 57, 64, 73, 74, 82 (top left, top right), 93, 97, 102, 105, 116, 121, 122, 129, 135, 144, 147, 154 (top left, top right, bottom right), 157, 160, 163, 170, 186, 188, 193, 194, 197, 200, 219, 228 (top right, bottom left), 230, 232, 240, 264, 274, 277, 278, 286 (top right), 295, 307, 312, 315, 320, 323, 328, 344 (top left, top right, bottom right), 346, 348, 356, 357, 359, 363, 365, 381, 385, 386, 391, 392, 401

MARTHA STEWART is the founder of Martha Stewart Living Omnimedia, as well as the author of dozens of bestselling books on cooking, entertaining, gardening, weddings, and decorating. She is the host of *The Martha Stewart Show*, the Emmy-winning daily TV show on Hallmark Channel. MSLO publishes several magazines, including *Martha Stewart Living;* produces Martha Stewart Living Radio on Sirius XM Channel 110; designs branded merchandise for a broad group of retailers; and provides a wealth of ideas and information at marthastewart.com.

Also available as an ebook